DISCARD

SAMUEL RICHARDSON

GARLAND REFERENCE LIBRARY
OF THE HUMANITIES
(VOL. 150)

SAMUEL RICHARDSON
*An Annotated Bibliography
of Critical Studies*

Richard Gordon Hannaford

GARLAND PUBLISHING, INC. • NEW YORK & LONDON
1980

Library of Congress Cataloging in Publication Data

Hannaford, Richard Gordon, 1941–
    Samuel Richardson, an annotated bibliography of
critical studies.

    (Garland reference library of the humanities ; v. 150)
    Includes indexes.
    1. Richardson, Samuel, 1689–1761—Bibliography.
I. Title.
Z8744.19.H36 [PR3666]   016.823′6   79-7916
ISBN 0-8240-9531-6

Printed on acid-free, 250-year-life paper
Manufactured in the United States of America

CONTENTS

PREFACE

This bibliography offers an annotated list of critical evaluations of Richardson from 1740 to 1978. Its six major divisions include the most recently determined canon of Richardson's works, the criticism from the eighteenth to the twentieth century, and a section on Masters and Doctoral theses. There are author and subject indexes, and an introduction that surveys the more important literary scholarship of nearly two and one-half centuries. Besides attempting to be as inclusive as possible, I have tried to make this bibliography as useful to Richardson studies as possible, and the following comments on some of its features may be useful to those using it.

Section I presents a complete, chronological list of Richardson's works, based upon William Sale's *Bibliographical Record* and upon subsequent additions to Richardson's canon. I have incorporated into this section a selected list of the more important editions of Richardson's works and novels (a selected list, since it soon became apparent that tracing every edition was beyond the scope of this bibliography), as well as subdivisions on Richardson's correspondence and the bibliographies referring to him or to special topics of particular importance.

Section II, divided into two parts, presents, first, a chronology of eighteenth-century criticism so that one may study the contemporary reaction to Richardson and his novels; the shifts in taste and degrees of praise or censure are not so clearly revealed in a more straightforward, alphabetical list. The chronology also illustrates how criticism surfaced in the fiction of the period: for example, in *The Virgin in Eden* (#125) Charles Povey digresses from his story of a "really" virtuous virgin to attack *Pamela*; in *The Stage-Coach* (#166) a character discusses how Richardson's fiction is worthy of serious attention; and in *The Peregrinations of Jeremiah Grant* (#204) a sea-captain asserts that Sir Charles Grandison is "the perfection of human invention." The second part of the eighteenth-century section is comprised of the many allusions to Richardson in letters, diaries, memoirs, biographies, and poems not easily set into a chronology. Here, alphabetically listed, can be found such important sources on Richardson as Samuel Johnson, Elizabeth Carter, and Hester Mulso, as well as the more trivial but often interesting anecdotes about and poetic tributes to Richardson.

Section III is simply an alphabetical listing of nineteenth-century criticism, but section IV on the twentieth century is sub-divided for greater ease in finding the kind of information desired. Primary works on Richardson, including a list of representative reviews, are listed separately, as are literary histories or general studies on the development of the novel; the remaining subdivisions separate work on Richardson into general literary and biographical criticism contained in periodicals, festschrifts, and chapters in books, and there are separate subdivisions on each of the novels. Because modern criticism is the most extensive, section IV is cross-referenced, and a title appears as many times as is appropriate, revealing through its annotation how it applies to that section.

Those interested in pursuing a special topic in Richardson criticism are invited to use the subject index, which lists items dealing with such concerns as Richardson's sentimentalism, epistolary technique, his influence or reputation, and themes found in the novels. Specific subtopics, such as "imagery" in *Clarissa* or "characterization" in *Sir Charles Grandison*, are further classified under headings for the respective novels.

· · · · ·

I began this project originally because students in my course on the eighteenth-century novel had no thorough bibliography on Richardson. I compiled this bibliography by examining the earlier lists noted in section ID of the present text; I have also relied heavily upon McKillop (#550) and Eaves and Kimpel (#537) by closely reading their texts and examining all footnotes. For the twentieth century, I have consulted the standard serial bibliographies such as those in *Philological Quarterly* and *PMLA*. Throughout my research I have been impressed with the range and diversity of studies on Richardson and his novels, and dismayed by the realization that I must have overlooked some; I hope there have not been many.

I would like to thank the Library and staff of Columbia University for the privilege of using the resources of their collection. I also wish to thank Ray Anderson, Interlibrary Loan Librarian at the University of Idaho, for his help and suggestions. The Pacific Northwest Bibliographic Center located at the University of Washington was especially helpful in locating materials—Ms. Nancy Grey even telephoned an author in order to find an obscure article. Several other individuals graciously took time to aid me in annotating items for the text. Ms. Lauren Brown, Special Collections Librarian at the Fondren Library, Rice University, described at some length the correspondence between Anne Richardson and Martha Richardson Brigden, which Alan Dugald McKillop once owned and which he asked to have deposited in the Library's collection. Ms. Carol Mazur, Reference Librarian at Mills Memorial Library, McMaster University, and Ms. Marcia Goerbe, Librarian for the Library Association of Portland, Multnomah County, Oregon, also wrote to me and described items from their collections which were otherwise impossible to find. I especially thank these highly professional people for taking time to respond so thoroughly and willingly to my inquiries.

Deserving more special thanks are, first, Carol Parshall for her invaluable help as an initial research assistant. Second, Bill Pyle from the Computer User Services of the University of Idaho cheerfully introduced me to the complexities of computer indexing; he truly made the indexes possible. Finally, for awarding me a grant to prepare the final manuscript of this bibliography I especially thank the College of Letters and Science and the Office of the Coordinator of Research of the University of Idaho.

Richard Hannaford
Moscow, Idaho

INTRODUCTION

A lengthy argument stormed in the pages of *Notes and Queries* (#469) for 1879, precipitated by an ardor to determine, at last, which was the "right" and which the "left" when describing Richardson's house at Hammersmith. William Sale quipped some years later that the furor could have been avoided if only everyone *faced the same direction*. Alas, Richardson has seldom enjoyed balanced or dispassionate appraisal. When he published *Pamela*, the novel's popularity swept through England and the Continent, inspiring one commentator in the *Gentleman's Magazine* (#306) to remark that it was "judged in Town as great a Sign of Want of Curiosity not to have read *Pamela*, as not to have seen the *French* and *Italian* dancers." The *Pamela* phenomenon and the subsequent successes of *Clarissa* and *Sir Charles Grandison* sparked a still-continuing debate regarding the merit of these novels. On the one hand, Richardson has been heralded a second Christ (his novels inspired moral revelations), and on the other, he has been accused of being tediously verbose and of writing disguised but dangerous licence. He is also acclaimed as a shrewd psychologist, and his novels are considered to be masterpieces of subtly intricate, epistolary technique.

A brief review of Richardson's reputation from the 1740's to the 1970's will further demonstrate how readers and critics have perceived his achievement. Although readers like Freval (#63) immediately praised *Pamela*, Fielding parodied the novel in *Shamela* (#114), and other attacks quickly appeared. "Remarks on PAMELA. By a PRUDE" (#337) comically burlesqued Mr. B for not taking the heroine by force when he could, suggesting that Pamela should never be expected to forgive him such weakness; *Pamela Censured* (#121), written by a moral opponent of the novel, quoted at length the more offensive passages. *Pamela: or, the Fair Imposter* (#377), one of a long line of anti-*Pamela*s, also focused on Pamela's questionable morality:

> Keep but your Honour spotless from Reproach;
> Think on the Charms of Wealth, a Title, and a Coach.

Richardson's advocates, however, were equally vehement. A contributor to the *London Magazine* (#339) denounced such scoffers at the novel, and he insisted that her character was a "shame" and a "reprove" to them. Similarly, Aaron Hill (#379) defended *Pamela* against the unfounded censure of "Infidels and Rakes." How successful Richardson was may be inferred from the notices of a fan which went on sale in fan-shops and china-shops of London, celebrating Pamela's life and adventures, of the sale of Highmore's engravings of *Pamela*, and of the curious waxworks presenting Pamela's life.

During the 1750's *Critical Remarks* (#168) considered Richardson responsible for corrupting public taste as well as the English language (because of coined words) and for encouraging a debilitating romantic temperament; *A Candid Examination* (#172) believed Richardson's verbosity a serious fault, as were his lapses from good taste. On the whole, however, most of the English reaction to Richardson appears in correspondence and memoirs of this period. Richardson circulated his manuscripts among his friends, requesting advice, and if he often ignored it, his letters to and from Aaron Hill, Mrs. Sarah Chapone, Mary Granville, Frances Grainger, and Hester Mulso are full of details of his novels and discussions of questions of morality and decorum. Lady Bradshaigh was, perhaps, his favorite correspondent, and these letters are often the most interesting and entertaining; other important letters were exchanged between Richardson and Young. The correspondence with Johannes Stinstra (#87) is particularly significant because there Richardson gave us the one biographical sketch of his own life. Among his friends, Dr. Johnson was the most prestigious; he perceived Richardson's knowledge of the human heart, his sensibility, and his originality, comparing him favorably with Shakespeare.

Two other English notices during the latter part of the eighteenth century deserve special notice. One, by James Beattie, "On Fable and Romance" (#239), considered Richardson's narrative technique to have been derived from the epic and drama, and Beattie suggested how the epistolary form kept the reader in much the same degree of suspense as it did the teller. The other notice was the sketch of Richardson's life published in the *Universal Magazine* (#245), a sketch authorized by Richardson's daughters.

By far the most significant eighteenth-century criticism of Richardson was written by French and German writers. Foreign critics paid as much attention as their English counterparts to the question of "morality" or "suitability"; but, this Ur-Podsnappery aside, beginning with Desfontaines', critiques focused more fully and thoughtfully upon Richardson's technique of writing fiction: the epistolary form, style, characterization, description, minute and detailed realism. Desfontaines (#129), Haller (#149), Gellert (#155), Dorat (#213), and Mercier (#217) should be carefully considered by any student of Richardson. The most important of the eighteenth-century critics, however, was Diderot. In his "Eloge de Richardson" (#197), he anticipated the work of later, twentieth-century critics who emphasize Richardson's probing of the psyche, especially its emotional, sexual nature. But Diderot also discussed Richardson's technique of molding minute details to create the subtle structure of his novels, and he studied how the morality of the books lies not so much in codes or doctrines as in the emotions they inspire.

Despite an increasing fussiness over Richardson's "propriety," nineteenth-century criticism emphasized Richardson's achievement through several significant contributions. In 1804, Mrs. Barbauld (#62) edited Richardson's correspondence and prefixed to it a memoir still valuable since she had access to some materials which have since disappeared. McKillop has suggested that she "selected, abridged, and combined, often obscuring dates and suppressing personal references," but it is necessary to remember that Richardson had tampered with his correspondence, especially that with Lady Bradshaigh, so he may be responsible for the confusion in the text of the correspondence in its early years (see Eaves and Kimpel [#537] and Pettit [#61] for a fuller discussion, especially of the Richardson-Young letters). Most nineteenth-century critical appraisals, such as Chalmer's (#402), Drake's (#419), Hunt's (#441), and Mrs. Oliphant's (#470), relied heavily upon Mrs. Barbauld's *Life* and *Correspondence* of Richardson. Lord Jeffrey's review in the *Edinburgh Review* (#443) quoted lengthy passages from it; later, Jeaffreson "appropriated" Jeffrey's account in his commentary, *Novels and Novelists* (#442).

In the nineteenth century, reviewers noted that the novels were seldom read, but Richardson's achievement and reputation were carefully analyzed by Scott in his critique for the Ballantine Novels Series (#489) and by Hazlitt in his *Lectures on the English Comic Writers* (#438). Hazlitt's short but incisive analysis noted Richardson's combination of romance and realism which creates the novels' underlying ambiguities, considered the minute details which authenticate the novels' essentially confessional nature, and studied his carefully delineated characterization and skills for building novelistic structure. Richardson's stature by 1859 is reflected in David Masson's "British Novelists" (#458) and by 1863 in Taine's *History of English Literature (* #502). Masson looked most carefully at *Pamela, Clarissa,* and the contrast between Richardson and Fielding; Taine generally examined Richardson's art with an emphasis upon the novelist as a moralist, suggesting that morality becomes a disadvantage when applied so thoroughly to a character like Clarissa.

Although Richardson's reputation clearly waned during the nineteenth century, such writers as Austen, Balzac, Coleridge, Carlyle, Thackeray, Stendhal, Eliot, Ruskin, and Hardy acknowledged his importance. Austen, for example, had read *Sir Charles Grandison* so thoroughly that she made the most recondite allusions to it in her novels. If Coleridge disliked Richardson's "vile" and "canting" mind, he appreciated, nevertheless, the "loaded feeling in the whole flux and reflux of [that] mind, in short the self-involution and dreamlike continuity" of Richardson's fiction. Thackeray satirized Richardson in *The Virginians*, sketching the novelist's love of admiration and his coterie of female devotees. Ruskin, on the other hand, believed Grandison and Quixote were the greatest characters of prose fiction, and if Eliot and Hardy were less enthusiastic, they did admire Richardson's morality and structural skills, respectively.

In the last decades of the nineteenth century new editions of the novels encouraged some reappraisal of Richardson as an artist, and his achievement was given useful scrutiny by Saintsbury and Stephen (#482 and #499). Texte (#504) also initiated research on Richardson's influence upon the French novelists, a topic which has become a major subject of twentieth-century criticism. Perhaps Birrell's "Samuel Richardson" in *Res Judicatae* (#396) characterized the approach to Richardson at the turn of the century. He summarized the novelist's achievement in a good-natured and sometimes shrewd lecture, concluding that nineteenth-century critics are actually "annoyed with Richardson because he violates a tradition": that of the novelist as either a drunk or an impoverished struggler.

As the twentieth century began, studies by Thomson (#574) and Dobson (#533) attemped to evaluate Richardson and interpret his novels not from the earlier preoccupation with his vanity, propriety, or alleged prurience, but from such data as the unpublished letters in the Forster Collection of the Victoria and Albert Museum, and from close reading of the texts of the novels. If neither author dramatically alters our understanding of Richardson's efforts, each began to see him not as an instinctive genius who penetrates the secret hearts of his characters, but as a conscious literary artist who deserves objective, critical analysis. Downs (#536) continued this kind of analytic study of Richardson, considering his life, novels, art, the milieu of an age characterized by "sentiment," and his influence upon the writers who came directly after him.

Modern scholarship derives from two major works of the 1930's. Sale's *Samuel Richardson: A Bibliographical Record* (#107) catalogues and discusses Richardson's work, thereby making possible a thorough study of specific texts. McKillop's *Samuel Richardson, Printer and Novelist* (#550) concentrates not so much on Richardson's "life and times" as on "the origins, publication, and reception" of the novels; for the first time Richardson is documented as a conscious literary craftsman. The book contains an important chapter on Richardson's reputation through the nineteenth century and a major bibliography of collected and first editions of the novels, abridgments, and parodies, as well as contemporary and modern criticisms. During this period, some other basic approaches to Richardson were also explored. Morgan (#556) connected Richardson with the novel of manners, and Hornbeak (#752 and #753) with the conventions of the domestic conduct books and letter-writing traditions. Singer (#568) examined Richardson's development of the epistolary form, as did Black (#525), who showed how the tradition developed after Richardson. Birkhead (#672) determined how Richardson used and understood the terms "sentiment" and "sensibility," and Utter and Needham in *Pamela's Daughters* (#1000) studied the novel in terms of contemporary social conventions and novelistic practices; they isolated such motifs as the love plot, delicacy, prudery, tears and hysteria, virginity and the wages of sin, and the Cinderella story, tracing these motifs through to Victorian times.

A second notable surge in Richardsonian studies occurred in the 1950's with an increasing emphasis upon three topics: Richardson as a literary artist or craftsman, as a psychological novelist, and as a novelist understood best in terms of the social and economic forces of the eighteenth century. Once again McKillop led the scrutiny of Richardson's technique with his analysis of epistolary form (#789). Frye's essay "Towards Defining an Age of Sensibility" (#735) further examined Richardson's craftsmanship, emphasizing his art as a "process," a technical feature of narrative closely allied to the personal and biographical rather than to the unfolding of a "story." Van Ghent's analysis of *Clarissa* (#1116) inaugurated considerable critical attention upon Richardson as a psychological novelist who often exposes a character's deviant urges and drives. Perhaps the most extensive analysis of this kind was written by Golden (#539), who believes that Richardson and his characters operate as fantasists in search of domination. Crucial to an understanding of social and literary backgrounds, with perceptive chapters as well on *Pamela* and *Clarissa*, is Watt's *The Rise of the Novel* (#577). Along with Watt's study, one should consult Humphrey's *The Augustan World* (#541), which contains chapters on social life, business, public affairs, religion, and moral and natural philosophy, thereby providing highly necessary information for understanding the milieu from which Richardson's novels emerge.

McKillop wrote in 1936 that Richardson needed "not so much rehabilitation or ardent defense as candid reëxamination." Since then, Richardson has received just this kind of thoughtful analysis. Reprints have now appeared of Mrs. Barbauld's edition of Richardson's correspondence, of the Prefaces and Postscripts to *Clarissa*, *Pamela*, and *Sir Charles Grandison*, and of critical pamphlets written during the eighteenth century. Additions have been made to Sale's canon of Richardson's works, and the texts of the novels have been minutely collated and critically analyzed. Richardson's theories on fiction have been discussed (#521), and his relationship to earlier narrative forms has been summarized by Day (#532) and Richetti (#563). The extensive biography by Eaves and Kimpel (#537) documents thoroughly and exhaustively what is known of Richardson's life and circle of acquaintances, and it includes a catalogue of all known correspondence. As never before, scholars in books and articles pursue the nature of Richardsonian "realism," of his sympathetic and revolutionary feminism, of his sentiment, and of his theology.

To discuss the scholarship in the literary journals today reevaluating Richardson's achievement would require a separate essay of its own, so thorough and extensive has the interest in Richardson become. However, the following selective survey may provide some idea of what is being done. *Pamela* has been scrutinized by Roussel (#973) and Dussinger (#924) for its epistolary technique and by Needham (#961) and Folkenflik (#932) for its characterization. Kreissman (#944) probed the full nature of the *Pamela* phenomenon, tracing the many criticisms, parodies, and theatrical adaptations of the novel in England and on the Continent. Both Sacks (#974) and Kearney (#941) see the novel from new perspectives generated by examining the action in the novel as it determines the book's morality and by rethinking how style and narration determine the book's aesthetics. *Clarissa* has received even more attention with studies by Brissenden (#1020) on sentimentalism, by Moynihan (#1086) and Steeves (#992) on feminism and the significance of women in Richardson's novels as a whole, and by Copeland (#698) and Wendt (#1124) on imagery and figurative language. The special relationship between Richardson's epistolary technique, characterization of Clarissa, and the theme of an individual's power to act is considered by Braudy (#1019), Cohan (#1033), Napier (#1088), and Preston (#1097): they suggest that in an evil world Clarissa can find her only security in a self-willed isolation in which she seeks power to control her own destiny. Preston particularly believes the epistolary form reveals Clarissa's search to be part of a continuing existential crisis; on the other hand, another group of scholars interprets the novel as essentially tragic drama: see Carroll (#1029), Dussinger (#1042), Park (#1093), and Sacks (#1103). *Sir Charles Grandison* inspires less commentary, but Harris has analyzed the novel's text, edited the recent Oxford edition (#48), and written an extensive introduction to it. Levin (#1144) also discusses the novel, exploring Sir Charles' fantasy of "physical mastery" and "polygamy" hidden in the narrative where a number of love-stricken women are fated to share him only as "sisters."

This survey of Richardson scholarship is most fittingly concluded by examining the four major works to appear since Eaves and Kimpel's authoritative biography in 1971. Preston notes that these books "have the character of 'second-generation' criticism. . . . They all start from the assumption that Richardson was a conscious artist who perfected his own technique for his own deliberate purposes. This discovery of the real Richardson is a rediscovery, a retort to the established critics and a redirection of our attention." Wolff (#582) focuses upon Richardson as a psychological novelist, but she redirects attention from neurotic deviations to show how "his genius lay in his ability to capture the dynamics of character under stress"; she also studies characterization in all three novels in terms of Puritan attitudes and social identity and carefully considers Richardson's sources. Kinkead-Weeks (#544) makes perhaps the most sustained effort to reinterpret Richardson's achievement by examining how Restoration drama and dramatic techniques underlie Richardson's unique imaginative vision. In each novel he reviews specific dramatic situations and explores "the implications of each in a flexible, changing and complex process"; multiple points of view determine how we eventually must interpret what happens in any situation. Doody (#534) is more concerned with tracing the contexts of Richardson's fiction, seeking out the sources in heroic plays and novels of love and seduction. The reviews of her book have been mixed, suggesting that her doctoral dissertation needed greater editing, that she should have studied and incorporated the insights of other Richardson scholars, or that her work opens new and unexplored facets of Richardson's work and that her book is "ambitious—and brilliant." Certainly, her special contribution is her focus upon imagery in the novels, especially visual and emblematic imagery. Finally, Brophy (#527) renews a necessary study of Richardson's technique of fiction, demonstrating how his novelistic theory "accurately describes the artistic structure of the novels and accounts for their effect."

To summarize briefly, Richardson's influence has been extensive. Rival publishers pirated his work, Fielding and others parodied *Pamela*, theatrical adaptations appeared throughout England and Europe, and subsequent novelists imitated his style and adapted his characters and themes to their own purposes. His system of ethics was early commended for providing appropriate instruction to the young and innocent or deplored for portraying a shockingly immoral hypocritical virtue. Today his morality is more evenly assessed from the perspective of his Puritan milieu and the dramatic contexts of the novels themselves. During the eighteenth century, some initial interest was given his technical prowess as a writer, but ackowledgment of his achievement as a craftsman has had to wait for the sustained work of twentieth-century critics. Richardson himself wrote to Johannes Stinstra on 29 March 1754, "You wonder, Sir, that I appeared not as a writer earlier. . . . My Business till within these Ten or Twelve Years past, filled up all my Time. I had no Leisure; nor, being unable to write by a regular Plan, knew I, that I had so much Invention, till I, almost accidentally slid into the writing of Pamela." Few would now argue that Richardson's skill is "accidental" or that his writing is without a "plan." Psychological realism in the novel begins with Richardson's conscious art, and with the dispassionate analyses of the last forty years, his lasting reputation as one of the most important originators of novelistic theory and technique seems assured.

ABBREVIATIONS

AUMLA	*Journal of the Australasian Universities Language and Literature Association*
BNYPL	*Bulletin of The New York Public Library*
CE	*College English*
CL	*Comparative Literature*
EA	*Etudes Anglaises*
ECS	*Eighteenth Century Studies*
ELH	*Journal of English Literary History*
ELN	*English Language Notes*
JEGP	*Journal of English and Germanic Philology*
JNL	*Johnsonian News Letter*
MLN	*Modern Language Notes*
MLQ	*Modern Language Quarterly*
MLR	*Modern Language Review*
MP	*Modern Philology*
N&Q	*Notes and Queries*
NCF	*Nineteenth Century Fiction*
NM	*Neuphilologische Mitteilungen*
PLL	*Papers on Language and Literature*
PMASAL	*Papers of the Michigan Academy of Sciences, Arts, and Letters*
PQ	*Philological Quarterly*
RAA	*Revue Anglo-Americaine*
REL	*Review of English Literature*
RES	*Review of English Studies*
SAQ	*South Atlantic Quarterly*
SB	*Studies in Bibliography*
SEL	*Studies in English Literature, 1500–1900*

I.
Richardson's Works

A. NOVELS AND MISCELLANEOUS WORKS

1. *The Apprentice's Vade Mecum: or, Young Man's Pocket-Companion.* 1733 (dated 1734).

2. *A Seasonable Examination of the Pleas and Pretentions of the Proprietors of, and Subscribers to, Play-Houses.* 1735.

3. *Gentleman's Magazine.* "Verses," 6 (Jan. 1736), 51.

4. *The Christian's Magazine.* 1737. Rev. and printed by Richardson, 1748.

   Richardson's revising or correcting must have been done before the book was first published since (except for the title page) the 1748 edition is printed from the same setting of type.

5. *The Complete English Tradesman.* Daniel Defoe. 4th edn. 1737 (dated 1738).

6. *A Tour thro' the Whole Island of Great Britain.* Daniel Defoe. 1724–27. Ed. and rev. by Richardson and others. 2nd and following edns. 1738, 1742, 1748, 1753, and 1761–62.

7. *AEsop's Fables.* 1739 (dated 1740).

   A revision, meant especially for children, of Sir Roger L'Estrange's translation of the fables.

8. *The Negotiations of Sir Thomas Roe.* Ed. by Richardson and others. 1740.

9. *Pamela.* I, 1740 (dated 1741); II, 1741.

10. *Letters Written to and for Particular Friends.* [*Familiar Letters.*]

11. *Clarissa.* Vols. I, II, 1747; III, IV, 1748; V-VII, 1748.

12. *Answer to the Letter of a Very Reverend and Worthy Gentleman, Objecting to the Warmth of a Particular Scene in the "History of Clarissa."* 8 June 1749.

     See #725 for a description and analysis of this rare pamphlet.

13. *Meditations Collected from the Sacred Books ... Being Those Mentioned in the "History of Clarissa."* 1749 (dated 1750).

14. *Rambler.* No. 97. 19 Feb. 1751.

15. *Letters and Passages Restored from the Original Manuscripts of the "History of Clarissa."* 1751.

16. *The Case of Samuel Richardson.* 1753.

17. *Sir Charles Grandison.* Vols. I-VI, 1753; VII, 1754 (duodecimo, all dated 1754); I-V, 1753; VI, 1754 (octavo "second" edition published simultaneously with duodecimo, all dated 1754).

18. *An Address to the Public.* 1 Feb. 1754.

19. *The Centaur Not Fabulous.* Edward Young. 1755. Rev. by Richardson.

20. *A Collection of the Moral and Instructive Sentiments, Maxims, Cautions, and Reflexions, Contained in the "Histories of Pamela," "Clarissa," and "Sir Charles Grandison."* 1755.

21. *Conjectures on Original Composition. In a Letter to the Author of "Sir Charles Grandison."* Edward Young and Richardson. 1759.

22. *The Life and Heroic Actions of Balbe Breton.* Trans. from Marguerite de Lussan's *Vie de Balbe-Berton.* 2 vols. 1760. Rev. slightly by Richardson.

23. *Candid Review.* "Six Original Letters upon Dueling," 1 (March 1765), 227-31.

24. *The History of Sir William Harrington.* Anna Meades. 4 vols. 1771. Rev. by Richardson.

25. "History of Mrs. Beaumont, a Fragment. In a Letter from Dr. Bartlett to Miss Byron." MS in the Pierpont Morgan Library; partly printed in Mrs. Barbauld (#62), V, 301-48.

B. SELECTED EDITIONS

1. Collected Works

26. *The Paths of Virtue Delineated; Or, the History in Minia-ture of the Celebrated Pamela, Clarissa Harlowe, and Sir Charles Grandison.* London, 1756.

   This edition is adapted for children, and it is es-pecially important because eighteenth-century English and American abridgements closely follow this text. A "new edition" appeared in London in 1813, entitled *Beauties of Richardson.*

27. *The Works of Samuel Richardson.* With a Sketch of His Life and Writings, by the Rev. Edward Mangin, M.A. 19 vols. London: W. Miller, 1811.

   This text apparently follows the duodecimo edition published shortly after Richardson's death, with some variants from earlier editions of 1742 and 1762.

28. *The Novels of Samuel Richardson, Esq.* ... To Which is Prefixed a Memoir of the Life of the Author. [Sir Walter Scott.] Ballantyne's Novelist Library. 3 vols. London, 1824.

29. *The Works of Samuel Richardson.* With a Prefatory Chapter of Biographical Criticism by Leslie Stephen. 12 vols. London: Sotheran & Co., 1883-84 (1, 9-12, 1883; 2-8, 1884, all dated 1883).

   This text seems to be primarily derived from the Mangin edition.

30. *The Novels of Samuel Richardson.* With a Life of the Author, and Introductions by William Lyon Phelps. 19 vols. 1901-02; rpt. New York: AMS Press, 1970.

31. *The Novels of Samuel Richardson.* With an Introduction by Ethel M.M. McKenna. 20 vols. London: Chapman and

Hall, 1902.

This text seems to be primarily derived from the Mangin edition.

32. *Richardson.* Sheila Kaye-Smith. The Regent Library. London, 1911.

Includes selections from the three novels.

33. *The Novels of Samuel Richardson.* Shakespeare Head Edition. 18 vols. Oxford, 1929-31.

Although there is no standard edition of the novels, this is the edition most often referred to by scholars. The texts are those of the octavo edition of *Pamela* (1742), *Clarissa* (1750), and *Sir Charles Grandison* (1754).

2. Individual Novels

34. *Pamela.* 6th edn. London, 1742.

The third edition of Volumes III and IV was published with the sixth edition of Volumes I and II, making this the first time the novel was published as a work in four volumes. Richardson corrected this text in many ways; he also deleted the congratulatory "letters to the editor" which had caused adverse criticism, but restored them in subsequent editions.

35. *Pamela.* London, 1801; rpt. 1810.

This is Richardson's last corrected edition of the novel (long thought to have been lost). There are over 8400 changes made in the texts of Volumes I and II. See #928 for a complete analysis of this edition.

36. *Pamela.* Ed. George Saintsbury. Everyman's Library. 2 vols. 1914; rpt. London: J.M. Dent and Sons, 1960-61.

There is no indication of what edition this text follows. See #928, pp. 61-62.

37. *Pamela.* Introduction by William Sale, Jr. New York: W.W. Norton, 1958.

There is no indication of what edition this text follows. See #928, pp. 61-62.

38. *Pamela*. Introduction by Mark Kinkead-Weekes. 2 vols. London: J.M. Dent and Sons, 1962.

    The same text as in the earlier Everyman edition.

39. *Pamela*. Ed. with an introduction by T.C. Duncan Eaves and Ben D. Kimpel. Boston: Houghton Mifflin, 1971.

    A reprint of the first edition of *Pamela I* (with the misprints corrected); it includes the Introduction to the second edition of the novel.

40. *Clarissa*. 3rd edn. London, 1751 (dated 1751-1750).

    This is Richardson's most thoroughly revised text of the novel which includes a new Preface, additions to the *Conclusion* (clarifying the Harlowe family's recognition of Clarissa's excellence and telling the fates of Sally Martin and Polly Horton), and a restoring of letters and passages earlier deleted from the text.

41. *Clarissa*. Ed. and abridged by E.S. Dallas. 3 vols. London: Tinsley Brothers, 1868.

    A mid-nineteenth-century edition which caused some renewed interest in Richardson as a novelist. See #406, #424, #480, and #519.

42. *Clarissa Harlowe*. Ed. and abridged by Mrs. Ward. Railway Library. London: George Routledge, and Sons, 1868.

    Severely abridges the novel, emphasizing the last three months of Clarissa's life.

43. *Clarissa*. Ed. and abridged with an introduction by John Angus Burrell. New York: Modern Library, 1950.

    This text does not identify the edition it follows, but it seems essentially to be based on some version of the 3rd edition. See #1119, pp. 107-08.

44. *Clarissa*. With an introduction by John Butt. Everyman's Library. London: J.M. Dent and Sons, 1962.

    This text does not identify the edition it follows, but it seems essentially to be based on some version of the 3rd edition. See #1119, pp. 107-08.

45. *Clarissa*. Ed. and abridged by George Sherburn. Riverside Edition. Boston: Houghton Mifflin, 1962.

This is basically an "eclectic" text which reprints
the faulty text of the Everyman Library edition, but
collates it with the 1759 edition of *Clarissa* and with
the texts of 1748 and 1751 ("chiefly for misprints,
omissions of essential words, etc.").

46. *Clarissa*. Ed. and abridged by Philip Stevick. San
     Francisco: Holt, Rinehart, and Winston, 1971.

     Reprints the text of the first edition; includes in
     the appendices selections from *Familiar Letters* and from
     the Preface to the first edition of *Clarissa*.

47. *Letters from Sir Charles Grandison*. Selected with a
     Biographical Introduction and Connecting Notes. Ed.
     George Saintsbury. 2 vols. London: G. Allen, 1895.

     There is no indication of what text this edition fol-
     lows.

48. *The History of Charles Grandison*. Ed. Jocelyn Harris.
     3 vols. Oxford: Oxford Univ. Press, 1972.

     Reprints the text of the first edition.

                    3. Miscellaneous Works

49. *The Apprentice's Vade Mecum (1734)*. Ed. Alan Dugald
     McKillop. Los Angeles: William Andrews Clark Memorial
     Library, Univ. of California, 1975.

     Reprints and discusses in an introduction Richardson's
     little manual of good advice.

50. *Familiar Letters on Important Occasions*. Ed. Brian W.
     Downs. London: George Routledge and Sons, 1928.

     Includes an introduction by Downs, a note on the text
     by J. Isaacs, as well as Richardson's Preface and a table
     of contents to the letters themselves.

C. CORRESPONDENCE

51. *Answer to a Letter from a Friend.* 10 April 1754. British
     Library Add. MS. 32,557, II, fols. 176-77.

     Richardson printed this letter (and #60) in response to
     criticism of Sir Charles Grandison's Catholic compromise:
     that he will marry the Lady Clementina if their sons are
     brought up Protestant and their daughters Catholic. Both
     letters are reprinted in *A Collection of the Moral and
     Instructive Sentiments* (#20), pp. 401-10.

52. *Auswahl aus Klopstocks nachgelassenem Briefwechsel und
     übrigen Papieren.* Ed. C.A.H. Clodius. Leipzig, 1821.

     Prints the correspondence between Meta Klopstock and
     Richardson.

53. Benoist, Howard. "An Unpublished Letter of Samuel Richard-
     son." *Library Chronicle* (Univ. of Penn.), 36 (1970),
     63-66.

     Prints the complete text of Richardson's thanks to the
     Reverend Mr. Kennicott, in 1754, for the latter's Preface
     to Richardson's *A Collection of the Moral and Instructive
     Sentiments.*

54. Bishop, Alison. "Richardson Discusses His *Clarissa* and
     Grandison." *Boston Public Library Quarterly*, 4 (1952),
     217-221.

     Prints and discusses a hitherto-unpublished letter from
     the manuscript collection of the Boston Public Library:
     Richardson to Lady Echlin, 17 May 1754.

55. Bonnard, G.A. "Samuel Richardson and Guillaume-Antoine
     de Luc." *MLR*, 46 (1951), 440-41.

     A four-line note from Richardson about sending Luc a
     set of his novels, with a notation by Luc that he re-
     ceived them and sent to Richardson a medal from the city
     of Geneva, expressing love and admiration.

56. C., F.W. "Richardson's 'Clarissa.'" *N&Q*, 4th ser., 3
     (1869), 375-78.

     Prints a hitherto-unpublished letter of Richardson's
     (22 Jan. 1749-50) in which the novelist evaluates
     Clarissa. Among other points, Richardson suggests "that
     for a young Lady to become a Clarissa the Foundations of

Goodness must be laid early." He also compares Clarissa
with the more "common" Sophia Western, discusses Lovelace,
considers the responsibility of doing one's "Duty," and
notes that "a Sense of Duty for *Conscience*' sake can only
be the proper Security of a Child's Obedience."

57. ———. "Richardson's Novels." *N&Q*, 4th ser., 1 (1868),
      285.

      Prints an unpublished letter of Richardson's (9 Nov.
      1749) which berates a young lady correspondent for
      having displayed her temper; the letter is composed as
      a fictional argument, with dialogue.

58. Carew Hunt, R.N. "Letters from an Autograph Collection."
      Cornhill Magazine, 73 (1932), 474-75.

      Includes a letter from Sarah Fielding to Richardson
      (4 Dec. 1758), regarding her novel, *The Countess of
      Dellwyn*, which she hopes he will examine and even correct.

59. *Catalogue of the Collection of Autograph Letters and
      Historical Documents Formed ... by Alfred Morrison*.
      London: Privately printed by Strangeways & Sons, 1883-
      97.

      A catalogue printed in two separate series (second
      series, 1882-93) of Morrison's collection of epistolary
      documents, including important ones pertaining to
      Richardson; the second series is perhaps more useful
      in that it omits facsimiles but reproduces more fully
      the texts of the documents.

60. *Copy of a Letter to a Lady*. 10 April 1754.

      See #51.

61. *The Correspondence of Edward Young, 1683-1765*. Ed. Henry
      Pettit. Oxford: Clarendon Press, 1971.

      Prints the extant correspondence between Young and
      Richardson. See #82 for more details on this correspon-
      dence.

62. *The Correspondence of Samuel Richardson*. Ed. Anna
      Laetitia Barbauld. 6 vols. London: Lewis and Roden,
      1804.

      Still the standard edition of Richardson's correspon-
      dence, but it is incomplete and does not always print

the complete text of a letter.

Reviewed: *The Critical Review*, 3rd ser., 3 (1804), 155–65; 276–87.
   The Eclectic Review, 1 (Feb. 1805), 122–28.

63. De Fréval, Jean Baptiste. Prefatory letter to *Pamela*. London, 1740.

An enthusiastic letter, praising Richardson; it alludes to the "facts" underlying the Pamela story, but notes that Richardson changed the names of the characters and locations in order to avoid giving offense.

64. Dottin, Paul. "Du nouveau sur Richardson (Documents inédits)." *RAA*, 5 (1928), 557–61; 6 (1929), 258–61; 7 (1929), 55–59, (1930), 432–34.

Prints extracts from Richardson's correspondence, concerning his brother-in-law, James Leake, his housekeeping, his printing business, and his role in being a kind of marriage agent for the daughter of a friend.

65. Eaves, T.C. Duncan. "Dr. Johnson's Letters to Richardson." *PMLA*, 75 (1960), 377–81.

Dates more accurately a letter referring to *Grandison*, rejects one letter from the correspondence, and corrects a letter mistakenly attributed to the Earl of Orrery but actually to Richardson. See #76.

*   ————, and Ben D. Kimpel. "Appendix: Richardson's Correspondence." See #537, pp. 620–704.

A list of all letters located to or from Richardson, noting dates, correspondents, and locations, and including brief remarks on many of the letters, particularly on those that need dating.

66. *European Magazine and London Review*, 53 (1808), 370–72, 429; 54 (1808), 10–13, 94–98, 190–92; 55 (1809), 101–04.

Prints correspondence between Sarah Wescomb (Mrs. John Scudamore) and Richardson.

67. Garrick, David. *Some Unpublished Correspondence of David Garrick*. Ed. G.P. Baker. Boston, 1907. P. 23.

Prints a letter to Richardson (12 Dec. 1748), thanking him for the gift of *Clarissa* and reaffirming his friendship for the novelist.

68. *Gentleman's Magazine*. "Original Letters to and from the
     Rev. Dr. Isaac Watts, James Harris, Joseph Ward, Sir
     Edward Walpole, Rev. Dr. Richard Price, Samuel Richard-
     son, and Joseph Highmore, Esq. now in Possession of
     Anthony Highmore," 86 (1816), 10-11, 116-18, 201-04,
     300-04, 401-04, 505-08, 577-78.

     Letters to Miss Highmore (afterwards Mrs. Duncombe),
     to Joseph Highmore, and from the artist to his daughter
     relating his attendance upon the dying novelist.

69. Harris, Jocelyn. "A New Dating for a Johnson Letter."
     N&Q, N.S., 20 (June 1973), 219-220.

     A new date of April 1753 is suggested for Johnson's
     letter to Richardson (no. 49.2 in Chapman's Letters--
     see #76) regarding *Grandison*, with a brief discussion
     of Johnson's response to the progress of the novel. See
     #65.

70. Hill, Aaron. *The Works of the Late Aaron Hill*. 4 vols.
     London, 1753. I, 327; II, 68-69, 158-59, 164, 228,
     269, 294, 297-302; III, 348-50.

     Includes such items as Hill's reference to *Pamela* and
     Clarissa; he is impressed with Richardson's imagery and
     his "moral hints ... sudden, like short lightening."
     Hill's many other letters are in the Forster Collection
     of the Victoria and Albert Museum.

71. Hughes, Helen Sard. "A Letter to Richardson from Edward
     Young." *MLN*, 37 (1922), 314-16.

     Corrects Mrs. Barbauld's printing of a letter from
     Young to Richardson, based upon an original MS preserved
     in the Wellesley College library.

72. *Imperial Review*. "An Unpublished Letter; from Mr.
     Samuel Richardson, to his Nephew, Thomas Richardson,"
     2 (1804), 609-16.

     This letter, with considerable alterations, was even-
     tually published by the Company of Stationers as a model
     letter in the form of a small pamphlet, given to appren-
     tices along with a copy of the Bible and the Book of
     Common Prayer.

73. Isles, Duncan E. "Other Letters in the Lennox Collec-
     tion." *TLS*, 5 Aug. 1965, p. 685.

     Notes four items from Richardson, three regarding *The*

Female Quixote and one regarding his recommendation of
her to Robert Dodsley for what may have developed into
her translation of *The Age of Lewis XIV.*

74. Kaiser, C.B. See #550, pp. 254-55.

Kaiser's letter to Richardson of 10 July 1753 reveals
more of Richardson's German friends and in this case reveals their anticipation of *Grandison's* publication.

75. *The Letters of Dr. George Cheyne to Richardson (1733-43).*
Ed. with an introduction by Charles F. Mullett. 1940;
rpt. University of Missouri Studies, 18, No. 1.
Columbia: Univ. of Missouri Press, 1943.

Summarizes Cheyne's leading ideas in the introduction
to provide a context for his letters to Richardson;
Cheyne especially emphasized his dietary convictions to
Richardson.

Reviewed: *PQ*, 23 (1944), 174-76.

76. *The Letters of Samuel Johnson.* Ed. R.W. Chapman. 3 vols.
Oxford: Clarendon Press, 1952.

Includes some nine letters to Richardson; a full index
in volume three notes all references to the novelist.
See #65 and #69.

77. *The Letters of Tobias Smollett.* Ed. Lewis M. Knapp.
Oxford: Clarendon Press, 1970.

Prints the six (?) possible letters to Richardson,
1756-60; includes notes and some commentary.

78. *The Letters of Tobias Smollett, M.D.* Ed. Edward S.
Noyes. Cambridge: Harvard Univ. Press, 1926.

Prints five letters from Smollett with Noyes' notes
and comments. See #77 above.

79. McKenzie, D.F. "Samuel Richardson, Mr. W., and Lady
T--." *N&Q*, N.S., 11 (1964), 299-300.

Gives the text of a recently discovered letter which
helps explain why Richardson severed his connection with
the *Daily Gazetteer* in 1746.

80. McKillop, Alan D. "A Letter from Samuel Richardson to
Alexis Claude Clairaut." *MLN*, 63 (1948), 109-13.

A letter, dated 5 July 1753, to the French mathematician.

81. *Monthly Magazine*. "Original Letters of Miss E. Carter
     and Mr. Samuel Richardson," 33 (1812), 533-43.

     Letters omitted from Mrs. Barbauld's *Correspondence*
     (#62) between Miss Carter and Richardson from 13 Dec.
     1747 to 13 Oct. 1753.

82. ————. "One Hundred and Fifty Original Letters between
     Dr. Edward Young ... and Mr. Samuel Richardson...," 36
     (1813), 418-23; 37 (1814), 138-42, 326-30; 38 (1814),
     429-34; 39 (1815), 230-33; 40 (1815), 134-37; 41 (1816),
     230-34; 42 (1816), 39-41, 331-35; 43 (1817), 327-29;
     44 (1817), 327-30; 45 (1818), 238-39; 46 (1819), 43-45;
     47 (1819), 134-37.

     Eaves and Kimpel (#537) note that "the text of Richard-
     son's correspondence with Young is in a confused state"; the
     text given by Mrs. Barbauld varies considerably from that
     in the *Monthly Magazine*. Pettit (#61) considers the
     latter text more reliable and even suggests that Mrs.
     Barbauld forged some alleged letters. Eaves and Kimpel
     point out, however, that the file of letters left by
     Richardson may well have been "tampered with," possibly
     by Richardson himself.

83. ————. 48 (1819), 326-28.

     Includes some of the correspondence between Richardson
     and Smollett.

84. Pettit, Henry. "The text of Edward Young's Letters to
     Samuel Richardson." *MLN*, 57 (1942), 668-70.

     Mrs. Barbauld's texts of the Richardson-Young corres-
     pondence (#62) are unreliable as shown by comparison with
     those published in the *Monthly Magazine* between 1813 and
     1819.

85. Richardson, Samuel. Forster Collection. Victoria and
     Albert Museum. MSS. 48 E5-48 E10.

     For locations of other collections in libraries and
     museums see Eaves and Kimpel, #537, pp. 630-704.

86. ————. "Private Thoughts on a Certain Proposal; and
     Narrative of the Transaction Consequent." MS, Yale
     Univ. Library, c. 1757.

     This is Richardson's commentary on his eldest, sur-
     viving daughter's marriage settlement, revealing much
     about his character. This manuscript has been printed

in Joseph W. Reed, Jr.'s "A New Samuel Richardson Manuscript," *Yale University Library Gazette*, 42 (1968),
215-31.

87. *The Richardson-Stinstra Correspondence and Stinstra's
     Prefaces to "Clarissa."* Ed. William C. Slattery.
     Carbondale: Southern Illinois Univ. Press, 1969.

     Reveals the warm friendship between the two men and
     Stinstra's obvious enjoyment of Richardson's fiction.

     Reviewed: *PQ*, 49 (1970), 375-76.
               RES, N.S., 22 (1971), 218-19.

88. *Selected Letters of Samuel Richardson.* Ed. John Carroll.
     Oxford: Clarendon Press, 1964.

     Provides an introductory history for the letters as
     well as a short discussion of Richardson's epistolary
     form and technique; letters are selected which bear
     directly on Richardson's art, themes, and characteriza-
     tion as well as on his personality.

     Reviewed: *JEGP*, 64 (1965), 740-42.
               MLR, 61 (1966), 499-501.
               MP, 64 (1966), 164-65.
               New Rambler, 17 (1965), 43-44.
               RES, N.S., 17 (1966), 323-26.

89. *Unpublished Letters from the Collection of John Wild.*
     Ed. R.N. Carew Hunt. London: Philip Allan & Co., 1930.
     Pp. 32-40.

     Includes (1) a letter from Frances Sheridan (5 Feb.
     1756) to Richardson, thanking him for his advice to have
     her *Memoirs of Mrs. Sidney Biddulph* published; (2) a
     letter from Miss Pennington (31 Oct. 1756) to Richardson,
     commenting on Mrs. Sheridan's news from Ireland ("is not
     this writing to the moment, the true place for corres-
     pondence Penny?") and giving Richardson an account of Mrs.
     Unwin and the latter's great respect for the novelist;
     and (3) Richardson's reply to Miss Pennington (10 Nov.
     1756) in which he comments on his being a "silent Person"
     at gatherings and thanking her for her account of Mrs.
     Unwin whom he believes reveals "the very Character that
     I would wish every ingenious Lady to aim at and deserve."

90. Vachell, H.A. "A Literary Find." *Spectator*, 160 (14
     Jan. 1938), 54.

     Prints a letter from Richardson to Beau Nash and Ralph

Allen concerning contributions to the rebuilding of the
"Mineral Water Hospital" at Bath.

91. *Weekly Miscellany.* "To My Worthy Friend, the Author of
     Pamela," 11 Oct. 1740.

     This is a printed, anonymous letter (probably written
     by Richardson's friend, William Webster, editor of the
     Weekly Miscellany) which is also the first notice of
     Pamela. It praises the novel for its truthfulness, sim-
     plicity, suspense, instruction, and morality. When *Pamela*
     was eventually published on 6 Nov. 1740, this letter
     (with slight alterations) was included as part of the
     prefatory material, as was Freval's letter (#63), and
     Richardson's own comments under the guise of "Editor."

92. Williams, I.A. "Two Kinds of Richardsons." *London
     Mercury*, 7 (1923), 382-88.

     Prints a conclusion to Richardson's letter to the Rev.
     John Stinstra heretofore unpublished; rejects other
     material as belonging to Jonathan Richardson (the portrait
     painter).

                          D. BIBLIOGRAPHY

93. Bartholomew, A.T. "Richardson." In *The Cambridge
     History of English Literature*. Ed. A.W. Ward and
     A.R. Waller. New York: Putnam's, 1913. X, 411-13.

     An early general survey of Richardson scholarship.

94. Bell, Inglis F., and Donald Baird. *The English Novel
     1578-1956: A Checklist of Twentieth-Century Criticisms*.
     Denver: Swallow, 1958. Pp. 107-10.

     A very selected number of the most general criticism.

95. Carroll, John. "Richardson." In *The English Novel:
     Select Bibliographical Guides*. London: Oxford Univ.
     Press, 1974. Pp. 56-70.

     A critical survey of Richardson's career and reputation.

96. ⸺⸺. "Samuel Richardson." In *The New Cambridge
     Bibliography of English Literature*. Ed. George Watson.
     Cambridge: Cambridge Univ. Press, 1969-74. II, 917-25.

The most recent revision and updating of this survey
of Richardson material.

97.   Cordasco, Francesco. *The 18th Century Novel: A Handlist
      of General Histories and Articles of the Last Twenty-
      Five Years with a Notice of Bibliographical Guides.*
      Brooklyn: Long Island Univ. Press, 1950. Rpt. in
      Eighteenth Century Bibliographies. Metuchen, N.J.:
      Scarecrow Press, 1970.

      A brief and often unreliable list of references.

98.   ———. *Samuel Richardson: A List of Critical Studies
      Published from 1896 to 1946.* 1948; rpt. Metuchen,
      N.J.: Scarecrow Press, 1970.

      Errors and a lack of annotation make this often in-
      complete listing less useful than it might have been.

      Reviewed: *PQ*, 29 (1950), 294-96 (unfavorable).

99.   Clifford, J.L. "The Eighteenth Century." In *Con-
      temporary Literary Scholarship: A Critical Review.*
      Ed. L. Leary. New York: Appleton-Century-Crofts,
      1958. Pp. 83-168.

      A concise, analytical survey of the critical scholar-
      ship in this period, with a short bibliography on
      Richardson criticism.

100. Downs, Brian W. "Samuel Richardson." In *The Cambridge
      Bibliography of English Literature.* New York: Mac-
      millan Company, 1941. II, 514-17.

      A useful but general survey of Richardson materials.

101. Draper, John W. *Eighteenth Century English Aesthetics:
      A Bibliography.* 1931; rpt. New York: Octagon Books,
      Inc., 1968.

      Often useful for discovering items concerning the
      background during Richardson's period.

102. Ewen, Frederic. *Bibliography of Eighteenth Century
      English Literature.* New York: Columbia Univ. Press,
      1935.

      A selective but incomplete list of Richardson
      references.

103. Gettman, Royal A. "Samuel Richardson." In *The Cambridge*

Bibliography of English Literature. Cambridge: Cambridge Univ. Press, 1957. V, 450-51.

A revision and updating survey of Richardson materials.

104. Hannaford, Richard. "Samuel Richardson: A Checklist of Criticism, 1945-1976." *Bulletin of Bibliography,* 34 (1977), Pt. I, 14-20, 51; Pt. II, 105-114.

A briefly annotated listing of modern Richardson criticism.

* McKillop, Alan D. *Samuel Richardson, Printer and Novelist.* See #550, pp. 321-333.

A detailed bibliography compiled in the 1930's which includes a list of first editions as well as adaptations, abridgements, and parodies of the novels.

105. Palmer, Helen H., and Anne Jane Dyson. *English Novel Explication: Criticisms to 1972.* Hamden, Conn.: The Shoe String Press, 1973. Pp. 321-33.

Covers very general criticisms from 1958 to 1972 updating Bell and Baird's *The English Novel* (#94).

106. Rochedieu, Charles A. *Bibliography of French Translations of English Works 1700-1800.* Introduction by Donald F. Bond. Chicago: Univ. of Chicago Press, 1948.

A brief introduction describes French methods of translation; includes a bibliography of Richardson's translated works.

107. Sale, William M., Jr. *Samuel Richardson: A Bibliographical Record of His Literary Career with Historical Notes.* 1936; rpt. Hamden, Conn.: Archon Books, 1969.

A descriptive bibliography of Richardson's works, including a chronology of his work and books inspired by his novels. The three-part bibliography lists the novels, edited works, pamphlets and works written in collaboration, and the contributions Richardson made to periodicals; it also notes those works which capitalized on the popularity of Richardson's novels up to Richardson's death.

Reviewed: *JEGP,* 36 (1937), 438-42.
        YWES, 17 (1936), 220-21.

108. Sherbo, Arthur. "Eighteenth-Century British Fiction in
     Print: An Uncritical Census." *CE*, 21 (1959), 105-11.

   A review of eighteenth-century anthologies and texts
   with an analysis of the reasons for studying eighteenth-
   century literature; provides a list of titles in print,
   including Richardson's.

109. Tobin, James E. *Eighteenth Century English Literature
     and Its Cultural Background.* 1939; rpt. New York:
     Biblo and Tannen, 1967.

   A general study of the period, covering such items
   as criticism, memoirs, poetry, and prose.

II.
Eighteenth-Century Criticism

A. CHRONOLOGY

1740

110. *The History of the Works of the Learned.* "The Negotia-
        tions of Sir Thomas Roe," 1 (May 1740), 346-60.

        A review article, praising Richardson's work as an
        editor of Roe's papers and letters.

111. ————. "*Pamela; or Virtue Rewarded,*" 2 (Dec. 1740),
        433-39.

        A review of *Pamela* which finds the work moving and
        entertaining, but considers that the "Language is not
        altogether unexceptionable, but in several Places sinks
        below the Idea we are constrained to form of the Heroine
        who is supposed to write it."

*   *Weekly Miscellany.* "To My Worthy Friend, the Author of
        Pamela." See #91.

        This first prominent notice of *Pamela* praises the
        novel for its truthfulness, simplicity, suspense, in-
        struction, and morality.

112. ————, 13 Dec. 1740.

        Published the "Preface by the Editor [Richardson]" of
        Pamela.

1741

113. *Bibliothèque britannique,* 17 (April-June 1741), 27-60;
        esp. 59-60.

        A summary of *Pamela* which also announces that the
        French translation is soon to be published.

114. [Fielding, Henry.] *An Apology for the Life of Mrs.*

Shamela Andrews. London, 1741.

Shamela is a travesty of the moral code found in
Richardson's novel. Fielding parodies the "warm" scenes
in *Pamela*, dislikes Richardson's "low," detailed realism,
and criticizes the idea of a serving maid marrying a
gentleman.

115. [Giffard, Henry.] *Pamela. A Comedy.* London, 1741.

Although not specifically criticism of Richardson,
this and the other dramatizations do help reveal the
popularity of the *Pamela* vogue. Giffard's play was
performed seventeen times in 1741 and again in 1742; it
was advertised in the *London Daily Post and General
Advertiser* for 23 Sept., 6 Nov., 9 Nov. 1741; *Daily Post*
for 17 Nov. 1741; and in the *Daily Gazetteer* for 17 Nov.
1741. A Mr. Edge revised this play into an opera, *Pamela:
Or, Virtue Rewarded* (Newcastle, 1742), and a second play
which followed Richardson's text more closely than
Giffard's (though apparently never performed) was published on 16 Nov. 1741.

116. *Göttingische Zeitungen von Gelehrten Sachen*, 23 Feb.
       1741, pp. 129-30.

Asserts that Marivaux's *Marianne* must have been a
model for *Pamela*.

117. [Haywood, Eliza.] *Anti-Pamela: or, Feign'd Innocence
       Detected; In a Series of Syrena's Adventures.* London,
       1741.

This is a parody of *Pamela* in which Syrena reveals,
again, the alleged hypocrisy and false modesty inherent
in Richardson's novel. This is one of the first of the
anti-*Pamela*s which often included Richardson's heroine
in the title in order to capitalize on his success.
For a more thorough discussion and list of the anti-
*Pamela*s see Kreissman (#944) and McKillop (#550).

118. [Kelly, John.] *Pamela's Conduct in High Life.* 2 vols.
       London, 1741 (I, May; II, Sept.).

This is the first of the spurious continuations of
Pamela. Of special interest are Kelly's remarks about
Pamela; he notes that only lechers criticize the book,
that *Shamela* is "low Humour," and that *Pamela Censured*
is a "Piece of Curlism."

119. *The Life of Pamela*. London, 1741.

An imitation of *Pamela*, retelling the story in the
third person. References in the notes to the narrative
criticize Richardson for his self-praise, for "monstrous
Inconsistencies" in Pamela's language, for his tedious
details, and for his lack of understanding for "the
Behavior and Conversation of the Nobility."

120. *Memoirs of the Life of Lady H-- The Celebrated Pamela*.
London, 1741.

A simple imitation of *Pamela*, utilizing the popular
identification of the heroine with Lady Hesilrige, and
patterning Pamela upon the literary type of a Patient
Griselda. Moralists could have little objection to
this story since, here, Pamela is a model of decorous
virtue and refined manners. The story is written "to
enforce the Practice of Virtue by an Example of the
Reward attending it."

121. *Pamela Censured*. London, 1741.

This is written by a moral opponent of the novel who,
characteristically, quotes at length the most objec-
tionable passages; the writer also suggests that Richardson modeled his novel after French romances in which
moral virtue is more honestly encouraged.

122. *Pamela in High Life: or, Virtue Rewarded*. London,
1741.

One of the other continuations of Richardson's novel
which takes up Pamela's adventures where the *High Life*
left off.

123. *Pamela; ou La Vertu Récompensée*. Traduit de l'anglois.
2 vols. London, 1741; 4 vols. Amsterdam, 1743.

This is the first French translation of *Pamela*; it is
especially significant because the translator's Preface
asserts that the work was done with Richardson's advice
and assistance; indeed, the sketches of the "fine" ladies
who visit Pamela first appear in this French version before being added to later English revisions.

124. Parry, James. *The True Anti-Pamela; or, Memoirs of Mr.
James Parry*. London, 1741.

Another of the productions which tried to capitalize
upon the success of *Pamela*; the book bears no resemblance

to Richardson's novel, but the Preface does note that
the original Pamela "is a virtuous Character" and "a
poor innocent Virgin, [who] withstood all the Attacks
of a Person of Fortune."

125.   [Povey, Charles.]   *The Virgin in Eden: or, The State
       of Innocency.*   London, 1741.

This conscientious Puritan develops his story about a
really virtuous virgin, but takes time to attack *Pamela*
at length: pages 68-79 are devoted specifically to an
exposure of *Pamela*. He especially decries licence
dressed as virtue, and he therefore wrote his story to
offset Richardson's inflammatory tale.

                              1742

126.   *L'anti-Pamela, Ou la fausse innocence découverte dans
       les avantures de Syrène.*   Amsterdam, 1742.

This French version of Haywood's novel includes a
French Preface which discusses the inconsistency and
complexity of Pamela's character.

127.   *Bibliothèque françoise*, 35, No. 2 (1742), 319-23.

Finds *Pamela* interesting and even ingenious, but
criticizes the current notion that the novel reflects
English virtue as opposed to French licence.

128.   *Bibliothèque raisonnée*, 28 (April-June 1742), 417-27.

A hostile review of *Pamela*, criticizing morally and
artistically Pamela's character.

129.   Desfontaines, Pierre F.G.   *Observations sur les écrits
       modernes*, 29 (June 1742), 70-71, 193-214.

An important early critic of Richardson who understood
the part the letter-form plays in Richardson's technique;
he found Pamela a complex character, and he admired the
difference between letters "written to the moment" and
memoirs recalled years later. Two years later, however,
his appreciation of Richardson diminished; he placed
Don Quixote and *Joseph Andrews* above Richardson's work.
[See his "Lettre d'une dame anglaise," prefixed to the
Avantures de Joseph Andrews [Amsterdam, (1744).]

130. [Fielding, Henry.] *The History of the Adventures of
      Joseph Andrews, and of His Friend Mr. Abraham Adams.*
      London, 1742.

      Fielding renews his attack on *Pamela* through his
      concept of "The Ridiculous." Fielding most effectively
      parodied Richardson's novel by revealing, through the
      careful delineation of his characters, the unethical
      basis of Richardson's supposed morality. Joseph's
      virtue is demonstrated to be affectation, and he is
      only less culpable than Pamela because she is hypo-
      critical as well. Fanny also contrasts Pamela in that
      her open avowal of love reveals clearly her counterpart's
      concealed preoccupation with sex.

131. *Lettre à Monsieur l'Abbé Des Fontaines sur "Pamela."*
      Amiens, 7 Aug. 1742.

      The author considers that Richardson is a rival of
      French novelists and that he learned several lessons
      from them. He also attacks Desfontaines for submitting
      to the Anglophiles by supporting a novel which, in the
      prefatory letter (by Freval), insults France.

132. *Lettre sur "Pamela."* Londres, 1742. Rpt. The Life &
      Times of Seven Major British Writers. Richardsoniana
      VIII. New York and London: Garland Publishing, Inc.,
      1975.

      This French critic (McKillop suggests it was Abbé
      Marquet) notes how readers of the novel are later
      ashamed of themselves for being affected. A jeering
      review of the novel's plot is made, and considerable
      fun is also made of Pamela's staying on to finish Mr.
      B's waistcoat at the risk of being violated. The
      novel's improprieties of language are noted, and the
      author hopes that the novel does not give a true picture
      of English manners.

133. Stolpe, R.M. *Dagspressen i Danmark.* Copenhagen, 1881.
      IV, 131-32.

      Quotes two Danish reviews of *Pamela* from the *Laerde
      Tidender* of 1742 and 1743, exalting the heroine.

134. *Universal Spectator and Weekly Journal.* "Pamela the
      Second," 24 April 1742.

      The Introduction to this dramatic poem refers to
      Pamela as an example of a story which reaffirms "the

innate Virtue of a Sensible Maid," and which rightfully
attacks "that barbarous Part of Modish Gallantry, of
Gentlemen endeavouring to seduce Women of inferior
Fortune." See #550, pp. 68-69.

1743

135. Anchersen, J.P. *Pamela eller Den Belnønede Dyd, først
     skrevet i Engelsk, og nu i Dansk oversat af L.* 4 vols.
     Copenhagen, 1743-46.

     Anchersen's Preface to this translation especially
     deplores the severe judgments being made on *Pamela*; he
     notes that it has been praised from the pulpit.

136. Chesnaye-Desbois, François Alexandre Aubert de la. "III.
     Lettre." In *Lettres amusantes et critiques sur les
     romans en general, Anglois et François, tant anciens
     que modernes*. Paris: Gissey, Bordelet, David, 1743.

     A long discussion, focusing upon the flaws in *Pamela*;
     the author concentrates upon the maxims incorporated in
     the novel's Preface in order to demonstrate that these
     maxims actually reveal the novel's weaknesses.

137. Fielding, Henry. *Miscellanies.* 3 vols. London, 1743.
     I, 91 (compare the Preface, iii).

     Includes a brief reference to *Pamela* in "Part of
     Juvenal's Sixth Satire, Modernized in Burlesque Verse":

             But say you, if each private Family
             Doth not produce a perfect *Pamela*;
             Must ev'ry Female bear the Blame
             Of one low private Strumpet's Shame?

1744

138. *Freymüthige Nachrichten*, I (1744), 19-20, 106-07.

     Repeats an earlier criticism (see #313) that women
     should have their reading restricted to the Bible,
     religious books, cookbooks, and *Pamela*, and also com-
     ments critically upon the anti-*Pamela*s of France and
     England.

139. Holberg, Ludvig. *Moralske tanker*. Copenhagen, 1744.

Holberg recognizes the extremes to which critics and
defenders alike have gone in evaluating the novel, but
sides with defenders of *Pamela* by asserting that Pamela
should be considered a girl of religious convictions
who is not hypocritical. He believes the book demon-
strates "just Sentiments" and portrays "an Example of
Virtue and Honour." Dr. Peter Shaw appropriated Holberg's comments in *The Reflector* (1750) and published
them as his own.

1745

140. Miller, James. *The Picture*. London, 1745.

In this play an irate father criticizes *Pamela* as one
of those works which ruin young people, an example of
how Richardson could be criticized on moral grounds for
writing prose fiction.

141. W., A. *Enormous Abomination of the Hoop-Petticoat*.
London, 1745. P. 4.

The writer criticizes prose fiction on moral grounds
and includes *Pamela* as one of the works distracting
Christians from prayers and the Bible.

1747

142. Fielding, Henry. *Jacobite's Journal*, 2 Jan. and 5 March
1747-48. Rpt. in McKillop #550, pp. 167-68.

Fielding praises *Clarissa* for its penetration and
power to raise and alarm the "Passions."

1748

143. *The Parallel; or, Pilkington and Phillips Compared*.
London, 1748.

One of the first criticisms of *Pamela*, attacking the
book's principles of education and lamenting how servant
wenches will now wish to become fine ladies.

144. Warburton, William. Preface to Volumes III and IV
(1748) of Richardson's *Clarissa*. Rpt. *Prefaces to*

Fiction. Ed. with an introduction by Benjamin Boyce.
The Augustan Reprint Society, Pub. No. 32. Los
Angeles: William Andrews Clark Memorial Library, Univ.
of California, 1952.

Warburton claimed in this Preface that Richardson had
followed French writers in his construction of character
and manners; Richardson denied this and dropped the
Preface from subsequent editions.

1749

145. Fielding, Sarah. *Remarks on "Clarissa."* London: F.
Robinson, 1749. Rpt. *Three Criticisms of Richardson's
Fiction 1749-1754.* The Life & Times of Seven Major
British Writers. Richardsoniana XIII. New York and
London: Garland Publishing, Inc., 1974.

Recounts at length the contemporary criticisms of the
novel as the writer encountered them in coffee shops,
in families, and from acquaintances.

146. *Freymüthige Nachrichten*, 6 (1749), 107.

A critic answers Holberg's criticisms of *Pamela* (#139)
which had been circulating through Denmark, France, and
Germany.

147. *Die Geschichte der Clarissa, eines vornehem Frauenzimmers.*
"Vorrede." 2nd edn. Göttingen, 1749.

The author refers to Haller as the most capable judge
of art in Germany and the one who especially influenced
the publisher to translate *Clarissa*.

148. Hagedorn, Friedrich von. *Poetische Werke*. Hamburg,
1825. V, 110-11.

The poet noted in a letter of 28 Sept. 1749 that
Clarissa portrayed a heightened sense of virtue and
vice, and although secondary characters were understandable to ordinary readers, the same was not true
for such inspired creations as Clarissa, Anna Howe,
or Lovelace.

149. [Haller, Albrecht von.] "Clarissa." *Gentlemen's Magazine*, 19 (1749), 245-46, 345-49.

Prints an analysis of Clarissa's character, emphasizing
Richardson's style, power of description, and exalted

sentiments. This is essentially a translation from the
Bibliothèque raisonnée, 42 (1749), 324-36; a German
translation is in *Sammlung kleiner Hallerisher Schriften*,
2nd edn. (Bern, 1772), I, 293-315. Richardson's reply
to Haller's criticism was added through an extensive
footnote, published with the second installment, in
Gentleman's Magazine and headed "Answers to the Objections"; the whole discussion is incorporated into the
Postscript of *Clarissa*.

1750

150. *Freymüthige Nachrichten*, 7 (1750), 219-21, 227-28, 237-
38, 245-47.

A long debate of poetic justice in *Clarissa*, paral-
leling the discussion in Richardson's Postscript and
his correspondence.

151. ————, 7 (1750), 406.

Quotes from Brockes' poem (#274) praising *Pamela*, a
poem which represents the most extensive defense of the
novel in Germany.

152. *The History of Charlotte Summers*. London, 1750. I, 221.

A novel in imitation of Fielding, yet noting, with
exaggeration, Richardson's brand of melancholy--
especially as it appears in *Clarissa*.

1751

153. Clément, Pierre. *Les cinq années littéraires*. Berlin,
1756. II, 28, 435.

Clarissa is not as fully appreciated in France because
of the lengthy moral digressions, and he finds *Grandison*
"une histoire tour à tour amusante & ennuyeuse."

154. *Correspondance littéraire*. Paris, 1877. II, 24-25.

In a letter of 25 Jan. 1751, the writer compares
Richardson's characterization and subtle analysis with
his tediousness--a common French evaluation.

155. Gellert, Christian Fürchtegott. "Preface." From
Briefe. Leipzig, 1751. P. 117. Trans. *History of*

the Swedish Countess of G. London, 1757. P. ix.

Briefly praises Richardson's characterization in *Clarissa*; it is typical of criticism by Richardson's early German admirers. Gellert's praise is equivalent to Diderot's in *Éloge* (#197) and more fully represents the German response to Richardson than Diderot's does the French. Gellert later revised his material to include praise of *Grandison* in *Sämtliche Schriften* (Leipzig, 1839), IV, 75.

156.   La Porte, Joseph de. *Observations sur la littérature moderne*, 4 (1751), 109-24; 5 (1751), 290; 7 (1752), 116-38.

A sympathetic appraisal of *Clarissa* but considers English fiction, in general, too diffuse; Prévost should have reduced the text still more.

157.   Prévost d'Exiles, Antoine François. "Introduction." In *Lettres angloises; ou, Histoire de Miss Clarisse Harlove*. 12 parts in 6 vols. London [Paris], 1751; VII, supplement (Lyon, 1762).

Richardson had this Introduction translated (FM XV, 2, fols. 62-72) and was annoyed that Prévost had omitted from this French edition "some of the most affecting parts." Prévost explains in his Introduction that he adapted the novel to fit French taste: "Par le droit suprème de toute Ecrivain qui cherche à plaire dans sa langue naturelle j'ai changé ou supprimé ceque je n'ai pas jugé conforme à cette vûe."

1752

158.   Fielding, Henry. *Covent-Garden Journal*, No. 10 (4 Feb. 1752).

Fielding, who understood the difference between the questionable virtue of a Pamela and the heroicism of a Clarissa, praises Richardson in contrast with censure of Rabelais and Aristophanes.

159.   *Monthly Review*, 7 (1752), 470.

Reveals some condescension towards *Pamela* in a very brief and passing reference in a discussion of *The History of Betty Barnes*.

160. Stinstra, Johannes. "Preface." In *Clarissa. Of De
       Histoire van eene Jonge Juffer. Uit het Engelsch naar
       den Derden Druk vertaald door Joannes Stinstra.* 8
       vols. Harlingen, 1752-55.

   The Preface emphasizes the novel's ethical qualities,
   but it also focuses upon the characterization of Clarissa
   and her essential probability and naturalness.

                              1753

161. Collier, Jane. *Essay on the Art of Ingeniously Tor-
       menting.* Dublin, 1753. Pp. 42, 43, 105.

   A satirical discourse on conduct between husband and
   wife, parent and child, master and servant, friend and
   acquaintance, the book includes a comment on "old
   Harlowe" who enjoys showering upon Clarissa such items
   as money, clothes, or jewels when all she desires is
   "kind looks, and kind words!" Richardson and Fielding
   are equated as "good ethical" writers.

162. *Correspondance littéraire.* Paris, 1877. II, 248
       (1753).

   Reflects a shift in the critical appraisals of Richardson; his subtle shadings of style are now praised, and
   Clarissa is especially admired.

163. *Dublin Spy*, 5 Nov. 1753.

   Richardson tried to avoid Irish piracy of *Pamela* and
   sent 1500 sets of the novel to Ireland with Bacon,
   thereby incurring violent invective for having deprived
   Irish printers and stationers of their livelihood.

164. *Gentleman's Magazine*, 23 (1753), 466-67.

   A reprinting of an article from Arthur Murphy's *Gray's
   Inn Journal* (31 Oct. 1753) which defends Richardson
   against the Irish piracies.

165. ———, 23 (1753), 511-13.

   The first printed criticism of *Grandison*, the article
   discusses Richardson's understanding of the polite world,
   its men and manners; it commends the book for its interesting scenes and affecting situations.

166.   [Smythies, Miss, of Colchester.]   *The Stage-Coach.*
       London, 1753.   I, 71.

       A disciple of Richardson reveals through one of her
       characters that Richardson's and Fielding's fictions
       are both beginning to be considered worthy of serious
       attention.

                              1754

167.   *The Book of Conversation and Behavior.*   London, 1754.

       This is typical of the books published on the model
       of Richardson; the dedication was to Richardson, and
       the author typically admired the novelist's morality.

168.   *Critical Remarks on "Sir Charles Grandison," "Clarissa"*
       and "Pamela" ... *by a Lover of Virtue.*   London, 1754.
       Rpt. Alan D. McKillop, ed.   The Augustan Reprint
       Society, No. 21.   Los Angeles, 1950.   Also, *Three*
       Criticisms of Richardson's Fiction 1749-1754.   The
       Life & Times of Seven Major British Writers.   Richard-
       soniana XIII.   New York and London: Garland Publishing,
       Inc., 1974.

       This is a highly critical review of Richardson's
       novels, finding him responsible for corrupting the
       public taste and the English language (through coined
       words) and for encouraging a debilitating romantic
       temperament.

169.   Dodd, Dr. William.   *The Sisters.*   *Novelist's Magazine,*
       5 (1781), 103 (first published in 1754).

       Richardson's famous heroines and the precedents they
       set are discussed by silly novel-reading women.

170.   Lessing, Gotthold Ephraim.   *Sämtliche Schriften.*   Ed.
       Lachmann and Muncker.   Stuttgart, 1890.   V, 399, 433;
       VII, 18-19.

       He reviewed *Grandison* in 1754 and put it in the same
       high category with *Clarissa.*

171.   *Monthly Review.*   "Sir Charles Grandison," 10 (Jan. 1754),
       70-71.

       A review which stresses the book's good sense, admira-
       ble sentiment, and correct observations and moral com-

ments; it notes equally the absurdity of the letter-
writing scheme as well as Richardson's tedious verbosity.

172. Plummer, Francis. *A Candid Examination of the "History
      of Sir Charles Grandison."* London, 1754. Rpt. *Three
      Criticisms of Richardson's Fiction 1749-1754.* The Life
      & Times of Seven Major British Writers. Richardsoniana
      XIII. New York and London: Garland Publishing, Inc.,
      1974.

      This pamphlet praises the Italian portion of the novel
      and the scenes with Harriet Byron, but it criticizes
      Richardson's excessive length and the novel's lapses
      from good taste.

1755

173. Fielding, Henry. "Preface." In *The Journal of a Voyage
      to Lisbon.* 1755. Ed. Harold E. Pagliaro. New York:
      Nardon Press, 1963. Pp. 29-30.

      Fielding alludes to Richardson's practice of including
      self-praise in the prefatory material of his novels, and
      he comments also on Richardson's assertion that enter-
      tainment should be only a "secondary consideration in a
      romance."

174. Kennicott, Benjamin. "Preface." In *A Collection of the
      Moral and Instructive Sentiments.* See #20, pp. iii-x.

      He suggests that Richardson's works will be as lasting,
      as admired, and as beneficial as Plutarch's.

175. [Kidgell, John.] *The Card.* London, 1755. I, xii-xiv;
      II, 94, 295.

      Kidgell burlesques Richardson's epistolary technique
      and satirizes Sir Charles' attitude toward dueling; he
      intimates that Sir Charles would be a suitable escort
      for Dulcinea del Toboso.

176. *Monthly Review,* 12 (1755), 117-21.

      Notes that Kidgell's satire is directed primarily
      against the "exceptionable parts in the plan, characters,
      and stile" of *Grandison.*

177. Prévost d'Exiles, Antoine François. "Introduction." In

Nouvelles lettres angloises, ou Histoire du Chevalier Grandisson. 8 parts in 4 vols. Amsterdam, 1755-56.

He especially praises Richardson's genius and asserts that based upon his pleasure at translating *Clarissa*, he knows his time is not wasted in translating *Grandison*.

178. ———. "Spectacles. Paméla." *Journal étranger*, 1 (Feb. 1755), 176-200.

Primarily an analysis of Goldoni's play *Paméla*, this review also considers Richardson's work to be morally corrupt.

1756

179. *Critical Review*, 1 (April 1756), 224-25.

Discusses an extract from Fulke Greville's *Maxims, Characters, and Reflections* (1756), revealing Greville's severe evaluation of Richardson's work; Richardson is often "the most minute, fine, delicate observer of human nature ... but he often carries that refinement into puerility."

180. ———. "The Paths of Virtue Delineated; or, the History in Miniature of the celebrated *Pamela*, *Clarissa Harlowe*, and *Sir Charles Grandison*, familiarised and adapted to the Capacities of Youth," 1 (May 1756), 315-16.

A review article which esteems Richardson for his virtue and religion; it is happy to find the books now available in such a form, since few entertaining books are so well adapted to the instruction of young people. The compliments are possibly inserted at Smollett's request.

181. Greville, Fulke. *Critical, Satyrical, and Moral Maxims, Characters, and Reflections.* London, 1756.

Includes a commentary on Richardson, mingling praise with severe criticism. For example, Richardson "is in many particulars the most minute, fine, delicate, observer of human nature I ever met with, the most refined and just in his sentiments; but he often carries that refinement into puerility, and that justness into tastelessness."

182. *Journal encyclopédique*, 2 (Feb. 1756), 32-38.

     A rejoinder to the criticism in the *Mercure de France* (#183), pointing out that objections to *Grandison* apply to the original but not to Prévost's translation.

183. *Mercure de France*, 1 (1756), 50-78.

     Asserts that Richardson did create the new genre of the moral novel, but like the negative response in the *Monthly Review* (#184), it criticizes *Grandison* for being an obsolete romance.

184. *Monthly Review*, 14 (1756), 581-82.

     A review of an abridged edition of Richardson's three novels, *The Paths of Virtue Delineated*; the *Monthly Review* was usually critical of Richardson, and here refers negatively to his "twenty or thirty volumes (the Duce knows how many of 'em there are)."

185. Warton, Joseph. "Sect. V." In *An Essay on the Genius and Writings of Pope*. 2 vols. 4th ed., corrected. London, 1782. Rpt. New York: Garland Publishing, Inc., 1970. I, 286.

     Considers that Clementina's madness in *Grandison* is particularly well represented, perhaps better portrayed than Lear's and comparable to Orestes' in Euripides. Richardson quoted this praise in an advertisement sheet for the fourth edition of the novel (see Sale, #107, p. 91).

1757

186. *Correspondance littéraire*. Paris, 1877. III, 161; IV, 24-25.

     This marks a further shift in French criticism, illustrating that for some, Prévost's abridged translations of Richardson's novels are no longer satisfactory; it also marks the only praise by a French critic of Monod's literal translation of *Grandison*.

187. Fielding, Sarah. *Lives of Cleopatra and Octavia*. London, 1757. Pp. ii-iii.

     In her introduction, Sarah Fielding applauds equally the "rural Innocence" of *Joseph Andrews* and "the

inimitable Virtues" of *Grandison* as examples which excite "our insatiable Curiosity for Novels or Romances."

188.   *Monthly Review*, 17 (July 1757), 47–50.

A review of Goldoni's comedy based on *Pamela*; suggests
Goldoni improves on Pamela's characterization by giving
her knowledge of her true father as a rebel Scotch nobleman and thus making her "virtue" understandable.

1758

189.   Marmontel, Jean François. "Essai sur les romans."
       Mercure de France (Aug. 1758), 79–95. Rpt. *Oeuvres*.
       Paris, 1819. III, 558–96.

A favorable review of *Grandison*, reversing the earlier
negative response in the same journal (#183).

1759

190.   "Jenny: Or, The Female Fortune Hunter." In *The Theatre of
       Love. A Collection of Novels, None of which were ever
       printed before*. London, 1759. Pp. 229–48.

This is a satire of *Pamela* in which Jenny reads the
novel, tries to imitate her, and finds herself ignored
by a baronet's son. This novel is, according to
McKillop, typical of the "female Quixote" theme fashionable in many novels of the eighteen fifties (#550, p.
83).

1760

191.   Diderot, Denis. *Oeuvres complètes*. Ed. Assezat and
       Tourneux. Paris, 1876. P. 514: to Mlle. Voland, 20
       Oct. 1760.

A balanced criticism of his reading of *Clarissa*, depre-
ciating the extremes to which other critics of the
novel have gone.

192.   Gottsched, Johann Christophe. *Handlexikon oder kurzge-
       fasstes Wörterbuch der schönen Wissenschaften und
       freyen künste*. Leipzig, 1760.

In an article on *Pamela*, only Goldoni's dramatization, *Paméla nubile*, is discussed; the latter was disseminated more widely throughout Europe than the novel itself.

193. *Imperial Magazine*, 1 (1760), 686-87.

A criticism of Richardson's novels, illustrating the reaction against his high popularity in the 1750's.

194. *Louisa; or, Virtue in Distress*. London, 1760. P. x.

The author admits following Richardson's pattern of plot and characterization.

195. Lyttleton, George, Lord. *Dialogues of the Dead*. London, 1760.

Richardson is praised for his characters and portrayal of domestic virtues; he is awarded greater merit than Marivaux or Fielding.

1761

196. *Critical Review* (Sept., 1761). Rpt. *Court Miscellany*, 2 (1766), 241-44; *Journal étranger*, 12 (1761), 201-11 [trans. Suard]; *London Chronicle*, 12 (20-22 Oct. 1761), 386-88.

A long comparison between Richardson and Rousseau, based upon a discussion of *Eloisa*; determines the slant of much later criticism, featuring Rousseau as more sentimental but refined and Richardson as more natural, interesting, and dramatic.

197. Diderot, Denis. "Éloge de Richardson." *Journal étranger*, 8 (Jan. 1761), 5-38. Rpt. *Oeuvres esthétiques*. Ed. Paul Vernière. Paris: Editions Garnier Frères, 1959.

The most important eighteenth-century criticism of Richardson, giving Diderot's observations on Richardson's genius and originality and an analysis of his novels: "Richardson ... qui élevent l'esprit, qui touchent l'ame, qui respirent partout l'amour du bien ..."; for the European response to Diderot's praise see McKillop #550 (fn. 151, p. 274) and for the background of the *Éloge* see Diderot's letters to Mlle. Volland: *Oeuvres*, XIX, 47, 49-50, 55, 61, 70 (letters of 17, 22, 28 Sept., 2, 19 Oct. 1761).

198. [Kenrick, William.] *Monthly Review*, 25 (1761), 260.

      A one-paragraph, general comparison of Richardson with
      Rousseau, holding the two evenly similar; the *Monthly*
      usually was inclined to criticize Richardson.

199. *London Chronicle*, 2-4 July 1761.

      One of the obituaries, emphasizing Richardson's
      generosity and benevolence.

200. Ridley, James. *James Lovegrove*. London, 1761. I, 171.

      Praises Richardson's "System of Ethicks."

201. Smollett, Tobias. *Continuation of the Complete History
      of England*. London, 1761. IV, 128.

      Appraises Richardson, finding his aligning of the
      passions with virtue meritorious in the three novels
      and noting in the novelist "a sublime system of ethics,
      an amazing knowledge, and command of the human nature."

                              1762

202. Hervey, James. *A Treatise on the Religious Education
      of Daughters*. Boston, 1762. P. 15.

      An acquaintance of Richardson's, Hervey was an evan-
      gelical Puritan who severely judged literature, and yet
      he included *Clarissa* in his program of education as "a
      Book admirably calculated to instruct and entertain."

203. *A New and General Biographical Dictionary*. London, 1762.
      X, 142-43.

      Recognizes Richardson's virtuous motives for writing,
      but finds the novels do not always have the effect
      intended; he puts too much reliance on Shaftesbury's
      system of human nature.

                              1763

204. *The Peregrinations of Jeremiah Grant*. London: 1763.
      P. 181.

      A sea-captain owns he is well acquainted with Richard-
      son's characters and believes Sir Charles "the perfection

of human invention"; a typical early response to Richardson.

205.   *The School for Wives*.   London, 1763.   Pp. 35-36.

Characters in *Grandison* are models for characters in
this story who also refer specifically to them.

1764

206.   *Anecdotes of Polite Literature*.   London, 1764.   II, ii,
       78-79.

Gives Rousseau much more merit as a novelist than
Richardson, who is considered "tedious," "trifling,"
"verbose," and "uninteresting."

1766

207.   [Jephson, Robert.]   *The Batchelor*.   No. 4, 12 April
       1766.   Rpt. Dublin, 1769.   I, 11.   Originally published
       under the pseudonym "Jeoffrey Wagstaffe" in the *Dublin
       Mercury*.

A description of a rich widow who, in writing a novel,
says she does so in the manner of a Clarissa or a Grandison; the writer shall be a Harriet Byron who blushes at
the escapades of a Clementina running after the virtuous
Sir Charles.

208.   *Universal Museum*.   "A Critical Examination of the Re-
       spective Merits of Voltaire, Rousseau, Richardson,
       Smollett, and Fielding," N.S., 2 (Aug. 1766), 391-93.
       Rpt. *London Chronicle*, 20 (6-9 Sept. 1766), 247;
       Royal Magazine, 15 (Sept. 1766), 146-49.

A comparison of Richardson with Rousseau: the one more
"pathetic," the other more "florid."

1767

209.   Kelly, Hugh.   *Memoirs of a Magdalen*.   London, 1767.   Rpt.
       Novelist's Magazine, 7 (1782), 33.

The hero-seducer of the story writes to his friend
how the latter is in fact imitating the character of

Belford, but that *he* should not consider *himself* "such
another contemptible blockhead as Lovelace."

1768

210. *High Life*. Dublin, 1768. P. 290.

The author laments the want of Richardson's genius
for describing a story of seduction and abduction;
another example (of many) of writers trying to imitate
Richardson's style and themes.

1769

211. Griffith, Mrs. Elizabeth. *The Delicate Distress*. Lon-
     don, 1769. II, 113-14.

Pamela is referred to as an example which, to "un-
tutored minds," may raise illusions of grandeur; Mrs.
Griffith warns against such behavior.

212. *The Masquerade*. London, 1769. I, 50-51.

An abducted heroine reads *Grandison* and is afraid her
abductor will turn out a Sir Hargrave.

1771

213. Dorat, Claude Joseph. "Idées sur le romans." Prefixed
     to *Les sacrifices de l'amour*. 1771; rpt. Avignon,
     1793. I, 3-14.

A more balanced appraisal of Richardson's genius for
carefully delineated characters and strong, concrete
detail.

1772

214. *The Feelings of the Heart*. London, 1772. I, 37.

A young rustic woman reads *Pamela* and then fears her
suitor resembles Mr. B.

215. *Letters Concerning the Present State of England*. "A

Catalogue of the Most Celebrated Writers of the
Present Age." London, 1772. Pp. 357-58, 393-94.

Praises Richardson and Fielding as the supreme writers
of "delineation of character" and "comic romance," respectively; the author boldly compares them with Shakespeare.

1773

216. *Letters by Several Eminent Persons Deceased.* Ed. John
Duncombe. London, 1773. II, 174-254.

Richardson's defense of his ending for *Clarissa* initiated a long discussion of poetic justice by William Duncombe, Joseph Highmore, and George Jeffreys.

217. Mercier, Louis Sébastien. *Du Théâtre.* Amsterdam, 1773.
P. 326. See also *Éloges et discours philosophiques.*
Amsterdam, 1776. Pp. 236-37 n. *Mon Bonnet de Nuit.*
Amsterdam, 1784. I, 206; II, 191, 234. *Fictions
morales.* Paris, 1792. III, 189-92, 200-02.

Even more enthusiastic than Diderot, he claims Richardson must always be the favorite reading of men of taste
and distinction and that *Clarissa* is superior to the
Aeneid.

218. *Pamela Howard.* London, 1773. I, 90-91; II, 112.

The character, Bouvery, is not only based upon Lovelace but alludes to him; he later meets the Grandisons
and prefers Lady G. to Harriet Byron.

1774

219. Brooke, Henry. *Juliet Grenville: or, The History of
the Human Heart.* London, 1774. III, 91-92.

The heroine of this novel especially criticizes
Richardson's portrayal of vice in *Pamela* and the idea
that virtue can ever be united with it. However,
Richardson is commended for possessing "much of nature"
and for portraying nice touches of passion.

1775

220. Aikin, J., and A.L. "An Enquiry into Those Kinds of
     Distress which Excite Agreeable Sensations." In
     Miscellaneous Pieces, in Prose. 2nd edn. London:
     J. Johnson, 1775. Pp. 206-07.

     In making pity agreeable, an author should not make
     the object of it disagreeable; Richardson admirably rends
     the heart but preserves Clarissa's grace and delicacy,
     and "Clarissa abandoned ... is the object ... of ...
     veneration."

221. *The Benevolent Man: Or, the History of Mr. Belville*.
     London, 1775. II, 4.

     The author originally set out to write a tragic novel
     similar to *Clarissa*, but recants and announces that he
     has abandoned his plan under the pressure of his friends'
     arguments, despite "the example of the author of Claris-
     sa."

1776

222. *Disinterested Love: Or, The History of Sir Charles
     Royston and Emily Lesley*. Dublin, 1776. I, 48.

     An imitative Lovelace disclaims against a Sir Charles
     Grandison.

223. *The Husband's Resentment*. London, 1776. I, 37-38.

     The heroine, Miss Belville, tries to suggest that
     no Richardsonian plot or characters now influence the
     times or novel writing.

224. Pratt, Samuel Jackson. *Pupil of Pleasure*. 1776; 2nd
     edn. London, 1777. I, 2.

     The hero, a swaggering imitator of Lovelace, cries
     out in his enthisiasm: "Richardson's a child, Grandison
     a monster, Lovelace a bungler"; a further imitation of
     this passage can be found in *Excessive Sensibility*
     (1787), I, 234.

225. ————. "A Criticism upon Modern Novels and Novel
     Writing." *Westminster Magazine*, 4 (1776), 521.
     Rpt. *Miscellanies*. Vol. 3. London: T. Becket, 1785.

Typical criticism of *Grandison*, censuring Sir Charles as a too perfect gentleman. For further criticism of this kind see McKillop #550, p. 230 n. 8.

1777

226. *Nouvelle bibliothèque d'un homme de goût.* Paris, 1777. IV, 81-82.

A balanced understanding of Richardson as a writer who combined moral sentiment with sharply accentuated types of character and vivid detail.

227. Priestley, Joseph. *Lectures on Oratory and Criticism.* London, 1777. P. 129.

An educationalist, critical of Richardson's social and moral code, Priestley believes characters like Lovelace might well teach the wrong lesson to the innocent.

228. Reeve, Clara. *The Old English Baron, a Gothic Story.* 1777; rpt. London: E. and C. Dilly, 1778. First published as *The Champion of Virtue, a Gothic Story.* London, 1777.

The Preface makes a brief reference to Richardson: "The business of Romance is, first, to excite the attention; and, secondly, to direct it to some useful, or at least innocent, end. Happy the writer who attains both these points, like Richardson."

1778

229. Le Harpe, Jean François de. "Des roman." In *Oeuvres.* Paris, 1778. III, 337-88.

A balanced evaluation of Richardson, revealing that the "querelle de *Pamela*" has been forgotten; it emphasizes the moral novel and novel of sensibility as derived from Richardson.

230. *The Unfortunate Union.* London, 1778. I, 4.

Sir Charles becomes a model which characters in the novel try to emulate.

1779

231. [Cavendish, Georgina, Duchess of Devonshire.]   *The*
      Sylph. London, 1779. II, 22-23.

      Pamela Andrews is called "pernicious" because it
      encourages young women to try to make their fortunes
      by marrying above them.

232. Sherlock, Martin. *Lettres d'un voyageur anglais*.
      Londres, 1779. Trans. John Duncombe. London, 1780.

      Especially praises Richardson for creating perfect
      characters.

233. *The Wedding Ring: Or, History of Miss Sidney*. London,
      1779. III, 103.

      A comparison of Rousseau's "soft eloquence" with
      Richardson's "heart-felt, refined language" and masterly
      descriptions of human passions.

                          1780

234. *Lady's Magazine*, 11 (1780), 375.

      A typical, quick reference to Richardson, noting that
      a clergyman might well chastize women who prefer
      Rousseau's fiction "to the chastest and most charming
      touches of a Richardson."

235. *The Relapse*. London, 1780. I, 24-25.

      A heroine is warned by referring her to Clarissa when
      the former hesitates to obey her father's will regarding
      her marriage.

                          1781

236. Sherlock, Martin. *Letters on Several Subjects*. 2 vols.
      1781; rpt. New York: Garland Publishing, Inc., 1970.
      I, 141-55.

      Discusses Richardson's moral principles and proclaims
      Clarissa to be a model for all women; includes an example
      from *Clarissa*, revealing its pathos.

1782

237. *London Magazine.* "Umbra's Dialogues. Dialogue III. Sir
      Charles Grandison, Tristram Shandy," 51 (1782), 211-
      13.

      Typical criticism of *Grandison* which helped obscure
      the novel's importance as a pioneer novel of manners.

238. Wolff, Elisabeth Bekker, and Agatha Deken. *Sara Burger-
      hart.* The Hague, 1782.

      These two Dutch writers adopted Richardson's form and
      created perhaps the best and most sustained performance
      of any novel modeled on Richardson, including *Evelina*;
      for further details on Wolff-Deken see McKillop #550,
      pp. 266-68; Ghijsen #1172; Moquette #1188; and Slattery
      #1203.

1783

239. Beattie, James. "On Fable and Romance." In *Disserta-
      tions Moral and Critical.* 2 vols. Dublin: Exshaw,
      Walker and Others, 1783. II, 311-15.

      Considers Richardson's narrative method to be derived
      from the epic and the drama, noting that the epistolary
      form keeps the reader in the same degree of suspense as
      the teller; the minute detail tends to become tedious,
      and pathetic scenes too overcharged, but Richardson's
      moral sentiments "are profound and judicious."

240. Blair, Hugh. "Philosophical Writing--Dialogue--Epis-
      tolary Writing--Fictitious History." In *Lectures on
      Rhetoric and Belles Lettres.* Lecture Thirty-Seven.
      2 vols. 1783; rpt. Ed. Harold F. Harding with a
      Foreword by David Potter, Carbondale and Edwards-
      ville: Southern Illinois Univ. Press, 1965. II,
      290-310.

      A brief notice stressing the moral teaching of
      Richardson's novels.

241. Brooke, Mrs. Frances Moore. *Rosina. A Comic Opera.*
      London, 1783. III, 41.

      Provides an example of a character who does not admire
      Pamela because she realizes how foolish it would be to
      model her behavior on Richardson's heroine.

1785

242. Le Tourner, Pierre. "Preface." In *Clarissa Harlowe,
      traduction nouvelle et seule complète*. Geneva and
      Paris, 1785-87.

      Calls attention to the errors and emendations made
      by Prévost and declares that this edition straight-
      forwardly and accurately reproduces the novel as
      Richardson wrote it. See McKillop (#550) for further
      details regarding translations during this period.

243. *The Rencontre: Or, Transition of a Moment*. Dublin,
      1785. Pp. 136-37.

      This novelist both attacks and defends Richardson's
      creation of "good" and "bad" characters by emphasizing
      his genius for portraying a character's psychology and
      manners.

244. Reeve, Clara. *The Progress of Romance through Times,
      Countries, and Manners*. 1785; rpt. New York:
      Garland Publishing, Inc., 1970.

      Notes how moral Richardson is and how capably he
      portrays the human heart; presents through her character
      of Hortensius the gratitude of women writers to Richard-
      son; also suggests that *Pamela* is his masterpiece.

                            1786

245. L. "*Memoirs* of the *Life* and *Writings* of Mr. *Samuel
      Richardson*, the celebrated author of *Pamela*, *Clarissa*,
      and *Sir Charles Grandison*: With his Portrait,
      elegantly engraved, from an original Painting by
      Highmore." *Universal Magazine of Knowledge and
      Pleasure*, 78 (Jan. 1786), 17-21, 73-77.

      A brief but significant sketch of Richardson's life
      authorized by his daughters; reviews his life, novels,
      and literary reputation.

246. [Seward, Anna.] *Gentleman's Magazine*, 56 (1786), 15-17.

      Discusses her distress at Clara Reeve's putting *Pamela*
      over *Clarissa* or *Grandison* as Richardson's chief work.
      See Clara Reeve, *Gentleman's Magazine*, 56 (1786), 117-
      18, for her rebuttal to Anna Seward, and also *Gentleman's*

Magazine, 56 (1786), 288-89, for "a Constant Reader's"
further analysis of Clara Reeve's "strange dissent" from
the traditional evaluation of Richardson's works,
ascribing personal motives as her reason for such a
judgment.

1787

247.   B.   "On Novel Writing."   *The Microcosm*, No. 26 (14 May
     1787), 294-306.

     Discusses the general distinctions between the terms
"novel" and "romance" with a few comments on *Grandison*
(a novel "too perfect to be imitated") compared with
Tom Jones.

248.   More, Hannah.   "Sensibility."   In *Sacred Dramas*.   Phila-
     delphia, 1787.   P. 186.

     Distinguishes between the "passions" and "feelings"
(or "sentiments") and considers Richardson's writing
distinct from sentimentalism; a later revision of the
poem drops the reference to Richardson as the reaction
against sentimentalism stiffened.

1788

249.   *Journal des savants* (Oct. 1788), 680.

     In discussing a play derived from *Clarissa*, this
French reviewer reveals again that the French believed
Richardson needed editing (despite the novelist's
strengths in characterization and sentiment).

250.   [Seward, Anna.]   *Gentleman's Magazine*, 58 (1788), 818,
     1005-06, 1168-71.

     Criticism of Richardson develops on the grounds that
Clarissa and Sir Charles Grandison are too idealized.

251.   ————.   *Variety: A Collection of Essays, Written in
     the Year 1787*.   London, 1788.   P. 215.

     Notes Johnson's evaluation of *Clarissa* as perhaps "not
only the first *novel*, but perhaps the first *work* in our
language, splendid in point of genius, and calculated to
promote the dearest interests of religion and virtue."

1789

252.   *The Triumph of Fortitude.* London, 1789. I, 129.

       A young woman is told to avoid Pamela's prudery when
       she is faced with the advances of a man of superior
       rank.

1790

253.   Macaulay, Catherine (Sawbridge) Graham. *Letters on
       Education.* London, 1790. Pp. 145-47.

       This is typical of the reaction against Richardson
       on moral grounds; it suggests his novels especially
       corrupt the manners of the young.

1792

254.   Smith, Charlotte. *Desmond.* London, [1792]. II, 214-15.

       Another depreciation of Lovelace and his plotting as
       examples of what can now be found in current literature.

1793

255.   Bennett, John. *Letters to a Young Lady.* Philadelphia,
       1793. II, 57-58.

       Indicates how those who read *Clarissa* or *Grandison* as
       conduct books often lapsed into sheer sentiment.

256.   Parsons, Eliza. *Woman As She Should Be.* London, 1793.
       I, 141-42.

       Characters in *Grandison* are models for the characters
       in this novel who also refer to them.

257.   Thomson, Alexander. *Essay on Novels.* Edinburgh, 1793.

       Considers Richardson (along with Rousseau and Goethe)
       as more "moving" than Homer, Virgil, or Milton.

1797

258.   Darwin, Erasmus. *A Plan for the Conduct of Female
        Education in Boarding Schools, Private Families, and
        Public Seminaries.* Derby: J. Drewry, 1797; Phila-
        delphia: John Ormrod, 1798. Ch. XIV, pp. 47–48.

        A passing commentary on Mrs. Macaulay's and Madame de
        Genlis's recommendation of Richardson's novels because
        his heroines command their passions unlike their counter-
        parts in mere romances; the author criticizes Richard-
        son's prolixity and feels there are objectionable
        passages in the books.

259.   Foster, Hannah Webster. *The Coquette, or the History
        of Eliza Wharton.* Boston, 1797; 2nd edn., Charles-
        town, 1802. P. 53.

        This work is based upon a Richardsonian plot and
        mingles fact with fiction; one correspondent warns
        Eliza not to be a Clarissa and to be wary of her own,
        second Lovelace.

260.   Godwin, William. "Of Choice in Reading." In *The En-
        quirer. Reflections on Education, Manners, and Litera-
        ture.* London, 1797. Pp. 134–35.

        In a discussion of the overt moral of a novel com-
        pared with its tendency, he remarks that few would wish
        to resemble Lovelace as compared with Grandison, although
        neither is exactly "calculated to produce imitation."

1798

261.   [Foster, Hannah Webster.] *The Boarding School.* Boston,
        1798. Pp. 160–61.

        Typical of writers on education who criticized
        Richardson's moral and social code because a character
        like Lovelace might teach wrong lessons to the young
        and innocent.

262.   [Murray, Judith Sargent.] *The Gleaner.* Boston, 1798.
        II, 64–67.

        Advises that daughters should read *Clarissa* as an
        initiation in virtue.

1799

263.   Mathias, Thomas J. *The Pursuits of Literature. A
       Satirical Poem*. 9th edn. London: T. Becket, 1799.

       In a lengthy note discussing novels, there is brief
       mention made of Richardson as "a man of virtue and
       genius" for his *Clarissa*.

1800

264.   Smith, Charlotte. *The Letters of a Solitary Wanderer*.
       London, 1800. I, 25-26.

       Considers the strength as well as the weaknesses of
       Richardson's art in contrast with the gothic spirit of
       the turn of the century; especially believes that
       creating a set of characters who act and speak appro-
       priately to real life, with an accompanying minuteness
       of description, represents Richardson's strength and
       makes him great despite the tedious length of his
       novels.

B. CRITICISM OF, REMARKS ABOUT,
AND TRIBUTES TO RICHARDSON IN LETTERS,
DIARIES, MEMOIRS, BIOGRAPHIES, AND POEMS

265.   *American Magazine, Monthly Chronicle for the British
       Colonies*. "A Poem. On the Invention of Letters and
       the Art of Printing*," 1, No. 6 (March 1758), 281-90.

       Praises Richardson for instilling virtue through
       his art and for being the incarnation of the moral
       Grandison he created.

266.   Arblay, Mme. d' [Fanny Burney]. *Diary and Letters of
       Madame d'Arblay*. Ed. Charlotte Barrett. London,
       1891. I, 520.

       Includes information regarding the Duchess of
       Portland's relationship to Richardson.

267.   Argenson, Marquis d'. *Memoires*. Ed. René Louis de
       Voyer de Paulmy. Paris, 1825. P. 437.

Typical of the enthusiastic admirers of *Grandison*
who believed the novel a second New Testament and Sir
Charles a Christ on earth.

268. Baretti, Giuseppe. *Lettere instruttive descrittive a*
      familiari. Syracuse, 1826.

      An Italian author, who had met Richardson by 1753, was
      grieved to hear of his death; he is said to have provided
      the Italian background for *Grandison*.

269. [Beattie, James.] Sir William Forbes. *An Account of*
      the Life and Writings of James Beattie. 2 vols.
      Edinburgh, 1806. I, 38-46: to Dr. John Ogilvie, 20
      Aug. 1759.

      Beattie had intended to write a criticism of *Clarissa*,
      but his ideas were anticipated by Richardson in the Post-
      script to the novel.

270. Bennet, George. *Pamela Versified: or, Virtue Rewarded*.
      London, 1741.

      One of three initial poems modeled on *Pamela*, it is an
      unfinished "Heroic Poem" which was to have retold Pamela's
      story in fifteen parts. Only one number appeared. See
      also #307 and #377.

271. [Birch, Thomas.] *The Orrery Papers.* Ed. Emily Charlotte
      Boyle (Countess of Cork and Orrery). London, 1903.
      II, 14, 49: from Thos. Birch, 19 Jan. 1747-48; 20 Dec.
      1748.

      Birch comments that *Clarissa* is too long and not as
      "relished" as *Pamela*, but believes the incidents of the
      last volumes are more various and interesting; he re-
      marks again that *Clarissa* is excellent and may do good
      "if the length and seriousness of it do not so much
      discourage an age of remarkable indolence and levity."

272. Bodmer, J.J., and J.J. Breitinger. *Der Mahler der*
      Sitten. Rev. edn. Zurich, 1746. II, 281-82.

      These authors include in their list for a ladies'
      library both *Pamela* and *Joseph Andrews*.

273. Boissy, Louis de. "Pamela en France, ou La Vertue
      Mieux Eprouvée." In *Oeuvres du Théâtre.* Vol. IX.
      Paris: Veuve Duchesne, 1766.

      This is not a serious treatment of the novel or story,

but really only a skit; the chief interest is the advice
in the play given to Pamela not to resist the advances
of B.   For more details on the dramatic adaptations of
Pamela, see Canby #908, Facteau #931, and Kreissman
#944.

274.   Brockes, B.H.   *Lobgedichte auf de Pamela*.   In *Irdisches*
       Vergnügen in Gott.   Hamburg, 1739-48.   IX, 553-58.

This poem represents the most thorough defense of
Pamela which appeared in Germany in the eighteenth
century.

275.   Burns, Robert.   *The Letters of Robert Burns*.   Ed. J.
       De Lancy Ferguson.   2 vols.   Oxford: Clarendon Press,
       1931.   I, 58-59: to Dr. John Moore, 28 Feb. 1791.

Burns notes that Richardson has a power to delineate
the human heart, but his characters are not of this
world.

276.   [Carter, Mrs. Elizabeth.]   *Memoirs of the Life of Mrs.*
       Elizabeth Carter.   Ed. Montagu Pennington.   London,
       1808.

Includes information regarding Mrs. Carter's relationship with Richardson, including the matter of Richardson's printing her "Ode to Wisdom" in *Clarissa*.

277.   ————.   *A Series of Letters between Mrs. Elizabeth*
       Carter and Miss Catherine Talbot from the Year 1741
       to 1770.   Ed. Montagu Pennington.   1809; rpt. 4 vols.
       in 3, London: F.C. and J. Rivington, 1819.

Includes evaluations of *Pamela*, *Clarissa*, and *Grandison*
from 1742, 1749, 1753, and 1754.   Mrs. Talbot especially
admired *Clarissa* just as she equally detested *Tom Jones*;
although Mrs. Carter felt Clarissa to be a fully credible
character, and although she, too, admired the novel,
she could not agree with her friend's analysis of
Fielding's novel.

278.   Chapone, Mrs. Sarah Kirkham.   *Remarks on Mrs. Muilman's*
       Letter to the Right Honourable The Earl of Chester-
       field. In a Letter to Mrs. Muilman.   London, 1750.
       P. 19.

Mrs. Chapone compliments Richardson for having written
Clarissa wherein are minutely pictured "Men of Honour
... drawn at full Length, by the most masterly intellectual Painter, that has adorn'd the Age and Nation."

279. Chateaubriand, François Auguste René. *Essai sur la littérature Anglaise et considerations sur le génie les temps, des hommes et des révolutions.* 1836; rpt. *Oeuvres Complètes de Chateaubriand*, Nouvelle edn., Paris: Librairie Garnier Frères, n.d. English trans. *Sketches of English Literature.* London: Henry Colburn, 1836.

A brief commentary on Richardson, his style, and the epistolary form; it includes passing references to Richardson and the development of the novel.

280. Chenier, André. "Elégies, II." In *Oeuvres complètes.* Ed. Gerard Walter. Pleiade Edition. [Paris, 1950.] P. 58.

Compares Julie with Clarissa and Clementina as "phantoms of poetic reveries."

281. Chesterfield, Philip Dormer Stanhope, fourth Earl of. *The Letters of Horace Walpole.* Ed. Peter Cunningham. Edinburgh: John Grant, 1906. IV, 305n–06n.

He writes to David Mallet (5 Nov. 1753) that *Grandison* "amuses" him: it is "too long, and there is too much mere talk in it"; he also suggests that Richardson errs when he tries to write about "high life" because he mistakes its "mode," although not its nature, since he has "knowledge" and "skill" in describing and interesting the heart. Richardson "deserves well of mankind, the object of all his writings being virtue."

282. ————. *The Letters of ... Chesterfield.* Ed. Bonamy Dobrée. King's Printer Edition. 6 vols. London: Eyre & Spottiswode Ltd., 1932.

Includes a brief reference to Richardson, who lacks stylistic "savoir," but who certainly knows the human heart.

283. Cobden, Edward. "Ode on E.C. alias Clarissa exemplified." In *Discourses and Essays.* London, 1757. Pp. 327-28 (second pagination).

He makes a comparison of Clarissa's story to the feigned account given by Elizabeth Canning in 1753 that she had been kidnapped and held prisoner.

284. Cowper, William. "An Ode on Reading Mr. Richardson's History of Sir Charles Grandison." Forster MS. XVI,

2, fol. 14.

This is an enthusiastic tribute to Richardson and his novel.

285. *Daily Advertiser.* "Advice to Booksellers (After Reading Pamela)," 8 April 1741.

An epigram on the authorship of *Pamela*. See the *Gentleman's Magazine* for a printing of a variant of this epigram: 11 (1741), 214; 50 (1780), 333.

286. ———, 28 April, 2 May, 1741.

Includes some brief poetry describing the fan which went on sale in fan-shops and china-shops of London, celebrating the life and adventures of Pamela.

287. ———, 23 April 1745.

Pamela's life was represented in a curious wax-work, containing over a hundred figures. See also the August 8th advertisement for "a Curious Representation of Pamela in High Life ... larger than the first Piece of wax-work of this kind, which was call'd the Low Life of Pamela."

288. [Donnellan, Anne.] *Elizabeth Montagu, The Queen of the Blue-Stockings, Her Correspondence from 1720 to 1761.* London, 1906. II, 46: 10 Nov. [1753] (misdated 1754).

Mrs. Donnellan wrote of *Grandison* that it "is too fine spun," even if "there are fine things and fine characters in it."

289. Du Deffand, Marie, Marquise. *Lettres de la Marquise du Deffand à Horace Walpole (1766-1780).* Ed. Mrs. Paget Toynbee. London, 1912. I, 591: to Walpole, 4 July 1769; also see I, 397; III, 575.

Although Richardson was most often appropriated by the sentimentalists in France, Mme. du Deffand more fully appreciated his realistic and domestic detail.

290. Duncombe, John. *An Evening Contemplation in a College.* London, 1753. P. 10.

Includes an early compliment on *Grandison*:

Reports attract the lawyer's parting eyes,
Novels Lord Fopling and Sir Plume require;
For songs and plays the voice of Beauty cries,
And Sense and Nature Grandison desire.

291.   ———.   *Feminiad*.   London, 1754.   P. 607.

>   Considers Richardson to be the "constant patron" of
>   the fair sex in a tribute of several lines.
>
>>   To these weak strains, O thou! the sex's friend
>>   And constant patron, Richardson! attend!

292.   ———.   "Ode to Health."   In *A Collection of Poems*.
       Ed. Robert Dodsley.   2nd edn.   4 vols.   London, 1748–
       55.   IV, 275–77.

>   This is typical of the sonnets and odes written by
>   Richardson's admirers; it invokes the muse on Richardson's
>   behalf as a writer who delights as he improves his fellow
>   man.   Miss Mulso also wrote an ode of the same title;
>   see #347, IV, 152–54.

293.   ———.   "To the Author of Clarissa."

>   These lines were added to the third edition of *Clarissa*
>   (VIII, 300–03) and assert that had Richardson written in
>   Athens, he would have had a statue constructed for him
>   on the banks of the Ilyssus, and he would have been in-
>   cluded by Plato in his Republic.   See Sale #107, P. 57.

294.   Easy, Charles.   *Gentleman's Magazine*, 18 (Dec. 1748),
       548.

>   This is a mock letter written under the signature of
>   Cibber's famous character, Sir Charles Easy, commenting
>   on *Clarissa*'s length and his own "tears" at reading the
>   novel; this is, apparently, an advertising puff for the
>   novel rather than serious criticism.

295.   [Edwards, Jonathan.]   Thomas H. Johnson.   "Jonathan
       Edwards and the 'Young Folks' Bible.'"   *New England
       Quarterly*, 5 (1932), 39–40.

>   Edwards was aware of Richardson's novels, and according
>   to his "Catalogue"—a notebook of jottings and comments
>   on books—he knew *Clarissa* to be "highly commended" and
>   *Pamela* to be "an *Interesting original worthy to be
>   spoken of in terms of high Respect*"; Edwards read
>   *Grandison* with particular pleasure.

296.   Edwards, Thomas.   Letters.   Bodleian Library.   MSS. Bodl.
       1011–12.

>   One of Richardson's extreme devotees, he defended
>   *Clarissa* by emphasizing Richardson's perceptive insight
>   into human nature.

297. ———. Sonnet.

> This sonnet Edwards sent to Richardson "which, if it
> should be thought worth publishing, I desire may be in-
> scribed to the author of Grandison ... and subscribed
> T.E."; Richardson included the sonnet in the second
> edition of *Grandison*, Vol. I, second issue. See Sale
> #107, p. 79.

298. ———. Sonnet. Forster MS. XII, 1, fol. 45.

> An unpublished sonnet referring to *Grandison*, assert-
> ing that this novel deserves "higher meed" than *Clarissa*.
> It is printed in McKillop #550, p. 196.

299. ———. "To the Author of Clarissa."

> These lines face the title page of Vol. I of the
> third edition of the novel; they praise Richardson for
> his skill in arousing, terrifying, and calming the mind
> while portraying virtue and morality.

300. Evans, Cadwallader. *Monthly Magazine*, 40 (1815), 512.

> In a letter (12 Feb. 1754) reprinted here from the
> *Port Folio*, Evans notes that *Grandison* has not been
> much read by his acquaintances, that some "accuse it
> of a prolixity," but that the novel nonetheless has
> many "strenuous advocates."

301. Fontanes, Louis de. *Les correspondants de J. Joubert*.
      Ed. Paul de Reynal. Paris, 1883. P. 30.

> In writing from London in 1785, he indicates with
> considerable exaggeration, that Richardson's work had
> fallen into disrepute.

302. Franklin, Benjamin. *The Autobiography of Benjamin
      Franklin*. Ed. Leonard W. Labarree and others. New
      Haven: Yale Univ. Press, 1964. P. 72.

> Franklin comments that Bunyan, Defoe, and Richardson
> (in *Pamela*) are the pioneers of agreeably mingling dia-
> logue with narration.

303. [Garrick, David.] "On Clarissa." Printed in McKillop
      #550, p. 161.

> McKillop suggests that this is the "Epigram on Cl[a].
> by Mr. Garrick" listed in the Index to the *Clarissa*
> material, Forster MS. XV, 3, fol. 2, which is no longer
> in the collection. The poem is inscribed on the

flyleaf of the first volume of a set of the third edition of *Clarissa* presented to Mrs. Garrick by Richardson. The lines commend *Clarissa* for its delight and
morality although "The tasteless Vulgar" slight the
novel's "Beauties."

304. Genlis, Madame de. *Mémoires*. Paris and Londres, 1825.
     III, 292-93, 360-61.

     Among her recollections of Richardson, she recalls
     seeing what was probably Highmore's third portrait of
     Richardson and describes it; she also notes how Edward
     Bridger showed her the corrected copy of *Pamela*, urging
     her to translate it into French.

305. ———. *Théâtre à l'usage des jeunes personnes*.
     Paris, 1783. IV, 85-86.

     Advises that *Clarissa* should be read by young women
     as an initiation in virtue.

306. *Gentleman's Magazine*, 9 (Jan. 1741), 56.

     This is a notice that the "encomiums" of last month
     on *Pamela* came out too late to be included in the maga-
     zine, but that a second edition of the novel is to
     appear soon since it is "judged in Town as great a Sign
     of Want of Curiosity not to have read *Pamela*, as not to
     have seen the *French* and *Italian* dancers."

307. ———. "To the Author of Pamela," 15 Feb. 1745, p.
     104.

     In this third poem (signed Belinda) upon *Pamela*, a
     Salisbury poet thanks Richardson on behalf of "instruc-
     ted country damsels," who, from the model of Pamela,
     learn "virtuous dignity." See Bennet #270, and J.W.
     #377.

308. ———, 19 (Jan. 1749), 38.

     Prints an elegiac couplet regarding *Clarissa* supposed-
     ly by Pamela B. Junior: "Scire hominum mores varios,
     bene scribere, si vis:/ Perlege Clarissam; mente fruare
     tuâ."

309. ———, 54 (1784), 488.

     Richardson's daughter, Martha Bridgen, denies that
     her father attended Christ's Hospital. See #331.

310. Gibbon, Edward. *Mémoires littéraires de la Grande
     Bretagne*. I (1767), 76.

     He compares Fielding with Richardson and considers
     both to have developed the novel "to its highest
     possible degree."

311. ————. *Miscellaneous Works*. London, 1814. II, 36:
     to Mrs. Porter, 1756.

     A brief comment which assesses *Grandison* to be
     "superior" to *Clarissa*.

312. *Göttlingische Zeitungen von Gelehrten Sachen* (1743),
     454.

     Although the *querelle de Pamela* was apparently not
     carried out among German critics, this author does
     restrict women's reading to the Bible, a catechism, a
     prayer book and hymn book, a cookbook, and *Pamela*.

313. [Goldsmith, Oliver.] Sir James Prior. *The Life of
     Oliver Goldsmith*. 2 vols. London, 1837. II, 111.

     Prior notes that Goldsmith "honoured" Richardson's
     morality, but he eschewed "his prolixity and sentimen-
     tal refinements."

314. Graham, Mr. *Journal britannique*, 3 (Dec. 1750), 438.

     He makes a complimentary epigram on *Clarissa* which
     is later included in the Dutch edition of the novel.

         This Work is Nature's; every tittle in't
         She wrote, & gave it Richardson to *print*.
         But He, (so loose to Trust Mankind is grown)
         The Goddess brav'd, & calls the book his own.

315. Grant, Mrs. Anne. *Letters from the Mountains Being the
     Real Correspondence of a Lady, between the Years
     1773 and 1807*. 2 vols. London: Longman, Hurst,
     Rees, and Orme, 1806.

     Comments upon *Clarissa*; her favorite heroine is drawn
     "uniformly consistent ... yet so judiciously kept
     within the bounds of nature and probability" [3 Oct.
     1778].

316. Granville, Mary (Mrs. Delany). *The Autobiography and
     Correspondence of Mary Granville, Mrs. Delany with
     Interesting Reminiscences of King George the Third*

and *Queen Charlotte*. Ed. Lady Llanover. 3 vols.
London: Richard Bentley, 1861. II, 523, 614; III,
244.

Two references to *Clarissa*, reflecting her high opin-
ion of his "capacity and excellent heart"; also comments
on *Grandison*: "what a soul that Richardson has."

317. Graves, Richard. "Trifling Anecdotes of the Late Ralph
Allen, Esq. of Prior Park, near Bath." *The Triflers*.
London, 1806. P. 68.

Recounts Richardson's desire to be known as a guest
of Ralph Allen's.

318. [Gray, Thomas.] Norton Nicholls. "Reminiscences of
Gray." In *Correspondence*. Ed. Paget Toynbee and
Leonard Whitely. London, 1935. III, 1298.

Thomas Gray agrees with Johnson's evaluation that
Richardson presents a sound morality in his novels; he
greatly admired *Clarissa*.

319. Haller, Albrecht von. *Göttingische Zeitungen von
Gelehrten Sachen* (1748), 274-75.

He welcomes the appearance of the first two volumes
of *Clarissa* and promises a translation.

320. Hawkins, Laetitia Matilda. *Gossip about Dr. Johnson
and Others, Being Chapters from the Memoirs of Miss
Laetitia Matilda Hawkins*. Ed. Francis Henry Skrine.
London: Eveleigh Nash and Grayson Limited, 1926.

Includes her comment how *Clarissa* was once placed in
the hands of children for moral purposes.

321. Hénault, C.J.F. *Le president Hénault et Madame du
Deffand*. Ed. Lucien Perey. Paris, 1893. Pp. 289-90.

In a letter of 30 Jan. 1751, he criticizes *Clarissa*
for its tediousness, but comments how everyone is
reading it.

322. Hervey, John Lord. "Frontispiece to the History of Sir
Charles Grandison." Forster MS. XV, 3, fols. 63-64;
European Magazine, 32 (1797), 412-13 (said to be
"now first printed").

An enthusiastic, poetic tribute to Richardson's
novel.

323. Hurd, Richard. Letter. British Library Add. MS.
      32,557, fol. 47: Richard Hurd to Cox Macro, 7 Nov.
      1742.

      An early letter evaluating *Pamela*; See McKillop
      #795, p. 63.

324. *Imperial Magazine*. "Sent to Miss C---, with Clarissa,"
      1 (1760), 269.

      This is a poem commending Richardson for striving
      "t'engage the soul in virtue's cause"; Richardson
      improves the heart by emphasizing and demonstrating
      the value of morality.

325. Johnson, Samuel. *The Rambler*. Ed. W.J. Bate and
      Albrecht B. Strauss. The Yale Edition of the Works
      of Samuel Johnson. Vols. III-V. New Haven and
      London: Yale Univ. Press, 1969.

      See the index in volume V for references to Richard-
      son's connection with and participation in *The Rambler*;
      includes Johnson's observations prefacing *Rambler* No.
      97 that Richardson "taught the passions to move at the
      command of virtue."

326. ———. "Rowe." In *Lives of the English Poets*. Ed.
      George Birkbeck Hill. 3 vols. 1905; rpt. New York:
      Octagon Books, Inc., 1967. II, 67.

      Richardson stimulates esteem and detestation simul-
      taneously in the character of Lovelace; an index in vol.
      III provides other references (primarily in notes) to
      Richardson.

327. [———.] Boswell, James. *Boswell's Life of Johnson*.
      Ed. George Birkbeck Hill. 6 vols. 1887; rev. and
      enlarged L.F. Powell, Oxford: Clarendon Press, 1934-
      64, 1971.

      A full index notes Johnson's many references to
      Richardson, from his appeal to the novelist when in
      debt to his criticism of the novels and comparison of
      Richardson with Fielding.

328. [———.] Hawkins, Sir John. *Life of Samuel Johnson*,
      LL.D. 1787; 2nd rev. and corrected edn., London: J.
      Buckland, 1787.

      Passing references to Richardson based on Johnson's
      knowledge and recollections; for example, the pronuncia-

tion of Pamela by Richardson's female pupils and a description of the "morose" Richardson at home with his family.

329. [————.] Piozzi, Hester Lynch. *Anecdotes of the Late Samuel Johnson*. London, 1786. P. 221.

Notes Johnson's statement regarding Clarissa: "You may observe there is something which she prefers to truth."

330. [————.] Clifford, James L. *Hester Lynch Piozzi*. Oxford, 1941. P. 437.

Records Johnson's assessment at one point of *Clarissa*: "a prodigious Work--formed on the stalest of all empty Stories"; also notes a version of Johnson's comment: "The heroine sometimes justified her Parents at the Expense of Truth."

331. [Jones, Rev. John.] "Mr. Samuel Richardson, Printer. (A Great Genius)." *Gentleman's Magazine*, 53 (1783), 924-25.

A letter from the Rev. Mr. Jones, telling how Richardson "expostulated" with an older widow who pretended to virtue but was always inciting trouble (*he* was eleven); it also includes information about Richardson's relationship to Young.

332. Laclos, Pierre Choderlos de. *De l'Éducation des femmes*, "Sur le roman 'Cecilia,'" *Les Liaisons dangereuses*. In *Oeuvres complètes*. Ed. Maurice Allem. Pléiade Edition. [Paris, 1959.] Pp. 262, 454, 521.

Reveals Richardson's influence upon the Continent; he called *Clarissa* "le chef-d'oeuvre du roman."

333. Le Blanc, Jean Bernard. *Lettres d'un françois*. 2 vols. The Hague, 1745. I, 279-80.

He argues that *Pamela* is propaganda, part of a program of one of the Societies for the Reformation of Manners, a curious analysis which nevertheless had its supporters in France, among them both Argenson and Prévost.

334. Lefanu, Alicia. *Memoirs of the Life and Writings of Mrs. Frances Sheridan*. London, 1824.

Includes anecdotes regarding Richardson's private life, derived at third hand from her mother; describes

Richardson's later moodiness but capacity for animated
wit and humor.

335. *Lettre à Madame de**** *sur l'Anti-Pamela*. 1742.

This is essentially an advertising puff for a French
anti-*Pamela*, but it also directly attacks Richardson's
novel.

336. *Lettres du Marquis de Roselle*. Amsterdam, 1764. II,
54-56.

He advises that young women should read *Clarissa* as
an initiation in virtue.

337. *London Magazine*. "Remarks on PAMELA. By a PRUDE," 10
(May 1741), 250-51. Also *Scots Magazine*, 3 (July
1741), 303.

A briefly comical treatment, suggesting that Mr. B
was foolish not to take the heroine by force when he
could, and she should never be expected to forgive
such weakness.

338. ————. "To the Author of SHAMELA," 10 (June 1741),
304.

This is an epigram, indicating some support for the
satirical attack against *Pamela* in *Shamela*.

339. ————. "An Apology for the Censorious," 10 (July
1741), 358.

The lines in this poem (signed "R.D.") defend *Pamela*
against scoffers who know too well that her character
is a "shame" and "reprove" to them.

340. *Le Magazin des événemens de tous genres*, 4 (May 1742),
76-80.

The writer criticizes Pamela's character through a
heroine who retells the story in doggerel verse.

341. [Malone, Edmond.] Sir James Prior. *Life of Edmond
Malone ... with Selections from His Manuscript
Anecdotes*. London, 1860. P. 439.

Comments upon Richardson's silence in company, his
vanity, and his "club of women" he had about him; he
also recalls the anecdote of the Bishop of Salisbury,
who said he could not get beyond the bailiff scene in

Clarissa because "it affected him so much that he was drowned in tears."

342. Mendelssohn, Moses. *Briefe, die neueste Litteratur betreffend*. Collected edition. Nos. 123-24. Berlin. VII (1760), 113-50; No. 168, X (1763), 287.

He unfavorably discusses a Wieland adaptation of *Grandison*, but praises Richardson and *his* powers in comparison; he further comments that Richardson had written a friend in Germany that he could not read Rousseau's *Héloise*. [Nichols in *Literary Anecdotes* (#467) says Richardson did read the novel and even made unfavorable marginal notes.]

343. Mirabeau, the Elder. *Letters of Eminent Persons Addressed to David Hume*. Ed. J.H. Burton. Edinburgh, 1849. Pp. 22-23.

Wrote to Hume in 1763 that the French were more devoted to Richardson than his own countrymen.

344. [Moncreiff, John.] *The Scale: or, Woman Weighed with Man*. London, 1752.

In this poem, the writer suggests in his tribute to Lyttleton's "Monody" that, whereas "artful wicked Lovelaces abound," Lyttleton comprehends and values the pious virtue of a Clarissa.

345. Montagu, Lady Mary Wortley. *The Complete Letters of Lady Mary Wortley Montagu*. Ed. Robert Halsband. 3 vols. Oxford: Clarendon Press, 1965.

Lady Mary considers Richardson's dullness, virtuous but unpleasant heroines, and his works in general; for example, "This Richardson is a strange Fellow. I heartily despise him and eagerly read him, nay, sob over his works in a most scandalous manner" (22 Sept. 1755).

346. More, Mrs. Hannah. *Memoirs of the Life and Correspondence of Mrs. Hannah More*. Ed. William Roberts. London, 1834. II, 78.

Records Johnson's anger at her reading of *Tom Jones* and his high commendation of Richardson; also recollects that Richardson once remarked that the Second Earl of Dartmouth would be an excellent nobleman who would be comparable to Sir Charles Grandison if the Earl were not a Methodist.

347. Mulso, Hester (later Mrs. Chapone). *The Posthumous Works of Mrs. Chapone*, 4 vols. London, 1808. II, 29–143.

      Information from perhaps the chief ornament of Richardson's feminine circle of admirers; she was, perhaps, a model for Harriet Byron in *Grandison*.

348. [————.] *The Letters to Gilbert White of Selborne from ... the Rev. John Mulso*. Ed. Rashleigh Holt-White. London, [1907]. P. 43.

      John Mulso writes on 6 Oct. 1750 how the Mulsos have become acquainted with Richardson who, he says, is a man of "Goodness and Sensibility."

349. Nichols, John. *Biographical and Literary Anecdotes of William Bowyer*. [Later expanded into *Literary Anecdotes*.] London, 1782.

      Provides an early account of Richardson's career, of a probable French *Pamela* printed in London, and of Richardson's connection with *The Daily Journal* and *The Daily Gazetteer*.

350. ["Philotimos."] *London Chronicle*, 13 (8–10 Feb. 1763), 143.

      A memorial on Richardson's death, suggesting a sculptor be employed to memorialize the novelist.

351. Pilkington, Laetitia. *Memoirs*. Dublin, 1748.

      Richardson met her through Dr. Delany, and she provides information about him, his family, and his generosity; the two corresponded over several years. She also provides some criticism of *Pamela* and *Clarissa*, especially in her correspondence with Cibber in Mrs. Barbauld's edition of Richardson's *Correspondence* (#62).

352. Piozzi, Hester Lynch. *Autobiography Letters and Literary Remains*. Ed. Abraham Hayward. London, 1861. I, 311.

      Records Johnson's remark that had Richardson waited till she "came out, my praises would have added two or three years to his life: For ... that fellow died merely for want of change among his flatterers."

353. ————. *Observations and Reflections Made in the Course*

of a Journey through France, Italy, and Germany.
London, 1789. I, 265-66.

Notes how Italy is exactly as Richardson depicted it
in *Grandison*; recalls Johnson's comment that Richardson
"had seen little and ... read little."

354. ————. *Thraliana*. Ed. Katherine C. Balderston. 2
      vols. Oxford: Clarendon Press, 1942; 2nd edn., 1951.

Gives an account of church bells ringing on the marriage of Pamela, Johnson's estimate of Richardson's
desire for praise, and other references noted in the
index to volume II.

355. Reich, Erasmus. Forster MS. XV, 3, fol. 56: 10 May
      1754. Rpt. McKillop #550, p. 255.

He includes in this letter information regarding the
German translations of *Grandison*; for further details
regarding *Grandison* in Germany and Richardson's knowledge of his Leipzig friends, Klopstock in particular,
see #550, pp. 255-65.

356. Relph, Rev. Josiah. "Wrote after Reading Pamela or
      Virtue Rewarded." In *A Miscellany of Poems*. Glas-
      gow, 1747. Pp. 133-34.

Idealizes Pamela as a heroine.

357. Richardson, Anne, and Martha Bridgen. Correspondence
      from 28 Dec. 1780 to 24(?) Aug. 1784. MSS, Special
      Collection, Fondren Library, Rice University.

This correspondence consists of ten letters, very
difficult to read and in most cases running to four
pages each. It includes recollections by the two
sisters of their father's schooling, his speaking
Latin with Edward Young, his account of some particulars about the mysterious patron who influenced him in
his early life, and their belief that Mrs. Beaumont
was a real person. The manuscript collection also includes a letter supposedly written by Anne to her
parents (6 Feb. 1757) and a draft letter by Anne to
the *Gentleman's Magazine* concerning Dr. Young. There
are fifteen letters written by Anne to her niece Sally
Crowther Moodie, covering the period 12 April 1792 to
Oct. 1802.

358. [Robson, James.] George Smith and Frank Benger. *The*

Oldest London Bookshop. London, 1928. P. 80.

Recounts Robson's comments about a friend who had read *Grandison* and who believed the novel was an idealization and not an account of real life.

359. Rousseau, Jean-Jacques. *Lettre à M. D'Alembert.* In *Oeuvres complètes.* 2nd edn. Paris, 1826. II, 125n.

See also *Julie, ou la Nouvelle Héloïse,* III, xviii, for his comment on love at first sight in *Grandison,* and his conversation with Bernadin Sainte-Pierre, *La vie et les ouvrages de Jean-Jacques Rousseau,* Ed. Maurice Souriau (Paris, 1907), p. 140; Rousseau's earliest notices of Richardson are generous and only in his novel does he become disparaging, reflecting the later sentimentalism which criticized Richardson's imposing of a rigid code upon human nature.

360. Sade, Marquis de. *Les Crimes de l'amour* [1800]. In *Oeuvres complètes.* Paris, [1961]. III, 26-28.

Praises Richardson for his knowledge of the human heart and the tearful ending of *Clarissa.*

361. Salley. His. MSS Comm., MSS. of Lady Du Cane (1905), p. 327. See McKillop #550, p. 97.

In 1742 Salley wrote to the Chevalier de Caylus that he had read *Pamela,* and for him the novel was not always boring, but that many of his women friends had found it so; nevertheless, the latter had, in public, applauded the heroine's virtue and modesty and considered the novel "un livre plus beau que l'évangile."

362. Seward, Anna. *Letters of Anna Seward.* 6 vols. Edinburgh: George Ramsay & Company, 1811.

Includes comments and judgments upon Richardson and his novels from 1786 to 1799: for example, "I have always considered the Clarissa and Grandison of Richardson, as the highest efforts of genius in our language, next to Shakespeare's plays."

363. Seward, William. *Anecdotes of Distinguished Persons.* London, 1798. II, 91.

Records that Johnson thought Richardson had modeled Sir Charles Grandison upon the non-juror, Robert Nelson.

364. Shenstone, William. *Letters of William Shenstone.* Ed.

Duncan Mallam. Minneapolis: Univ. of Minnesota Press, 1939.

Contains numerous references to Richardson (see the index), including Shenstone's preference for *Clarissa* as well as his belief that Richardson "wants the Art of Abridgement in every Thing he has yet wrote."

365. Skelton, Philip. *Complete Works.* Ed. Robert Lynam. London, 1824. VI, 247.

One of Richardson's admirers for whom Richardson had done some printing; he especially loved *Clarissa* and, although critical of novel reading generally, excepted Richardson's novel from censure.

366. [Somerset, Frances Seymour, Duchess of.] *Select Letters between the Late Duchess of Somerset, Lady Luxborough, Mr. Whistler, Miss Dolman, Mr. R. Dodsley, William Shenstone, esq. and Others.* Ed. Thomas Hull. 2 vols. London, 1778. I, 187, 194.

Praises *Grandison* and places it above either *Pamela* or *Clarissa*; also notes Shenstone's belief that Richardson's verbosity is too extreme. See #364.

367. [Staal de Launay, Mme. de.] Henry Harrissee. *L'Abbé Prévost; histoire de sa vie et des oeuvres d'après des documents nouveaux.* Paris, 1896. Pp. 337-38.

Madame de Staal wrote to l'Hericourt in 1742 that she had read a badly written French translation of *Pamela*, full of boring and often disagreeable details. She adds, however, "j'ai lu les quatres tomes avec un attachement qui ne m'a pas permis de quitter que je ne fusse au bout que j'ai trouvé avec regret."

368. Stuart, Lady Louisa. *Gleanings from an Old Portfolio.* Ed. Mrs. Godfrey Clark. Edinburgh, 1898. III, 95.

A letter to her sister after reading *Grandison* aloud: notes how out of fashion Richardson currently is and how laughable some of the manners of his age (coaches and six), but comments as well on the worthy parts "worth very great attention."

369. Talbot, Mrs. Catherine. Journal. British Library Add. MS. 46,490.

This friend of Richardson's introduced him to Mrs. Carter; the journal includes observations of Richardson.

370. Theophila. *The "History of Sir Charles Grandison"
      Spiritualized*. London, 1760.

      A poem which finds a mystical meaning in the novel,
      arising from the marriage of Sir Charles and Harriet
      Byron.

371. Thomson, Alexander. "Vale of Pity." In *The Paradise
      of Taste*. London, 1796. Pp. 64-65.

      An indulgent tribute to Richardson's essential senti-
      mentalism: "BOLOGNA's melancholy maid" who "taught the
      world CLARISSA's fate to wail."

372. Tilly, Alexandre, Comte de. *Ouevres melées*. Berlin,
      1803. Reviewed and quoted in translation in *Monthly
      Review*, N.S., 42 (1803), 478.

      He was shocked that Shakespeare, but not Richardson,
      had a monument in Westminster Abbey.

373. Tscharner, J.B. von. *Le Poète Edward Young*. Ed. W.
      Thomas. Paris, 1901. P. 600.

      Thomas notes how in 1752 the Swiss, Tscharner, sent
      back to Haller a description of Richardson "as a senti-
      mental and melancholy genius overwhelmed by domestic
      bereavement."

374. [Turner, Thomas.] Charles Fleet. *Glimpses of Our
      Ancestors in Sussex*. Lewes, 1882.

      A Sussex shopkeeper, Turner responded to his wife's
      reading of Clarissa's funeral with the following: "Oh,
      may the Supreme Being give me grace to lead my life in
      such a manner as my exit may in some measure be like
      that divine creature's."

375. Uz, Johann Peter. "Lines to Grotzner" [22 Nov. 1753].
      In *Sämtliche poetische Werke*. Ed. Sauer. Stuttgart,
      1890. P. 361.

      The German poet (he translated Mrs. Carter's "Ode
      to Wisdom" from the pages of *Clarissa*) considered the
      idealized characterization of Clarissa to be monstrous.

376. Voltaire. *Oeuvres*. Paris, 1877-85. XL, 350; XLV,
      262-63.

      Reveals Voltaire's hostility toward Richardson which
      by and large was not common at the time.

377. W——————, J——————. *Pamela: or, the Fair Imposter*. Dub-
      lin, 1743; London, 1744.

      One of three initial poems modeled on *Pamela*, this
      one is an anti-*Pamela* written especially in the temper
      of *Shamela*, concluding with the following note on
      Pamela's morality:

      Keep but your Honour spotless from Reproach;
      Think on the Charms of Wealth, a Title, and a Coach.

      See #270 and #307.

378. Walpole, Horace. *Horace Walpole's Correspondence with
      Sir Horace Mann*. Vol. VI of *Horace Walpole's Corres-
      pondence*. Ed. W.L. Lewis. 36 vols. New Haven: Yale
      Univ. Press, 1937-73.

      In two letters, Walpole considers Richardson "deplor-
      ably tedious" (20 Dec. 1764) and dull (27 Sept. 1767).

379. *Weekly Miscellany*, 28 Feb. 1741.

      Prints one of Hill's eulogistic letters and his verses
      "for the Unknown Author" from the Introduction to the
      second edition of *Pamela*.

380. Whitehead, William. *On Nobility*. London, 1744. P. 6.

      In his lines of poetry, Whitehead associates Pamela
      with other lowly damsels who made great marriages.

381. Williams, Anna. "Verses to Mr. Richardson on his His-
      tory of Sir Charles Grandison." *Gentleman's Magazine*,
      24 (Jan. 1754), 40.

      Praises *Grandison* as a *succès d'estime* rather than as
      a novel, but she considers that all three novels are
      valuable for their morality.

382. Young, Edward. *Conjectures on Original Composition.
      In a Letter to the Author of "Sir Charles Grandison."*
      London, 1759. P. 78.

      Includes an oblique reference to Richardson's
      original genius.

383. Zachariä. *Die vier Stufen des weiblichen Alters.*
      Rostock, 1757. P. 14.

      Considers that the ideal young woman would read almost
      no novels except Richardson's.

III.
Nineteenth-Century Criticism

384. Allibone, S. Austin. "Samuel Richardson." In *A Critical Dictionary of English Literature and British and American Authors*. 3 vols. 1854; rpt. Philadelphia: J.B. Lippincott & Co., 1858-71. Supplement. 2 vols. Philadelphia, 1891. II, 1796-1801.

Discusses Richardson's literary career and reputation, based primarily upon many references to nineteenth-century critical appraisals.

385. Aquilius. "A Few Words about Novels--A Dialogue, in a Letter to Eusebius." *Blackwood's Magazine*, 64 (1848), 459-74; esp. 460.

Although *Pamela* was so successful that it could not be kept away from maids (who used it as a model for aspiring after and pursuing young gentlemen), and although *Clarissa* was disguised as a moral book suitable for young people, the writer concludes that Richardson's novels are really indecent.

386. *Argosy*. "On the History of the Novel in England," 14 (1872), 273-77.

Defines the novel and gives a short history of the form; considers Richardson and Fielding to be the founders of the English novel, emphasizing Richardson's style and his delineation of human nature, portrayal of "universal sentiments and passions," and analysis of the human heart.

387. *Athenaeum*, No. 2994 (Jan.-June 1884), 399-400.

A review of the Sotheran edition of Richardson's novels (#29), finding *Pamela* and *Grandison* tedious and negligible, but evaluating *Clarissa* as a work of genius, especially in the development of Lovelace.

388. Austen, Jane. *Jane Austen's Letters to Her Sister*

Cassandra and Others. Ed. R.W. Chapman. Oxford: Clarendon Press, 1932. Pp. 140, 322, 344, 486-87.

Records the references Austen made to Richardson's novels: for example, her criticism of "perfection" as found in *Grandison.*

389. [————.] Henry Austen. *The Novels of Jane Austen.* Ed. R.W. Chapman. 2nd edn. Oxford: Clarendon Press, 1926. V, 7.

Jane Austen's brother records in the Biographical Notice of 1817 (included here) that his sister especially delighted in *Grandison* and Richardson's power of creation, although she did not fall into the error, even in her admiration for him, of imitating "his prolix style and tedious narrative."

390. [————.] J.E. Austen-Leigh. *Memoir of Jane Austen.* Ed. R.W. Chapman. Oxford: Clarendon Press, 1926.

Jane Austen's nephew notes how her knowledge of Richardson was especially characterized by what she knew about the minutest detail of *Grandison.*

391. Barbauld, Anna L. "Life of Samuel Richardson, with Remarks on His Writings." See #62, I, vii-ccxii.

A biographical study, with critical material on the three novels and information on the correspondence; an important early work.

392. ————. "Richardson." In *The British Novelists; with an Essay and Prefaces, Biographical and Critical.* 50 vols. London: F.C. and J. Rivington, 1810. I, i-xlvi.

An introduction to *Clarissa* for *The British Novelists* series, providing a biography of Richardson and an evaluation of all three novels.

393. Balzac, Honoré de. *Oeuvres.* Ed. Marcel Bouteron and Henri Longnon. Paris: Louis Conard, 1912-32. The significant references can be found in the Avant-propos of the *Comedie humaine*, I, xxxv; *Illusions perdues*, XI, 276; *Mémoires de deux jeunes mariées*, I, 231-32; *Modeste Mignon*, II, 81; *Pierrette*, XI, 90; *Albert Savaurus*, III, 39; *Honorine*, IV, 351; *Correspondence 1819-1850* (Paris, 1876), I, 87; and *Lettres à l'étrangère* (Paris, 1899), I, 471, 476.

Balzac was disenchanted with the Protestant heroines
in *Pamela* and *Grandison* as well as with the tedium of
the latter; *Clarissa*, however, is one of the supreme
novels of the world.

394.   Bibb, Grace C. "The English Novel." *Western; a Journal
of Literature, Education and Art*, 2 (1876), 257-78.

Discusses Richardson's place in the development of
the novel in terms of his contribution to characterization.

395.   Billson, Charles J. "The English Novel." *Westminster
Review*, 138 (1892), 602-20.

A brief mention of Richardson as a founder of "that
school of genteel novelists" in a summary history of
the novel.

396.   Birrell, Augustine. "Samuel Richardson." In *Res
Judicatae*. 1892; rpt. New York: Charles Scribner's
Sons, 1916.

A good-natured, sometimes shrewd lecture on Richardson
and his novels, suggesting that nineteenth-century
critics are actually "annoyed with Richardson because he violates a tradition" of the novelist being
either a drunk or an impoverished struggler.

397.   Bowles, William Lisle. "An Answer to Some Observations
of Thomas Campbell, Esq. in His Specimens of British Poets." In *The Invariable Principles of Poetry*. Bath:
Richard Cruttwell, 1819.

Notes in passing how Richardson is a fine painter of
nature; his art is based upon the passions and its
chief characteristic is pathos; *Clarissa* is the novel
discussed.

398.   Brink, Jan Ten. *De Roman in Brieven 1740-1840*. Amsterdam: Elsevier, 1889.

Comments especially upon *Grandison*.

399.   *British Quarterly Review*. "British Novelists and Their
Styles," 30 (1859), 443-65.

A review of Masson's book (#458) which also briefly
considers Richardson's accomplishments in his three
novels; although Richardson's weakness lies in plot,

his strengths lie in his "minute homeliness" and "moral
sense." The writer compares him to Defoe, Fielding,
Smollett, and Sterne.

400.   Carlyle, Thomas. "Burns." In *Critical and Miscellaneous
       Essays. The Works of Thomas Carlyle*. 30 vols. Lon-
       don: Chapman & Hall, 1898-1901. XXVI, 277.

       Richardson is briefly compared with Homer and Defoe
       in terms of his descriptive power.

401.   Chalmers, Alexander. *The British Essayists*. London,
       1802-03. XIX, xiv.

       Reports that Richardson's contribution to Johnson's
       Rambler was the only successful paper and the one truly
       popular.

402.   ———. "Samuel Richardson." In *The General Biograph-
       ical Dictionary*. Rev. edn. 32 vols. London: J.
       Nichols and Son, 1816. XXVI, 191-97.

       Essentially a summary of Richardson's life and
       character, it includes a notice of Mrs. Barbauld's
       Life (#391) and a critical extract from Sherlock's
       evaluation of the novelist (see #236).

403.   Chambers, Robert. "Samuel Richardson." In *Chambers's
       Cyclopedia of English Literature*. 3rd edn. Rev.
       Robert Carruthers. 8 vols. New York: American Book
       Exchange, 1879. III, 244-48.

       A short evaluation of Richardson's achievement with a
       short extract from *Pamela* illustrating his technique.

404.   *Chambers's Biographical Dictionary*. "Samuel Richardson."
       Ed. J.O. Thorne. 1897; rev. edn. New York: St.
       Martin's Press, 1968. P. 1081.

       Summarizes Richardson's life and achievement with
       brief notices of nineteenth-century evaluations.

405.   *Chambers's Journal of Popular Literature, Science, and
       Arts*. "The Man of Men: According to Our Great-Grand-
       mothers," 30 (1858), 193-97.

       A plot summary of *Grandison* with an analysis that dis-
       covers the "vitality" of the novel in its minute render-
       ing of English life in the eighteenth century.

406. *The Christian Remembrancer.* "Richardson," 56 (1868),
      330-55.

      A review of Richardson stimulated by E.S. Dallas's
      edition of *Clarissa* (#41); special attention is given
      to the character of Lovelace, Dallas's introduction,
      and the critical positions taken toward *Clarissa* both
      in the eighteenth and nineteenth centuries.

407. Coleridge, Samuel Taylor. *Anima Poetae.* Ed. Ernest
      Hartley Coleridge. 1895; rpt. Folcroft, Pa.: Fol-
      croft Press, 1969. P. 166.

      Comments on Richardson's mind: for example, it is
      "vile," "hypocritical," and "canting."

408. ————. *Biographia Literaria.* 2 vols. London, 1817.
      Rpt. Everyman's Library Edition. London: J.M. Dent
      & Sons, Ltd., 1930.

      A brief comment in chapter 23, noting Richardson's
      "loaded sensibility, minute detail, the morbid con-
      sciousness of every thought and feeling in the whole
      flux and reflux of the mind, in short the self-involu-
      tion and dreamlike continuity" of his work.

409. ————. *Table Talk.* In *Coleridge's Miscellaneous
      Criticism.* Ed. Thomas M. Raysor. London: Constable
      & Co., Ltd., 1936. P. 437.

      Notes Coleridge's comment that "to take him [Fielding]
      up after Richardson is like emerging from a sickroom
      heated by stoves, into an open lawn on a breezy day."

410. *Critical Review*, 3rd ser., 3 (1804), 155-65, 276-87.

      A long, favorable review of Mrs. Barbauld's *Corres-
      pondence* and *Life* of Richardson (#62 and #391); com-
      pares Richardson with Defoe and the dramatists, printing
      extracts from Mrs. Barbauld's criticism as well as from
      the novels and correspondence.

411. Crompton, Samuel. "Richardson's 'Clarissa' Annotated."
      N&Q, 5th ser., 8 (1877), 101-03.

      Presents selections of the annotations by Lady
      Bradshaigh and Richardson inscribed in her first edi-
      tion of *Clarissa.*

412. Cross, Wilbur L. "The Eighteenth-Century Realists 1.

Samuel Richardson." In *Development of the English
Novel*. 1899; rpt. New York: Greenwood Press, 1969.
Pp. 31-42.

Studies Richardson's abandonment of the paraphernalia
of romance for a realistic concentration upon and exmina-
tion of "the heart," but suggests that as a psychologist,
Richardson is linked in several ways to the conventions
of romance.

413. Cumberland, Richard. "Observer." In *British Essayists*.
Ed. A. Chalmers. 45 vols. London: J. Johnson and
Others, 1802-03. No. 27, XLI (1803), pp. 179-86.

Although *Clarissa* is conceived of in the highest moral
terms, the thought is better than the execution; prudent
parents should forbid the novel to their daughters since
much mischief will arise from young ladies imagining
themselves a Clarissa.

414. Dallas, E.S. Introduction to *Clarissa*. See #41.

Briefly summarizes the novel and Richardson's achievement.

415. De Sevelinges. "Samuel Richardson." In *Biographie
Universelle, Ancienne et Moderne*. 52 vols. Paris:
L.G. Michaud, 1811-28. XXXVII (1824), 579-82.

Summarizes Richardson's life and accomplishment in
his novels, citing various French critics' judgments of
Richardson such as Diderot's and La Harpe's.

416. Dibdin, Charles. *Observations on a Tour* ... London,
[1803]. I, 142.

Believes enough in Richardson's "astonishing genius"
but censures him for creating exaggerated and morally
flawed characters imitated by other writers.

417. Disraeli, Isaac. *Curiosities of Literature*. New York,
1877. II, 227.

Notes Richardson's love of his own writing and gives
an anecdote from Mrs. Lennox, concerning Richardson
reading his voluminous letters to his guests.

418. Dobson, Austin. "Richardson at Home." In *Eighteenth
Century Vignettes*. Second series. 1894; rpt. London:
Oxford Univ. Press, 1923. Pp. 50-76.

Provides information regarding Richardson's personality,

habits, and friends. First printed in *Scribner's Magazine*, 14 (1893), 375-83.

419. Drake, Dr. Nathan. "Sketches Biographical and Critical
of the Occasional Contributors to *The Rambler*, *Adven-
turer*, and *Idler*." In *Essays, Biographical, Critical
and Historical, Illustrative of "The Rambler," "Adven-
turer," and "Idler."* 2 vols. London: J. Seeley,
Buckingham, 1809-10. II (1810), 47-73.

Reviews Richardson's life (based upon Mrs. Barbauld's
Life, #391), comments upon Richardson's contemporaries'
evaluations of the novels, especially analyzes
Clarissa, and summarizes Richardson's literary reputation.

420. Dunlop, John Colin. *History of Prose Fiction*. 2 vols.
1814; rpt. rev. with Notes, Appendices, and Index
by Henry Wilson. London: George Bell and Sons, 1906;
New York: AMS Press, 1969. II, 569-72.

A summary of Richardson's three novels, emphasizing
his delineation of character.

421. *Edinburgh Review*. "Lives of Edward and John Philips,
Nephews and Pupils of Milton, &c. By William Godwin,"
25 (1815), 485.

Richardson's popularity has waned in England but not
abroad; but if the blemishes in diction have been re-
moved in translation, so have been his distinctive
style and portrayal of English manners.

422. Eliot, George. *The George Eliot Letters*. Ed. Gordon
S. Haight. New Haven: Yale Univ. Press, 1954-55.
I, 240; II, 65; VI, 320.

Eliot's comments on Richardson, including her
sentiment regarding his perfect morality.

423. FitzGerald, Edward. *Letters and Literary Remains*.
London, 1902-03. II, 247; III, 321.

Notes Richardson's prolixity; recalls Tennyson commenting that *Clarissa* was one of "those large, still,
Books" which he loved.

424. Forman, H. Buxton. "Samuel Richardson, As Artist and
Moralist." *Fortnightly Review*, 12 (Oct. 1869), 428-43.

A thorough analysis of *Clarissa* treating especially

the characterization of Clarissa and Lovelace and the
theme of marriage (as applicable to the nineteenth century as to Richardson's era); the review was inspired
by Dallas's edition of *Clarissa* (#41), and it gives
some evaluation of the abridgement.

425. Forsyth, William. *The Novels and Novelists of the
     Eighteenth Century, in Illustration of the Manners
     and Morals of the Age.* 1871; rpt. Port Washington,
     N.Y.: Kennikat Press, 1970. Ch. 7, 213-57.

     Looks at the three novels and at the correspondence,
     especially a letter to Lady Bradshaigh; it is a sancti-
     monious review of the novels with an emphasis upon
     Grandison "to which the objection of immortality does
     not apply."

426. *Fraser's Magazine.* "British Novelists--Richardson,
     Miss Austen, Scott," 61 (1860), 20-38.

     An article signed "W.F.P." which summarizes Richard-
     son's achievement, concentrating upon his power of
     characterization in *Clarissa* and *Grandison.*

427. ————. "Richardson," 71 (Jan. 1865), 83-96. Also
     Littell's Living Age, 84 (1865), 215-26.

     Reviews Richardson's achievement and notes that he
     deserves to be read more than he is; it includes plot
     summaries and studies the characterization of Sir
     Charles and Clarissa, Richardson's morality, and the
     manners of the age portrayed in the novels.

428. Gassmeyer, Max. *Samuel Richardsons "Pamela." Ihre
     Quellen und ihr Einfluss auf die englische Literatur.*
     Leipzig: Druck von O. Schmidt, 1890.

     Not examined.

429. *Gentleman's Magazine*, 76 (1816), 577-78.

     Prints Highmore's account of Richardson's death.

430. ————. "Letters of the Earl of Dudley to the Bishop
     of Llandaff," 167 (1840), 339-48; esp. 342-43 and
     343n.

     Briefly mentions the dreary duty of reading such works
     as *Grandison* and *Clarissa*; the footnote calls attention
     to the criticism on the two novels in the *Memoirs* of
     Sir James Mackentosh, Vol. II, p. 237.

431. ————. "Piozziana," N.S., 34 (1850), 267.

    A brief notice which describes how the Italian scenes in *Grandison* best illustrate Richardson's genius.

432. Gosse, Edmund. *Modern English Literature.* 1897; rpt. New York: D. Appleton and Co., 1928. Pp. 241-42.

    A brief reference to Richardson, placing his contribution to the novel below that of Fielding, Sterne, or Smollett.

433. ————. "The Novelists." In *A History of Eighteenth Century Literature (1660-1780).* 1889; rpt. Freeport, N.Y.: Books for Libraries Press, 1972. Pp. 245-51.

    A brief and very general survey of Richardson's novels.

434. Gould, Elizabeth Porter. "Novel Writing." *The Literary World,* 15 (1884), 245.

    Primarily a discussion (in dialogue form) of the scope and form of the novel, with a reference to *Clarissa* to illustrate how important "a good reading atmosphere" is "to reflect an author's mind."

435. Green, Thomas. *Extracts from the Diary of a Lover of Literature.* Ipswich, 1810. P. 77.

    Notes how *Grandison* with its emphasis upon the "lesser manners" which formulate a civilized life justly rates its greater popularity than that of *Clarissa* which portrays "the higher morals, engrafted on the fiercer passions."

436. Griffin, Richard. *Specimens of the Novelists and Romancers.* London, 1810; 1st American from the 2nd Edinburgh edn., New York, 1831. II, 43-44.

    Indicates the impression *Pamela* made on the humble people late in the eighteenth century.

437. Hardy, Thomas. "The Profitable Reading of Fiction." *The Forum,* 5 (March 1888), 67.

    Briefly notes Richardson's constructive art in *Clarissa.*

438. Hazlitt, William. "On the English Novelists." In *Lectures on the English Comic Writers.* Centenary

Edition. Ed. P.P. Howe. 21 vols. 1819; rpt. J.M.
Dent and Sons, 1960. VI, 117-20.

A short but incisive analysis of Richardson's strengths
as a novelist; Hazlitt's other miscellaneous references
to Richardson should be checked in the index.

439. Henley, William Ernest. "Richardson." In *Views and
      Reviews. Works*. London: David Nutt, 1908. V, 257-65.

Typical criticism of Richardson's "fantastic" ideals,
with brief glances at the three novels, emphasizing the
brilliance of *Clarissa* and the masterly creation of
Lovelace.

440. Hill, George Birkbeck, ed. *Johnsonian Miscellanies*.
      2 vols. 1897; rpt. New York: Barnes & Noble, 1966.

Records various anecdotes about Richardson: Mrs.
Piozzi's recollection of Johnson's comment about Clarissa, "there is always something she prefers to truth";
Miss Frances Reynolds' remarks about Johnson's apparent
jealousy of Richardson's success with certain literary
ladies Johnson felt a paternal affection for; and
Hannah More's memory of Johnson's panegyric on Richardson's virtues. Also prints three of Johnson's letters
to Richardson; consult the index for all references to
Richardson.

441. Hunt, Leigh. *The Town. Its Memorable Characters and
      Events*. 2 vols. 1848; rpt. with an introduction
      by Austin Dobson. London: Henry Froude, 1907. Pp.
      58, 89-96.

Includes a comment upon Richardson's and his wife's
portraits in Stationers' Hall; he makes a biographical
summary based upon Mrs. Barbauld's *Life* (#391).

442. Jeaffreson, J. Cordy. *Novels and Novelists, from
      Elizabeth to Victoria*. 2 vols. London: Hurst &
      Blackett, 1858. I, 118-47.

Briefly treats Richardson by superficially scanning
critical and biographical information from the *Edinburgh
Review* (#443), appropriating it and transforming it
into an exaggerated critical analysis.

Reviewed: *New Quarterly Review and Digest of Current
            Literature*, 7 (1858), 259-64 (unfavorable).

443. Jeffrey, Francis Jeffrey, Lord. *Samuel Richardson.*
     1853; rpt. Folcroft, Pa.: Folcroft Press, 1969.
     Originally published *Edinburgh Review*, 5 (1804-05),
     23-44. Rpt. *Museum of Foreign Literature, Science
     and Art*, 32 (1838), 41-50.

     A lengthy review of Mrs. Barbauld's edition of
     Richardson's correspondence (#62). Jeffrey quotes and
     appreciates her comments on *Clarissa*, but laments, on
     the whole, that the letters were made public. Richard-
     son's copious detail is, perhaps, his most valuable
     contribution to the novel.

444. Jusserand, J.J. *The English Novel in the Time of Shake-
     speare.* Trans. Elizabeth Lee. Rev. and enlarged by
     the author, London: T. Fisher Unwin, 1890. Pp. 123,
     124, 127, 169, 249-50.

     Richardson and his novels are considered in the
     tradition of prose developed by such writers as Lyly
     and Greene; suggests the name, Pamela, was borrowed
     from Sidney.

445. ————. *Le Roman anglais; origine et formation des
     grandes écoles de romanciers du xviiie siècle.*
     Paris: Ernest Leroux, 1886.

     A summary of Richardson's artistic merit and his
     effect on French literature: "il révéla au monde tout
     le charme infini de l'analyse des mouvements du coeur."

446. Knight, Charles. "Samuel Richardson." In *Shadows of
     the Old Booksellers.* London: Bell and Daldy, 1865.
     Pp. 125-53.

     A general life of Richardson with brief commentaries
     on the novels; some greater attention paid to Richard-
     son's business life.

447. Lang, Mrs. Andrew. "Manners and Morals in Richardson."
     National Review, 14 (1889), 321-40. Also *Littell's
     Living Age*, 183 (1889), 771-82.

     A discussion of Richardson and the novels, emphasizing
     the different fashions and styles of the earlier era:
     the independence of his heroines, his views on duelling,
     his use of first names.

448. ————. "Richardson." In *Letters on Literature.*

London: Longmans, Green, & Co., 1889. Pp. 135-46.

A chatty discussion of *Grandison* (in the form of a letter), examining Richardson's characterization of Charlotte and Sir Charles and Richardson's naming of characters; some comparisons are made with the two earlier novels.

449. Lanier, Sidney. *The English Novel: A Study in the Development of Personality.* Rev. edn. New York: Charles Scribner's Sons, 1897. Pp. 176-81, 183-84.

Primarily a summary of Richardson's epistolary form with examples from *Pamela* and a plot summary of the book, noting its "moral mission" but "silly and hideous realization of it."

Reviewed: *Literary World*, 14 (1883), 204.

450. Larroumet, Gustave. *Marivaux. Sa vie et ses oeuvres.* Paris: Librairie Hachette et cie., 1910. P. 314, fn. 1.

Further discussion of the influence of Marivaux upon *Pamela*; modern scholarship considers direct influence unlikely.

451. Le Breton, André Victor. "Influence de Richardson." In *Le roman au dix-huitième siècle.* Paris: Société Française d'Imprimerie et de Librairie, 1898. Pp. 180-202.

Considers that until Rousseau, French taste in the novel depended upon Richardson.

452. Lee, Sophia. *The Life of a Lover.* London, 1804. I, 51.

A heroine is urged to avoid Pamela's prudery when a gentleman of greater rank makes advances to her.

453. *Library Journal.* "The Hundred Greatest Novels," 17 (1892), 55.

Includes *Pamela* in the list.

454. *Littell's Living Age.* "Clarissa," 87 (1865), 92-95.

The same article as in the *Spectator* for 1865, stimu-lated by a Leipzig edition of the novel; it studies Clarissa and Lovelace, emphasizing how thoroughly Richardson understood and portrayed them.

455. Lucas, Eliza. "An Essay in Criticism." In *A Library of American Literature*. Ed. E.C. Stedman and E.M. Hutchinson. 11 vols. New York: William Evarts Benjamin, 1889-90. II, 446-47.

A clever mock letter on *Pamela II*, noting the defect in Pamela of writing at length how others praise her.

456. Magnussen, Johannes. *Samuel Richardson; et afsnit af romanes historie*. Copenhagen, 1891.

This is a brief literary history, focusing upon the development of the novel, Richardson's achievement in his three novels, and his influence upon the novel's developing form. He relies primarily upon Mrs. Barbauld's *Life* of Richardson (#391) and Sir Walter Scott's life of the novelist published for *Ballantyne's Novelists Library* (#489). There is also a long note on Richardson's influence upon such writers as Goethe and Holberg.

457. Mangin, Edward. Introduction to *The Works of Samuel Richardson*. See #27, pp. vii-xxviii.

A sketch of his life and an evaluation of his achievement in the three novels.

458. Masson, David. "British Novelists of the Eighteenth Century." In *British Novelists and Their Styles*. Rev. edn. 1859; rpt. Folcroft, Pa.: Folcroft Press, 1969. Pp. 99-121.

A lecture, summarizing *Pamela* and *Clarissa* and contemporary reactions to them; it includes an evaluation and contrast of Richardson with his contemporaries, especially Fielding.

459. Minto, William. "The Decline of Poetry--the Novel." In *The Literature of the Georgian Era*. Ed. W. Knight. Edinburgh: William Blackwood and Sons, 1894. Pp. 103-110.

A two-page summary of Richardson's achievement, suggesting he is not now read, but that *Clarissa* "in favourable circumstances" evokes a kind of spell.

460. Mitford, Mary Russell. "Letters of Authors. Samuel Richardson." In *Recollections of a Literary Life; Or, Books, Places, and People*. London: Richard Bentley, 1852. Pp. 411-23.

Varied comments on Richardson's novels and personal

character, based upon Richardson's correspondence.

461. *Monthly Magazine.* "Eulogy on Richardson. An Original
      Letter," 3 (1800), 163-67.

      An article signed "R.P." arguing that Christ is the
      real prototype for the "*imaginary* beings that Richard-
      son *created*" for testifying to the salvation of all
      mankind.

462. ————. "Objections to Richardson's *Clarissa*," 3
      (1800), 321-23.

      A reply to #461 above, arguing that *Clarissa* and
      Grandison reveal many faults: virtue appears synonymous
      with rank and wealth; filial duty is not absolute; a
      too delicate nature is a chief calamity. As a work of
      art, *Clarissa* cannot be too much admired; as a model for
      right conduct, it is defective.

463. *Monthly Review.* "Standard Novels," 3 (Dec. 1844),
      533-58.

      A long analysis of German and French novels and
      novelists as well as a discussion of romance and
      historical romance; Richardson is mentioned in passing
      (538-39) with regard to his "English" morality, which
      was a check to foreign indecency and flippancy, but
      his books are "tedious" and naturally were supplanted
      by those of Fielding and Sterne.

464. More, Hannah. *Coelebs in Search of a Wife.* London,
      1808. II, 210-11.

      Considers Richardson's virtuous characters as por-
      trayals of "the triumph of religion and reason over
      the passions."

465. *New England Quarterly Magazine; Comprehending Litera-
      ture, Morals and Amusement.* "Answer to a Father's
      Inquiries Relative to the Education of Daughters,"
      3 (1802), 154-59.

      Richardson's novels are recommended above all others
      to a father perplexed about his daughter's reading,
      with special emphasis given to *Grandison*.

466. Nichols, John. *Illustrations of the Literary History of
      the Eighteenth Century.* 8 vols. 1817-58; rpt. New

York: Kraus Reprint Corp., 1966. VI, 798; VIII, 53.

Includes references to *Grandison* by Duncombe and comments on Mrs. Barbauld's *Life* of Richardson (#391) by Caldwell.

467. ————. "Samuel Richardson." In *Literary Anecdotes of the Eighteenth Century.* 9 vols. 1812-16; rpt. New York: AMS Press, 1966. IV, 578-98; also rpt. Colin Claire, ed. "Richardson." Carbondale: Southern Illinois Univ. Press, 1967. Pp. 296-303.

A brief summary of Richardson's life and reputation with copious notes from contemporaries on such subjects as *Clarissa* or the Dublin pirates of *Grandison*.

468. *North American Review.* "Thackeray, As a Novelist," 77 (1853), 199-219.

In this review article there is a brief notice of the pathos and sublimity of Richardson, but these are considered "smothered" by excessive sentiment and awkward phrasing.

469. *Notes and Queries.* "Richardson's House at the Grange, North End, Hammersmith," 5th ser., 12 (1879): F.G., 264-65; G.F.B., 295; O., 295; F.G., 318; G.F.B., 337-38; H. Fishwick, F.S.A., 358; W.P.B., 417; Charles Wylie, 437.

A spirited discussion of what is "left" or "right" when viewing Richardson's house in Fulham (near Hammersmith and thus so called). For William Sale's comment on this long exchange, see *N&Q*, 169 (1935), 133-34 (#844).

470. Oliphant, Mrs. "Historical Sketches of the Reign of George II. No. X.-- The Novelist." *Blackwood's Magazine*, 105 (March 1869), 253-76.

A lengthy review of Richardson's life and novels, based largely upon Mrs. Barbauld's *Life* (#391); it indicates the furor of reception given the novels.

471. Peet, William H. "Booksellers' Sales in the Eighteenth Century." *N&Q*, 7th ser., 9 (1890), 301-02.

An account is given of the copyright prices for the three novels in 1766: *Pamela* (£288); *Clarissa* (£600); *Grandison* (£480).

472. Perry, Thomas S. *English Literature in the Eighteenth
      Century.* New York: Harper & Bros., 1883. Pp. 316–
      19, 337–46.

      Richardson wrote in the spirit of his time and composed
      against the heroic romances while he taught the impor-
      tance of virtue.

473. Pooley, Charles. "Richardson's 'Choice of Hercules.'"
      N&Q, 1st ser., 6 (1852), 485.

      As an executor of Richardson's granddaughter, Sarah
      Moodie, Pooley owned the manuscript of a poem he thought
      was by Richardson; it is possibly a poem of the same
      title by Bishop Lowth.

474. Purbeck, Misses. *Neville Castle.* London, 1802. II,
      275–76.

      A character discusses Richardson's waning reputation
      and why Fanny Burney is preferred to him: she has the
      same morality but writes without his "coarseness and
      indelicacy."

475. *Quarterly Review.* "Growth of the English Novel," 163
      (1886), 34–64. Also *Eclectic Magazine*, 107 (1886),
      359; *Littell's Living Age*, 170 (1886), 771.

      Richardson's characters are "authentic," and Clarissa
      is the portrait of a "true woman"; comparisons are made
      with Fielding and Smollett.

476. Raleigh, Walter. "Richardson and Fielding." In *The
      English Novel.* 1894; rpt. St. Clair Shores, Mich.:
      Scholarly Press, 1970. Pp. 140–61.

      A brief biographical summary, using material from
      Richardson's letter to Lady Bradshaigh; a discussion
      of the three novels with primary emphasis on *Grandison*.

477. Rathery, E.J.B. "Richardson (Samuel)." In *Nouvelle
      Biographie Générale.* 46 vols. Paris: Firmin, Didot
      Frères, 1855–66. XLII, 194–95.

      A brief summary of Richardson's life, writings, and
      reputation.

478. Rowland, Percy Fritz. *A Comparison, Criticism, and
      Estimate of the English Novelists from 1700 to 1850.*
      The Chancellor's Essay. Oxford: B.H. Blackwell, 1894.

      A brief and superficial summary of Richardson's

achievement, commenting upon his "morbid effeminacy
and trivial exactitude" as well as upon his "genuine
gift of pathos ... [and] the truthful pourtrayal [sic]
of human character."

479. Ruskin, John. *The Complete Works of John Ruskin*. Ed.
E.T. Cook and Alexander Wedderburn. Library Edition.
39 vols. London: George Allen, 1903-12.

The index lists Ruskin's responses to the novels, to
his sense of Richardson as one of the greatest moral
story-tellers, and to Sir Charles as one of his favorite
heroes in fiction.

480. *St. James' Magazine*. "Richardson's 'Clarissa,'" N.S.,
2 (Oct. 1868-March 1869), 251-55.

A review, stimulated by Dallas's edition of *Clarissa*
(#41); it discusses the epistolary form which gives the
novel its *"vrai semblance,"* the manner in which Richardson deals with Clarissa's story, and the characterization of Clarissa and Lovelace.

481. Saintsbury, George. "The Eighteenth-Century Novel."
In *A Short History of English Literature*. 1898;
rpt. New York: Macmillan Company, 1960. Pp. 598-601.

A summary analysis of the novels with a summarizing
of Richardson's merits and faults: for example, vivid
if exaggerated scenes; real, if limp, grasp of conversation; knowledge of motive and sentiment; tedious
prose; dull story-telling and a lack of humor.

482. ————. Introduction to *Sir Charles Grandison*. See
#47, pp. xi-xxxiv.

Provides a biographical sketch, an analysis of the
novel, and notes connecting his selections from
Richardson's text.

483. Sand, George. *André*. Paris, 1868. P. 15.

Reveals further French Romantic response to *Clarissa*.

484. Sanford, Sir Daniel K. *On the Rise and Progress of
Literature*. Glasgow: Blackie & Son, 1847.

Originally composed to accompany the edition of the
"Popular Encyclopedia or Conversations Lexicon"; he
notes how Richardson created impossible characters
but elaborate detail.

485. *Saturday Review of Politics, Literature, Science and Art.* "Samuel Richardson," 55 (1883), 114-15.

    A review of Richardson's novels inspired by the Sotheran edition (#29); special attention is given to Lovelace, Clarissa, and Sir Charles.

486. Schlegel, Friedrich von. *Lectures on the History of Literature, Ancient and Modern.* Trans. J.G. Lockhart. Edinburgh: W. Blackwood, 1818. Pp. 261, 311.

    Lecture twelve merely notes his great admiration for Richardson's originality and power of representation.

487. Schmidt, Eric. *Richardson, Rousseau und Goethe. Ein Beitrag zur Geschichte des Romans im 18. Jahrhundert.* Jena: Frommann, 1875.

    Studies the impact of Richardson in Germany during the eighteenth century.

488. Scott, Sir Walter. "Henry Mackenzie." In *Lives of the Novelists.* Introduction by Austin Dobson. The World's Classics. London: Oxford Univ. Press, 1906. P. 168. Originally published as prefaces to Ballantyne's Novelists Library. 10 vols. London: Hurst, Robinson & Co., 1821-24. See #28.

    A contrast made between Richardson, Mackenzie, and Sterne, emphasizing Richardson's minutely traced events.

489. ————. "Samuel Richardson." In *Lives of the Novelists.* See #488, pp. 206-56. Rpt. *Museum of Foreign Literature, Science and Art,* 7 (1825), 104-22.

    Includes a short life of Richardson and analyses of the three novels as well as of Richardson's style and essential genius.

490. Seccombe, Thomas. "Samuel Richardson." In *The Age of Johnson, 1748-1798.* 1899; rpt. London: G. Bell and Sons, Ltd., 1932. Pp. 156-63.

    A general summary of Richardson's achievement in his three novels, referring to contemporary opinions about Richardson; an analytic review.

491. *A Sequel to the "History of Sir Charles Grandison." In a Series of Letters Discovered after the Death of the Late Mr. Richardson.* London, 1878.

    An extravagant burlesque which portrays Sir Charles

and Dr. Bartlett as hypocrites and villains; it reveals Harriet's relief when Grandison Hall burns, whereby are lost "1173 letters and copies of letters, besides 47 memoranda, schedules, and shorthand reports given me by my poor husband, and all his notes and reflections upon them."

492. Simonds, William Edward. "The Rise of the Novel." In *An Introduction to the Study of English Fiction*. Boston: D.C. Heath & Co., 1894. Pp. 45-47.

A brief summary of Richardson's interest in letters with a look at *Pamela* and *Clarissa*; he especially notes that "Richardson's sympathy with womanhood was genuine and intelligent."

493. Smith, Sydney. *Edinburgh Review*, 14 (1809), 146.

A review of Hannah More's *Coelebs* (#464), evaluating in passing Sir Charles as less agreeable than Tom Jones but more so than Sherlock or Tillotson.

494. Smyth, Albert H. *The Philadelphia Magazines and Their Contributors 1741-1850*. Philadelphia, 1892. Pp. 35-37.

Discovered a tribute to Richardson in the *American Magazine* for 1758 (see #265).

495. *Spectator*. "Samuel Richardson," 56 (1883), 1284-85.

Criticism of Richardson's fondness for flattery and his inability to judge others--like Fielding--justly; the new Sotheran edition (#29) may, however, tempt readers to read *Clarissa*, an effort worthwhile because of Richardson's creative power in that novel.

496. Stendhal [Marie Henri Beyle]. *De l'amour*. Paris: Editions de Cluny [1938]. P. 103.

Eaves and Kimpel suggest that Stendhal "must have been betrayed by his memory" (#537, p. 275) when he commented that Clarissa dies because of her offended feminine pride. Also see where Stendhal comments about weeping over *Grandison* in *Henri Brulard*, ch. 32.

497. Stephen, Sir Leslie. "The Cosmopolitan Spirit in Literature." In *Studies of a Biographer*. 4 vols. 1898-1902; rpt. New York: G.P. Putnam's Sons,

1907. IV, 230-59.

Discusses and evaluates Texte's thesis regarding the mutual influence of the French and English upon each other's literature, especially with regard to Richardson (see #504).

498. ————. *History of English Thought in the Eighteenth Century*. 2 vols. 1876; rpt. with a preface by Crane Brinton, London: Hart-Davis, 1962. II, 376-80.

Passing references to Richardson in a discussion of the literature of the period.

499. ————. "Richardson's Novels." *Cornhill Magazine*, 17 (1868), 48-69. Published as the Preface to the Sotheran Edition of Richardson's novels (see #29). Rpt. *Hours in a Library*. 4 vols. 1892; rpt. New York and London: G.P. Putnam's Sons, 1904.

A somewhat condescending review of Richardson, but it emphasizes his power of observation in his detailed settings and his sensitivity to feminine psychology.

500. ————. "Samuel Richardson." In *Dictionary of National Biography*. Ed. Leslie Stephen and Sidney Lee. 63 vols. London: Smith, Elder, & Co., 1885-1900. XLVIII, 243-47.

A general summary of Richardson's life and achievement.

501. Stockdale, Percival. *Lectures on the Truly Eminent English Poets*. London: D.N. Shruy, 1807. I, 181-89.

A reply to criticism censuring Richardson for creating too idealized characters in Clarissa or Sir Charles.

502. Taine, Hippolyte Adolphe. "The Novelists." In *History of English Literature*. 4 vols. 1863; rpt. New York: Frederick Ungar Publishing Co., 1965. III, 271-88.

A discussion and summary of Richardson's three novels; his art consists of his ability to combine while he observes, and "his meditation develops the ideas of the moralist," but his morality becomes a disadvantage when applied so thoroughly to the character of Clarissa.

503. Talfourd, Sir T. Noon. "On British Novels and Romances, Introductory to a Series of Criticisms on the Living

Novelists." In *Critical and Miscellaneous Writings*.
3rd edn. New York: D. Appleton and Co., 1872. Pp.
5-8.

An analysis reprinted from the *New Monthly Magazine*,
suggesting that Richardson's emotive power lies in his
minute detail compared with the "bright and breathing
world" of Fielding's novels.

504. Texte, Joseph. *Jean-Jacques Rousseau and the Cosmo-
      politan Spirit in Literature*. Trans. J.W. Matthews,
      1899; rpt. New York: B. Franklin, 1970. Esp. 144-51,
      155-241.

An analysis, arguing that Richardson changes the destiny of the French novel; a complete chapter evaluates
Richardson's novels, considering their defects, their
kind of realism, and Richardson's delineation of character, moral ideas, and sensibility.

505. Thackeray, William Makepeace. *The English Humorists*.
      In *Works*. Cornhill Edition. New York: Scribner,
      1911. XXI, 346.

Considers that Richardson's muse "was attended by
old maids and dowagers, and fed on muffins and bohea."

506. ————. "Nis Nisi Bonum." *Cornhill Magazine*, 1 (1860),
      129-34.

Records Macaulay's interest in *Clarissa*, his sense
of being infected by it while reading it, and the
incident in India when Macaulay was there, regarding
the impact of the novel among his acquaintances.

507. ————. *The Virginians*. In *Works*. Cornhill Edition.
      See #505, XVII, 129.

A famous sketch of Richardson, emphasizing his love
of admiration and the coterie of his female devotees.

508. Titherington, Richard H. "Development of the Novel."
      Munsey's Magazine, 8 (1892-93), 281-97.

Brief mention of Richardson in a summary history of
the novel; the emphasis is upon *Pamela*.

509. Traill, H.D. "The Novel of Manners." In *The New
      Fiction and Other Essays on Literary Subjects*. London:
      Hurst and Blackett, 1897. Pp. 137-69. Originally

published *Nineteenth Century, a Monthly Review*, 18
(1885), 561-76; also *Eclectic Magazine*, 105 (1885),
729-39; *Littell's Living Age*, 167 (1885), 323-32.

Discusses the "essential unsoundness" of Johnson's
distinction between Richardson and Fielding, emphasizing
instead that both exhibit human nature; primarily a
study of the novel of manners after Richardson.

510.   ———. "Richardson and Fielding." In *The New Lucian
        Being a Series of Dialogues of the Dead*. London:
        Chapman and Hall, 1884. Pp. 200-15. Rpt. *English
        Dialogues of the Dead; a Critical History, an Anthol-
        ogy, and a Check List*. Ed. Frederick M. Keener.
        New York: Columbia Univ. Press, 1973.

        A dialogue between the two novelists, Fielding
        charging Richardson with a love of ladies' foolery and
        flattery, Richardson lamenting Fielding's coarseness,
        and the two discussing each other's faults and merits.

511.   ———. "Samuel Richardson." In *The New Fiction and
        Other Essays on Literary Subjects*. London: Hurst
        and Blackett, 1897. Pp. 104-36. Originally published
        in *Contemporary Review*, 44 (Oct. 1883), 529-45; also
        Littell's Living Age, 159 (1883), 343-54.

        A review article, stimulated by the Sotheran edition
        of the novels (#29); a prosy discussion primarily of
        Pamela and *Clarissa* in terms of the central motive of
        each respective heroine.

512.   Tuckerman, Bayard. *A History of English Prose Fiction*.
        New York: G.P. Putnam's Sons, 1882. Pp. 193-203.

        A general but balanced survey of Richardson's novels
        and reputation; he stirred the heart and moved the
        passions, and with his novels "English fiction took a
        long step forward."

        Reviewed: *Literary World*, 13 (1882), 421.

513.   Ward, Mrs. Introduction to *Clarissa*. See #42, pp. iii-
        iv.

        She severely abridges the novel and emphasizes es-
        pecially the last three months of Clarissa's life.

514.   Ward, Wm. C. "Samuel Richardson." *Gentleman's Magazine*,
        N.S., 44 (1890), 74-86. Also *Littell's Living Age*,
        184 (1890), 459-66.

Richardson discussed in the context of his predecessors such as Mrs. Behn, Swift, and Defoe; his chief
contribution to the novel was in making his characters
live: analyses of Clarissa, Lovelace, and Sir Charles.

515. Watt, Robert. "Samuel Richardson." In *Bibliotheca
Britannica or a General Index to British and Foreign
Literature*. 4 vols. 1824; rpt. New York: Burt
Franklin, 1965. II, 803b.

A brief catalogue of his works.

516. Wells, Benjamin W. "Richardson and Rousseau." *MLN*,
11 (1896), 225-32.

A careful summary of the social and political conditions which made Richardson popular in France as well
as an analysis of his novelistic strengths and ideas
which so inspired Rousseau.

517. West, Jane. *The Infidel Father*. London, 1802. III,
334.

Richardson's famous heroines and the precedents they
set are discussed by silly novel-reading women.

518. ————. *Letters to a Young Lady*. London, 1811. II,
453-54.

Praises *Clarissa* and *Grandison* for moral excellence,
pathetic and descriptive power, and devout and pious
sentiment.

519. *Westminster Review*. "Richardson's *Clarissa*," 91 (1869),
48-75.

A review of Richardson's life, reputation, and technique, stimulated by Dallas's abridged edition of
Clarissa (#41); a brief análysis of the novel is
included.

IV.
Twentieth-Century Criticism

A. PRIMARY WORKS ON RICHARDSON
AND HIS PERIOD

520. Allen, B. Sprague. *Tides in English Taste, 1619-1800:*
     A Background for the Study of Literature. 2 vols.
     Cambridge: Harvard Univ. Press, 1937.

     Refers to Richardson and his three novels in relation
     to the milieu of the eighteenth century: for example,
     the "passion for porcelain" and Richardson's scoffing
     at it in *Grandison.*

521. Ball, Donald L. *Samuel Richardson's Theory of Fiction.*
     The Hague: Mouton, 1971.

     Discusses Richardson's theory of fiction implied
     in passages throughout his writing with analyses of
     narrative structure, epistolary technique, characteriza-
     tion, and moral doctrine.

     Reviewed: *PQ*, 52 (1973), 569.
               RES, N.S., 27 (1976), 81-84.

522. Bayne Powell, Rosamond. *Eighteenth-Century London Life.*
     New York: E.P. Dutton & Co., 1938.

     Does not deal with Richardson, but provides good back-
     ground for understanding the London scenes in his
     novels.

523. ———. *English Country Life in the Eighteenth Century.*
     London: John Murray, 1935.

     Not on Richardson specifically, but provides a good
     background to social customs.

524. Birnbaum, Johanna. *Die Memoirs um 1700. Eine Studie*
     zur Entwicklung der realistischen Romankunst vor
     Richardson. Halle: M. Niemeyer, 1934.

     This is a discussion which considers how memoirs in-
     fluenced the development of the realistic novel.

525.   Black, Frank G. *The Epistolary Novel in the Late Eigh-*
       teenth Century: A Descriptive and Bibliographical
       Study. Eugene: Univ. of Oregon Press, 1940.

       A study which carefully considers the epistolary novel,
       its conventions and techniques, as it develops after
       Richardson.

       Reviewed: *JEGP*, 40 (1941), 588-89.
                 YWES, 21 (1941), 201.

526.   Brissenden, R.F. *Samuel Richardson*. London and New
       York: Published for the British Council by Longmans,
       Green, 1958.

       A concise summary of Richardson's life and his three
       novels. A general introduction.

       Reviewed: *YWES*, 39 (1958), 215-16.

527.   Brophy, Elizabeth B. *Samuel Richardson: the Triumph*
       of Craft. Knoxville: Univ. of Tennessee Press, 1974.

       A formulation of Richardson's artistic precepts based
       upon his own comments on his correspondence, prefaces,
       and novels.

       Reviewed: *ECS*, 9 (1976), 454-56.
                 ELN, 13 (1975), 61-63.
                 JNL, 34 (1974), 8.
                 RES, N.S., 27 (1976), 81-84.

528.   Bullen, John Samuel. *Time and Space in the Novels of*
       Samuel Richardson. Monograph Series, 12, No. 2,
       July, 1965. Logan: Utah State Univ. Press, 1965.

       A discussion of how time and space create a special
       fictional world in Richardson's novels, especially in
       Clarissa where they blend to form a unified dramatic
       development.

       Reviewed: *YWES*, 46 (1965), 247.

529.   Chandler, Frank W. *The Literature of Roguery*. 2 vols.
       1907; rpt. New York: Burt Franklin, 1958.

       Not strictly on Richardson but provides a significant
       critical background for an understanding of Lovelace.

530.   Collins, Arthur Simons. *Authorship in the Days of*
       Johnson, Being a Study of the Relations between
       Author, Patron, Publisher and Public, 1726-1780.
       London: Robert Holden & Co., 1927.

References to Richardson with relation to "Author and Bookseller," "The Copyright Struggle," and "The Growth of the Public"; primarily background material on the status of writers in the eighteenth century.

531. Danielowski, Emma. *Die Journal der frühen Quaker.* Berlin, 1921.

Argues that Richardson's technique can be discovered by a minute inspection of Quaker autobiographies; does not actually say Richardson was influenced by them, but that they represent a vital background to his Protestant, religious life.

532. Day, Robert Adams. *Told in Letters: Epistolary Fiction before Richardson.* Ann Arbor: Univ. of Michigan Press, 1966.

What Richardson's predecessors lacked in artistic prowess they made up for in inventiveness; he traces epistolary and psychological fiction before Richardson, but notes that no developed or evolved tradition simply waited for Richardson's genius to exploit it. Early fiction "was too amorphous and was written too haphazardly to develop as [such] a literary form."

Reviewed: *MP*, 65 (1968), 389–91.
         Novel, 1 (1967), 83–85.
         SAQ, 66 (1967), 121–22.
         TLS, 18 Aug. 1966, p. 738.

533. Dobson, Austin. *Samuel Richardson.* 1902; rpt. Detroit: Gale Research Co., 1968.

An early analytical evaluation of Richardson's life, correspondence, novels, and literary reputation.

Reviewed: *Athenaeum* (17 Jan. 1903), 71–73.
         Bookman, 17 (March 1903), 98–99.
         Lamp, 26 (1903), 216–17.
         Nation, 76 (26 Feb. 1903), 177.

534. Doody, Margaret Anne. *A Natural Passion: A Study of the Novels of Samuel Richardson.* Oxford: Clarendon Press, 1974.

Special attention given to *Clarissa* and *Grandison*, but three chapters deal with *Pamela*; studies the background, sources and analogues as well as the achievement of the novels, but focuses primarily upon imagery, particularly visual imagery.

Reviewed: *EA*, 29 (1976), 611-12.
    ECS, 10 (1976-77), 262-64.
    PQ, 55 (1976), 515-18.
    RES, N.S., 27 (1976), 81-84.

535. Dottin, Paul. *Samuel Richardson, 1689-1761: Imprimeur
   de Londres, Auteur de "Pamela," "Clarisse," "Grandison."*
   Paris: Perin, 1931.

   A biography, showing how Richardson and his work were
   looked at condescendingly by Europeans in the early
   1900's.

   Reviewed: *English Studies*, 14 (1932), 37-40.
      MLN, 47 (1932), 120-22.
      PQ, 10 (1931), 320.
      RAA, 9 (1931), 151-52.

536. Downs, Brian W. *Richardson.* 1928; rpt. London: Frank
   Cass, 1969.

   Primarily biographical, but also contains critical
   information on the novels; analysis of Richardson's
   influence and biography.

   Reviewed: *PQ*, 8 (1929), 199.
      TLS, 31 Jan. 1929, p. 77.
      YWES, 9 (1928), 273-74.

537. Eaves, T.C. Duncan, and Ben D. Kimpel. *Samuel Richardson: A Biography.* Oxford: Clarendon Press, 1971.

   The now standard biography of Richardson's life; includes chapters on his printing years, his circle of
   friends, criticism of the three novels, analyses of the
   receptions given the novels, Richardson's general ideas,
   reading and criticism, and a full list in the Appendix
   of Richardson's known correspondence.

   Reviewed: *EA*, 26 (1973), 296-308.
      ECS, 6 (1973), 518-20.
      JNL, 31 (1971), 1-2.
      New York Review of Books, 10 Feb. 1972, pp.
       27-31.
      PQ, 51 (1972), 752-54.
      RES, N.S., 23 (1972), 504-08.
      SSNTS, 5 (1973), 110-16.
      TLS, 6 Aug. 1971, p. 945.

538. Foster, James R. *History of the Pre-Romantic Novel in England*. New York: The Modern Language Association of America, 1949.

A brief section on Richardson's novels and multiple references to him in terms of the general analysis of the pre-Romantic novel and of sentimentalism.

Reviewed: *MLN*, 68 (1953), 42–46.
           PQ, 29 (1950), 253–54.
           RES, N.S., 2 (1951), 187–89.
           TLS, 7 Oct. 1949, p. 645.

539. Golden, Morris. *Richardson's Characters*. Ann Arbor: Univ. of Michigan Press, 1963.

Richardson and his characters operate as fantasists in search of domination; chapters on such topics as "Richardson and the Bold Young Men," "Girls," "The Conflict of Wills," and "The Individual and Society."

Reviewed: *ELN*, 2 (1964), 136–38.
           JEGP, 63 (1964), 797–800.
           PQ, 43 (1964), 380–81.
           TLS, 18 June 1964, p. 529.

540. Huffman, Charles H. *The Eighteenth-Century Novel in Theory and Practice*. 1920; rpt. Folcroft, Pa.: Folcroft Press, 1969.

He discusses aesthetic principles with numerable passing references to Richardson, especially in chapter four, "Means of Reaching the Inner Life": unity of meaning is achieved through careful presentation of narrated material.

541. Humphreys, A.R. *The Augustan World: Society, Thought, and Letters in Eighteenth-Century England*. 1954; rpt. New York: Harper & Row, 1963.

Only an occasional reference to Richardson, but a sound work providing necessary background to an understanding of the novels; contains chapters on "social life," "business," "public affairs," "religion," "moral and natural philosophy," and the "visual arts."

Reviewed: *MLR*, 51 (1956), 103–05.
           PQ, 34 (1955), 259.
           RES, N.S., 7 (1956), 82–83.
           TLS, 3 Dec. 1954, p. 780; see reply, 17 Dec., p. 821.

542. Iser, Wolfgang. *Der implizite Leser; Kommunikations-
     formen des Romans von Bunyan bis Beckett.* Munchen:
     W. Fink, 1972. Trans. *The Implied Reader: Patterns
     of Communication in Prose Fiction from Bunyan to
     Beckett.* Baltimore: The Johns Hopkins Press, 1974.

     Passing references to Richardson, but no specific
     chapters or sections.

543. Kearney, Anthony M. *Samuel Richardson.* The Profiles
     in Literature Series. London: Routledge & Kegan
     Paul, 1968.

     A general introduction to Richardson's life and works
     with a more elaborate study of situation, character
     portrayal, setting and atmosphere, epistolary technique,
     and Richardson's range and achievement.

     Reviewed: *TLS*, 23 May 1968, p. 529.
               YWES, 49 (1968), 254.

544. Kinkead-Weekes, Mark. *Samuel Richardson: Dramatic
     Novelist.* Ithaca, N.Y.: Cornell Univ. Press, 1973.

     An interpretive analysis of Richardson's novels,
     examining them situation by situation and "exploring
     the implications of each in a flexible, changing and
     complex process"; also probes the form of the novels
     and considers Richardson as a conscious artist.

     Reviewed: *ELN*, 12 (1974), 146-49.
               JNL, 35 (1975), 4-5.
               PQ, 53 (1974), 785-87.
               RES, N.S., 27 (1976), 81-84.
               SEL, 4 (1974), 465-67.
               TLS, 25 Jan. 1974, p. 75.

545. Konigsberg, Ira. *Samuel Richardson & the Dramatic
     Novel.* Lexington: Univ. of Kentucky Press, 1968.

     Argues that Richardson utilized "subject matter and
     techniques developed in the drama" and combined them
     with earlier techniques of fiction to produce the
     modern form of the novel; includes chapters on "Maidens
     and Libertines," and "Sentimental Literature and
     Static Sensibility."

     Reviewed: *ECS*, 3 (1970), 562-63.
               JNL, 28 (1968), 7.
               PQ, 48 (1969), 385-86.

546. Leavis, Q.D. *Fiction and the Reading Public.* 1932;
     rpt. Folcroft, Pa.: Folcroft Press, 1974.

     Passing references to Richardson in relation to the
     growth of the reading public.

547. Levin, Gerald. *Richardson the Novelist: the Psycho-
     logical Patterns.* Costerus: Essays in English and
     American Language and Literature, New Series, 9.
     Atlantic Highlands, N.J.: Humanities Press, 1978.

     Includes chapters on psychological criticism, "Richard-
     son's Art," and "Richardson and Lawrence." It is essen-
     tially a Freudian interpretation which adds little to
     an understanding of Richardson's novels.

548. Longaker, Mark. *English Biography in the Eighteenth
     Century.* 1931; rpt. New York: Octagon Books, 1971.

     Summarizes how biography closely resembles what
     Richardson did with characterization.

     Reviewed: *MLR*, 27 (1932), 484-86.
               MP, 29 (1932), 381-82.
               RES, 8 (1932), 491-93.

549. McBurney, William H., ed. *Four Before Richardson:
     Selected English Novels, 1720-1727.* Lincoln: Univ.
     of Nebraska Press, 1963.

     A critical introduction connects the work of earlier,
     minor novelists with the themes and techniques Richard-
     son will adopt and exploit.

     Reviewed: *YWES*, 44 (1963), 248.

550. McKillop, Alan Dugald. *Samuel Richardson, Printer and
     Novelist.* 1936; rpt. Hamden, Conn.: The Shoe String
     Press, 1960.

     One of the most important critical and biographical
     evaluations of Richardson as a literary artist, examining
     his reputation and assessing his achievement.

     Reviewed: *MLR*, 33 (1938), 77-79.
               JEGP, 36 (1938), 438-40.
               RES, 14 (1938), 106-07.
               TLS, 10 April 1937, p. 270.

551. Major, J.C. *The Role of Personal Memoirs in English
     Biography and Novel.* Philadelphia: Univ. of Penn-

sylvania, 1935.

This is a discussion which deals primarily with re-
viewing memoirs before 1740, but provides background
for an understanding of Richardson's novels.

552. Markun, Leo. *Mrs. Grundy: A History of Four Centuries
      of Morals Intended to Illuminate Present Problems in
      Great Britain and the United States.* New York: D.
      Appleton and Company, 1930.

      Richardson and his novels are put into the context of
      Puritanism and the emphasis upon virtue; a brief analy-
      sis.

      Reviewed: *Saturday Review of Literature*, 9 Aug. 1930,
                 p. 34.

553. Mason, John E. *Gentlefolk in the Making: Studies in
      the History of English Courtesy Literature and
      Related Topics 'from' 1531 'to' 1774.* Philadelphia:
      Univ. of Pennsylvania Press, 1935.

      Occasional references are made to Richardson and his
      novels as they are discussed in their cultural milieu.

      Reviewed: *MLN*, 52 (1937), 593-96.
                 RES, 12 (1936), 350-51.
                 TLS, 19 Sept. 1935, p. 577.

554. May, Georges Claude. *Le dilemme du roman au XVIIIe
      siècle: Étude sur les rapports du roman et de la cri-
      tique (1715-1761).* New Haven and Paris: Yale Univ.
      Press, 1963.

      An analysis of the esthetic and moral attacks against
      the novel in the eighteenth century; many passing
      references to Richardson and especially to *Pamela*.

      Reviewed: *MLR*, 60 (1965), 624-25.

555. Moore, Cecil Albert. *Backgrounds of English Literature
      1700-60.* Minneapolis: Univ. of Minnesota Press, 1953.

      Places Richardson briefly in the tradition of "the
      English malady"; comments on Richardson's "nervous
      paroxysms" and "paralytic tremmors."

      Reviewed: *MLQ*, 15 (1954), 374-75.
                 PQ, 33 (1954), 252-53.
                 RES, N.S., 6 (1955), 91-92.
                 TLS, 4 Dec. 1953, p. 783.

556. Morgan, Charlotte E. *The Rise of the Novel of Manners.*
      1911; rpt. New York: Russell & Russell, Inc., 1963.

      Passing references to Richardson and his novels in
      the tradition of manners and popular literature; pri-
      marily explores pre-Richardson materials.

      Reviewed: *JEGP*, 11 (1912), 626-35.
                Nation, 93 (7 Dec. 1911), 550.

557. Noyes, Robert G. *The Neglected Muse. Restoration and
      Eighteenth-Century Tragedy in the Novel (1740-1780).*
      Brown Univ. Studies, Vol. 24. Providence: Brown
      Univ. Press, 1958.

      Passing references to Richardson and the novels in
      terms of eighteenth-century theories of tragedy and the
      effect of specific tragedies, such as *The Fair Penitent*,
      upon a novel like *Clarissa*.

      Reviewed: *JEGP*, 58 (1959), 533.
                PQ, 38 (1959), 294-95.

558. Paulson, Ronald. *Satire and the Novel in Eighteenth-
      Century England.* New Haven: Yale Univ. Press, 1967.

      Richardson's "writing to the moment" and its effect
      of immersing the reader in the life of the protagonist
      are contrasted with Fielding's "alternative form that
      never for a moment left the reader in doubt about the
      author's intention as to who was good and who evil."
      Commentary on all three novels.

      Reviewed: *JEGP*, 68 (1969), 182-86.
                MLQ, 29 (1968), 222-29.
                Novel, 2 (1969), 284-86.
                PQ, 47 (1968), 340-42.
                RES, N.S., 20 (1969), 232-35.

559. Perry, Bliss. *A Study of Prose Fiction.* 1902; rpt.
      and rev. Boston: Houghton Mifflin, 1930.

      Several passing but very general comments given to
      Richardson.

560. Poetzsche, Erich. *Samuel Richardsons Belesenheit. Eine
      literarischen Untersuchung.* Kiel: R. Cordes, 1908.

      This is a discussion which notes and analyzes the
      many quotations found in Richardson's works and cor-
      respondence in an effort to prove that Richardson was a
      well-read author; discusses Richardson's comments on

his contemporaries, and considers the impact of
dramatic literature upon *Clarissa*.

561. Pons, Christian. *Richardson et la littérature bour-
     geoise en Angleterre*. Aix-en-Provence: Publications
     des Annales de la Faculté des Lettres, 1971.

     Searches out sentimental and bourgeois literary back-
     grounds and reads them into Richardson.

     Reviewed: *PQ*, 51 (1972), 754.

562. Quinlan, Maurice James. *Victorian Prelude. A History
     of English Manners 1730-1830*. 1941; rpt. Hamden,
     Conn.: Archon Books, 1965.

     Considers the changing taste toward Richardson on
     the part of the evangelical editors of the *Eclectic
     Review*; two references to *Pamela* in relation to changing
     temperaments in the nineteenth century.

     Reviewed: *JEGP*, 42 (1943), 137-41.
               MLQ, 4 (1943), 386-88.
               RES, 19 (1943), 220-22.

563. Richetti, John J. *Popular Fiction before Richardson:
     Narrative Patterns 1700-1739*. Oxford: Clarendon
     Press, 1969.

     Provides a crucial background for an understanding of
     Richardson's novels.

     Reviewed: *ECS*, 5 (1971), 192-95.
               MP, 68 (1971), 312-15.
               PQ, 49 (1970), 318.
               RES, N.S., 22 (1971), 87-89.

564. Saintsbury, George. *The Peace of the Augustans: A
     Survey of Eighteenth Century Literature As a Place
     of Rest and Refreshment*. 1916; rpt. New York:
     Russell & Russell, 1970.

     Richardson, and especially *Pamela*, are discussed in
     terms of the eighteenth-century "nascent taste for
     'sensibility.'"

565. Sale, William M., Jr. *Samuel Richardson: Master Printer*.
     Ithaca, New York: Cornell Univ. Press, 1950.

     A standard work, making a systematic and extensive
     analysis of Richardson as a printer; includes lists of

books printed by Richardson.

Reviewed: *MLN*, 67 (1952), 484-85.
         MP, 48 (1952), 274-75.
         TLS, 29 June 1952, p. 412.

566. *Samuel Richardson, His Writings and His Friends.* Stan-
      dard Authors' Booklets. New York: Croscup & Sterling
      Company, 1901.

An interesting review of Richardson's life with brief
descriptions of the novels; it includes chapters on
"Richardson and Fielding," "Richardson's Friends," and
"Richardson's Correspondents" as well as illustrations
of Richardson, Lady Bradshaigh, and Richardson's house
at Hammersmith. It also excerpts items of praise from
eighteenth- and nineteenth-century personalities.

567. Schücking, Levin L. *Die Familie im Puritanismus.* Leip-
      zig, 1929. Trans. Brian Battershaw. *The Puritan*
      Family; A Social Study from the Literary Sources.
      New York: Schocken Books, 1970.

Includes a chapter on Richardson (pp. 145-58) which
argues that he refused to adopt romantic, literary
traditions regarding marriage and dealt instead with
the difficult problems he saw arising out of parental
authority exercised against the desires of children to
marry for love; contains sections on Clarissa and the
Puritan family, Richardson's morality, and the religious
problems in the family of the period. Consult the index.

568. Singer, Godfrey F. "Samuel Richardson and His Develop-
      ment of the Epistolary Novel." In *The Epistolary*
      Novel: Its Origins, Development, Decline, and
      Residuary Influence. Philadelphia: Univ. of Penn-
      sylvania Press, 1933. Pp. 60-98.

Discusses Richardson's importance and influence in
terms of epistolary form; examines each of the novels
and gives plot summaries.

Reviewed: *RES*, 11 (1935), 356-57.
         YWES, 14 (1933), 34, 304.

569. Slagle, Kenneth Chester. *The English Country Squire*
      As Depicted in English Prose Fiction from 1740 to
      1800. 1938; rpt. New York: Octagon Books, 1971.

Alludes throughout to Richardson, especially referring

to *Pamela* and to *Grandison*.

Reviewed: *JEGP*, 39 (1940), 151.
         YWES, 19 (1938), 204.

570. Stephen, Sir Leslie. *English Literature and Society
      in the Eighteenth Century*. Ford Lectures, 1903.
      1904; rpt. New York: Barnes & Noble, 1962.

      A summary review of Richardson and his novels,
      noting Richardson's "genius" but finding it impossible
      to determine "its precise quality." Also relates
      Richardson to the rise of sentimentalism.

571. Straus, Ralph, ed. *Tricks of the Town, Being Reprints
      of Three Eighteenth Century Tracts*. London: Chapman
      and Hall, 1927.

      A collection of materials, giving an account of
      life in eighteenth-century London and providing a good
      background for understanding Richardson's novels; in-
      cludes "Tricks of the Town Laid Open" (1747), "A Trip
      through the Town" (1735) and "A Trip from St. James to
      the Exchange" (1744).

572. Taylor, Gordon R. *The Angel-Makers: A Study in the
      Psychological Origins of Historical Change 1750-1850*.
      London: Heinemann, 1958.

      Passing references to Richardson in a psychological
      analysis of English history, emphasizing the role of
      sexuality on morality and social ideas.

      Reviewed: *Spectator*, 30 May 1958, p. 706.
               TLS, 11 July 1958, p. 390.
               Twentieth Century, 164 (1958), 201-02.

573. Thomsen, Ejnar. *Studier i Richardsons romaner*. Copen-
      hagen, 1928.

      Not examined.

574. Thomson, Clara L. *Samuel Richardson; a Biographical
      and Critical Study*. 1900; rpt. Folcroft, Pa.: Fol-
      croft Press, 1969.

      An early biography of Richardson with essays on the
      development of the novel, Richardson's three novels, his
      art, and his influence.

      Reviewed: *Athenaeum*, 22 Sept. 1900, pp. 369-70.

575. Tieje, Arthur Jerrold. *The Theory of Characterization
      in Prose Fiction Prior to 1740*. Minneapolis: Univ.
      of Minnesota Press, 1916.

      An analysis of the aims of fiction, specifically
      characterization, prior to Richardson as contained in
      prefaces and epilogues to works of fiction, first, in
      order to understand pre-Richardsonian purposes and
      methods, and, second, in order to provide a basis for
      understanding Richardson's (as well as Prévost's or
      Fielding's) place in the development of the novel.

576. Uhrström, Wilhelm. *Studies on the Language of Samuel
      Richardson*. 1907; rpt. Folcroft, Pa.: Folcroft
      Press, 1969.

      This is a discussion which studies the most important
      ways in which "the language of Richardson's time differs
      from modern English."

577. Watt, Ian. *The Rise of the Novel: Studies in Defoe,
      Richardson and Fielding*. 1957; rpt. Berkeley: Univ.
      of California Press, 1971.

      An important, seminal work on the eighteenth-century
      novel, providing insight into social and literary back-
      grounds and containing perceptive chapters on *Pamela*
      and *Clarissa*.

      Reviewed: *Essays in Criticism*, 8 (1958), 428-38.
                MLN, 72 (1957), 622-24.
                MP, 55 (1958), 208-10.
                PQ, 37 (1958), 304-06.
                Yale Review, 46 (1957), xviii-xxiv.

578. Weibel, Kathryn. *Mirror Mirror: Images of Women
      Reflected in Popular Culture*. New York: Anchor Books,
      1977.

      Links Richardson's invention of the popular novel and
      the fictional formulas of romance, courtship tales, and
      domestic melodrama to the popular image of the house-
      wifely, passive, wholesome, and pretty woman. Some
      discussion of both *Pamela* and *Clarissa*.

      Reviewed: *Booklist*, 74 (1977), 253.
                Library Journal, 102 (1977), 1668.

579. Whittuck, C.A. *The "Good Man" of the XVIIIth Century:
      A Monograph on XVIIIth Century Didactic Literature*.

London: George Allen, 1901.

Richardson is excluded from this work; he is "didactic enough" "but not *human* enough."

580. Willey, Basil. *The Eighteenth-Century Background: Studies on the Idea of Nature.* 1940; rpt. New York: Columbia Univ. Press, 1962.

Not on Richardson, but a standard work providing background information on the eighteenth-century milieu of his novels.

Reviewed: *JEGP*, 41 (1942), 246-48.
          PQ, 21 (1942), 188-90.
          RES, 18 (1942), 118-21.

581. Williams, Ioan. *Novel and Romance 1700-1800: A Documentary Record.* New York: Barnes & Noble, 1970.

A collection of statements and prefaces by eighteenth-century writers; includes selections from the introductory material to *Pamela* (1740) and (1741), from the 1747, 1748, and 1751 Prefaces to *Clarissa*, and from "An Account of *Clarissa* and Richardson's Reply."

Reviewed: *JNL*, 30 (June 1970), 5.
          PQ, 50 (1971), 401.

582. Wolff, Cynthia Griffin. *Samuel Richardson and the Eighteenth-Century Puritan Character.* Hamden, Conn.: Archon Books, 1972.

Focuses on Richardson as a psychological novelist, his concept of character and the literary devices for exhibiting character, and the sources for both: "his genius lay in his ability to capture the dynamics of character under stress."

Reviewed: *RES*, N.S., 26 (1975), 85-87.
          YWES, 54 (1973), 298-99.

583. Würzbach, Natascha, ed. *The Novel in Letters. Epistolary Fiction in the Early English Novel, 1678-1740.* London: Routledge & Kegan Paul, 1969.

Reprints nine early epistolary stories; summarizes the letter as a literary convention, using examples from *Clarissa* for criticism and explication.

B. LITERARY HISTORIES AND COLLECTIONS
ON THE DEVELOPMENT OF THE NOVEL

584. Allen, Walter. *The English Novel: A Short Critical History*. New York: E.P. Dutton and Company, 1955. Pp. 31-44.

   A summary review of Richardson's life and novels, especially *Pamela* and *Clarissa*; points out Richardson's general qualities, emphasizing that Richardson focuses upon "arbitrary and irresponsible power."

585. Baker, Ernest A. *Intellectual Realism: From Richardson to Sterne*. Vol. 4 of *The History of the English Novel*. 10 vols. 1936; rpt. New York: Barnes & Noble, 1966. Pp. 13-76.

   Examines the three novels in some detail.

586. Barnhart, Clarence L. "Samuel Richardson." In *The New Century Handbook of English Literature*. Rev. edn. New York: Appleton-Century-Crofts, 1967. Pp. 930-31.

   A one-paragraph summary.

587. Bloor, Robert H. "Richardson, Fielding, and Smollett." In *The English Novel from Chaucer to Galsworthy*. 1935; rpt. Folcroft, Pa.: Folcroft Press, 1970. Pp. 144-52.

   A short, unsympathetic and generalizing summary.

588. Borinski, Ludwig. "Richardson." In *Der englische Roman des 18. Jahrhunderts*. Bonn: Athenäeum, 1968. Pp. 98-148.

   Examines the three novels with an emphasis upon Richardson's personality and theology, with sections on various techniques such as the inner monologue and on the ideal of the gentleman.

   Reviewed: *Die neueren Sprachen*, 68 (1969), 151-53.

589. Bradbrook, Frank. "Samuel Richardson." In *From Dryden to Johnson*. Vol. 4 of *The Pelican Guide to English Literature*. Ed. Boris Ford. Baltimore: Penguin Books, 1957. Pp. 293-312.

   A good general introduction to Richardson.

590.   Bredvold, Louis I. "The Sentimental Novel: Richardson."
       In *The Literature of the Restoration and the Eighteenth
       Century 1660-1798.* Vol. 3 of *A History of English
       Literature.* Ed. Hardin Craig. 5 vols. 1950; rpt.
       New York: Collier Books, 1962. Pp. 119-23.

       A brief summary of Richardson's achievement, em-
       phasizing that his "real distinction and strength" de-
       pended upon "his identification with the popular
       sentimental trend."

591.   Browning, David C. "Samuel Richardson." In *Everyman's
       Dictionary of Literary Biography English and American.*
       London: J.M. Dent & Sons, 1958. Pp. 558-59.

       A one-paragraph summary.

592.   Burton, Richard. "Eighteenth Century Beginnings: Richard-
       son." In *Masters of the English Novel: A Study of
       Principles and Personalities.* 1909; rpt. Freeport,
       N.Y.: Books for Libraries Press, 1969. Pp. 23-47.

       A brief general summary critical of Richardson's
       tedious prose, but aware that his genius was psychologi-
       cal development.

593.   Cazamian, Louis. "Richardson." In *The Cambridge
       History of English Literature.* Ed. A.W. Ward and
       A.R. Waller. 14 vols. Cambridge: Cambridge
       Univ. Press, 1913. X, 1-19.

       Provides a view of the literary world in 1740; includes
       a brief biography and discusses the novels and the ways
       in which Richardson affected both British and Continen-
       tal literature.

594.   *Chambers's Cyclopedia of English Literature.* "Samuel
       Richardson." Ed. David Patrick. 3 vols. Rev. edn.
       J. Liddell Geddie. Philadelphia and New York: J.B.
       Lippincott Company, 1938. III, 294-300.

       An evaluation of Richardson's life and novels with
       extracts from each.

595.   Chatterjee, Ambarnath. "Around the Mid-Century: The
       Progress of the Novel (Richardson)." In *A Study of
       English Novel in the 18th Century.* Masters of English
       Literature Series, No. 24. Allahabad, India: Kitab
       Mahal, 1970. Pp. 35-43.

       An uncritical summary of the plots of the three novels

and of the epistolary form; points out Richardson's chief distinctions: subjectivity, minute recording of detail, and portrayal of emotion.

596. Church, Richard. *The Growth of the English Novel.*
     1951; rpt. London: Methuen & Co., 1957. Pp. 68-74.

     Places an emphasis upon Richardson's psychological fiction in *Pamela* and *Clarissa.*

597. Churchill, R.C. *English Literature of the Eighteenth Century.* London: University Tutorial Press, 1953.

     Richardson's three novels are briefly discussed in comparison with Defoe's and Fielding's novels; Richardson's waning popularity can in part be attributed to the skill of more modern novelists who have combined "his subtlety of analysis with Defoe's power of narration."

598. Compton-Rickett, Arthur. "Samuel Richardson." In *A History of English Literature, from Earliest Times to 1916.* 1918; rpt. London: Thomas Nelson and Sons, 1956. Pp. 247-51.

     Briefly summarizes Richardson's sentimentality and method of characterization with a note on his significance and influence.

599. Crawford, Jack R. "Samuel Richardson." In *What to Read in English Literature.* New York: G.P. Putnam's Sons, 1928. Pp. 191-93.

     A capsule summary of the three novels and of Richardson's significant contribution to the development of the novel.

600. Daiches, David. "The Novel from Richardson to Jane Austen." In *A Critical History of English Literature.* New York: Ronald Press Company, 1960. II, 700-13.

     Discusses Richardson from historical perspectives, with considerable plot summary of *Clarissa.*

601. ———. "Samuel Richardson." In *The Penguin Companion to English Literature.* New York: McGraw-Hill Book Company, 1971. Pp. 443-44.

     A brief evaluation of Richardson's life and achievement.

602. D[obson], A[ustin]. "Samuel Richardson." In *Encyclo-
      paedia Britannica*. 11th edn. 29 vols. New York:
      Encyclopaedia Britannica Company, 1910-11. XXIII
      (1911), 300-02.

      A careful review of Richardson's life and accomplish-
      ment in his novels, documenting the analysis with
      references from Richardson's contemporaries and presen-
      ting a good summary of Richardson's achievement.

603. Dyson, H.V.D., and John Butt. *Augustans and Romantics
      1689-1830*. Vol. 3 of *Introductions to English Litera-
      ture*. Ed. Bonamy Dobrée. 4 vols. 3rd rev. edn.
      London: The Cresset Press, 1961. Pp. 60-62, 228-29.

      A very brief, general criticism of Richardson's
      achievement.

604. Ebiike, S. *A Study of English Novels in the Eighteenth
      Century*. Tokyo, 1950.

      Not examined.

605. Edgar, Pelham. "Richardson and the Epistolary Novel."
      In *The Art of the Novel from 1700 to the Present Time*.
      1933; rpt. New York: Russell & Russell, 1965. Pp.
      46-51.

      Richardson combined domestic interests with love motifs
      derived from earlier writers; although the letter form
      does adapt well to the purpose of fiction, Smollett was
      more successful by varying the tone of his letters, and
      Fanny Burney's letters arise more naturally out of the
      occasions described.

606. Elton, Oliver. "The Novel: Samuel Richardson." In
      A Survey of English Literature, 1730-1780. 2 vols.
      1928; rpt. London: Edward Arnold, 1959. I, 160-81.

      A careful study of Richardson's style and technique
      in the three novels, emphasizing his contribution to
      the form of the novel.

607. Elwin, Whitwell. *Some Eighteenth Century Men of Letters*.
      Ed. Warwick Elwin. 2 vols. London: John Murray,
      1902.

      Passing references to Richardson in relation to other
      writers, such as his resentment against Fielding or his
      loyalty to Johnson.

608. Evans, B. Ifor. *A Short History of English Literature.*
      3rd edn. Harmondsworth, Middlesex: Penguin Books,
      1976. Pp. 132-34.

      Notes that Richardson, as a literary artist, was es-
      pecially in control of detail.

609. Fehr, Bernhard. *Die englische Literatur des 17. und 18.*
      Jahrhunderts. Vols. 15-16 of *Handbuch der Literatur-*
      wissenschaft. Ed. Oskar Walzel. Potsdam, 1928. Pp.
      245-49.

      Includes a general survey of Richardson's life and
      novels.

610. Ford, Ford Madox. *English Novel from the Earliest Days*
      to the Death of Conrad. 1930: rpt. Folcroft, Pa.:
      Folcroft Press, 1969. Pp. 71-75.

      Discusses Richardson's sentimentality and revels in
      it.

611. Freedman, Richard. *The Novel.* New York: Newsweek Books,
      1975.

      A survey of the novel from *Pamela* to the present;
      primarily for a general reader and for high school
      libraries.

612. Gerould, Gordon H. *The Patterns of English and*
      American Fiction: A History. 1942; rpt. New York:
      Russell & Russell, 1966. Pp. 74-81.

      Includes a general summary on Richardson.

613. Gillie, Christopher, ed. "Samuel Richardson." In
      Longman Companion to English Literature. London:
      Longman, 1972. Pp. 748-49.

      A brief summary of Richardson and his period with
      numerous cross references to Puritanism, Fielding,
      Defoe, and so forth; a review basically for under-
      graduates.

614. Gosse, Edmund. "Samuel Richardson." In *From Milton*
      to Johnson. Vol. 3 of *English Literature. An Illus-*
      trated Record. Ed. Richard Garnett and Edmund Gosse.
      4 vols. 1903; rpt. New York: Macmillan Co., 1935.
      Pp. 305-09.

      A summary analysis of Richardson's contribution to

the developing novel form and of his success in his
three novels; includes facsimiles of illustrations from
Clarissa by Stothard and a facsimile of a Richardson
letter to Dr. Cox Macro answering the latter's criticism
of *Grandison*.

615.   Harvey, Paul, ed. "Samuel Richardson." In *The Oxford
       Companion to English Literature*. 4th edn. Rev.
       Dorothy Eagle. Oxford: Clarendon Press, 1967. P.
       694.

       A one-paragraph summary.

616.   Hemmings, F.W.J. "Realism and the Novel: The Eighteenth-
       Century Beginnings." In *The Age of Realism*. Ed.
       F.W.J. Hemmings. Harmondsworth, Middlesex: Penguin
       Books, 1974. Pp. 9-35.

       Provides a useful background with bibliographies and
       chronological tables of the emerging realistic novel.

617.   Holliday, Carl. *English Fiction from the Fifth to the
       Twentieth Century*. New York: The Century Co., 1912.
       Pp. 219-28.

       A short general survey of Richardson's contribution
       to the development of the novel, emphasizing Richard-
       son's ability to portray states of mind rather than
       deeds.

618.   Houston, Percy Hazen. "Samuel Richardson." In *Main
       Currents of English Literature: A Brief Literary His-
       tory of the English People*. New York: F.S. Crofts &
       Co., 1926. Pp. 237-40.

       A summary analysis, emphasizing Richardson's scrutiny
       of action and emotion.

619.   Johnson, Reginald Brimley. "Samuel Richardson." In
       *The Comedy of Life from Richardson, Fielding,
       Smollett, Goldsmith, Sterne*. London: John Lane, 1928.
       Pp. 1-45.

       A brief summary with illustrative selections from the
       three novels.

620.   Kettle, Arnold. "Richardson, Fielding, Sterne." In
       An Introduction to the English Novel. Rev. two volumes
       in one. New York: Harper & Row, 1968. Pp. 59-79.

       Considers *Pamela* and *Clarissa* briefly and assesses

Richardson's contribution to the novel: "titillation of emotion for its own sake and the explicit recommendation of a bogus philosophy of life." Richardson's true genius was his portrayal of subtle and contradictory feelings in human beings.

621. Knight, Grant C. "Richardson." In *The Novel in English*. New York: Richard R. Smith, 1931. Pp. 32-41.

A superficial summary; comments that Richardson deserves the "indictment" for dullness and prolixity.

622. Körting, Gustav. "Samuel Richardson." In *Grandriss der Geschichte der englischen Literatur von ihren Anfängen bis zur Gegenwart*. Münster: H. Schöningh, 1905. Pp. 343-44.

A biographical sketch, a listing of the novels, and a brief bibliography.

623. Korninger, Siegfried. "The Novel from 1740 to 1760." In *English Literature and Its Background: The Restoration Period and the Eighteenth Century 1660-1780*. Vienna: G. Gistel, 1964. Pp. 182-92.

Two and one-half pages which summarize the three novels and Richardson's achievement.

624. Krutch, Joseph Wood. "Samuel Richardson." In *Five Masters: A Study in the Mutations of the Novel*. 1930; rpt. Bloomington: Indiana University Press, 1959. Pp. 109-73.

A general summary, stressing Richardson's middle-class respectability, efficient if mechanical virtue, and the pattern of sentimentalism in the novels.

625. Kunitz, Stanley, and Howard Haycraft. "Samuel Richardson." In *British Authors Before 1800: A Biographical Dictionary*. New York: H.W. Wilson, 1952. Pp. 434-36.

A summary of Richardson's life, achievement, and his literary reputation and influence.

626. Legouis, Émile. "Richardson." In *A Short History of English Literature*. Trans. V.F. Boyson and J. Coulson. Oxford: Clarendon Press, 1934. Pp. 235-37.

A summary analysis of Richardson's achievement.

627. ———, and Louis Cazamian. "The Novel of Sentiment."
      In *A History of English Literature*. 2 vols. Rev.
      edn. with additional chapters by Raymond Las Vergnas.
      New York: Macmillan Company, 1971. Pp. 843-50.

      Richardson's sentiment is allied with middle-class
      instincts; considers his art of description and his
      talent for an "austere concentration of interest."

628. Lovett, Robert Morss, and Helen Sard Hughes. "Richard-
      son and Fielding." In *The History of the Novel in
      England*. Cambridge, Mass.: Houghton Mifflin, 1932.
      Ch. 4, 52-63.

      A general, depreciating introduction to Richardson.

629. McCutcheon, R.P. "The Major Novelists: Richardson,
      Fielding, Smollett, Sterne." In *Eighteenth-Century
      English Literature*. 1950; rpt. London: Oxford Univ.
      Press, 1958. Pp. 49-53.

      A summary analysis.

630. McKillop, Alan Dugald. "Samuel Richardson." In *English
      Literature from Dryden to Burns*. New York: Appleton-
      Century-Crofts, 1948. Pp. 262-67.

      A brief but sound general introduction to Richardson's
      life and novels.

631. Millar, J.H. *The Mid-Eighteenth Century*. Vol. 9 of
      Periods of European Literature. Ed. George Saints-
      bury. New York: Charles Scribner's Sons, 1902. Pp.
      147-51.

      Briefly discusses Richardson in a chapter on prose
      fiction; chiefly about *Clarissa*, an extraordinary book.

632. Moody, William Vaughn, and Robert Morss Lovett. "The
      Eighteenth Century: The Novel." In *A History of
      English Literature*. Enlarged edn. Ed. Fred B.
      Millett. New York: Charles Scribner's Sons, 1943.
      Pp. 241-43.

      A summary analysis of Richardson's method, character,
      and purpose.

633. Myers, Robin. "Samuel Richardson." In *A Dictionary of
      Literature in the English Language from Chaucer to*

1940. 2 vols. New York: Pergamon Press, 1970. I, 718.

Briefly lists Richardson's works and editions.

634. Neill, S. Diana. *A Short History of the English Novel*. Rev. edn. New York: Collier Books, 1964. Pp. 58-68.

A short, general survey.

635. Nicoll, W. Robertson, and Thomas Seccombe. "The Rise of the Novel: Richardson and Fielding." In *A History of English Literature*. 3 vols. New York: Dodd, Mead & Company, 1907. II, 635-62.

Richardson's contribution to the novel is placed into the history of prose fiction with special attention given to the distinctions between him and Fielding.

636. Osgood, Charles Grosvenor. "Novels: Richardson, Fielding, Smollett, Sterne." In *The Voice of England. A History of English Literature*. 1935; rpt. New York: Harper and Bros., 1952. Pp. 332-34.

A summary of the three novels, emphasizing the importance of *Clarissa*.

637. Otis, William Bradley, and Morriss H. Needleman. "The Eighteenth Century: The Novel." In *A Survey-History of English Literature*. New York: Barnes & Noble, 1938. Pp. 388-90, 395-96.

An outline summary of Richardson's life and works with lists indicating his merits and defects; it also compares him with Fielding.

638. Otten, Kurt. *Der englischen Roman vom 16. zum 19. Jahrhundert*. Berlin: E. Schmidt, 1971.

Suggests that *Pamela* and *Clarissa* are derived from the persecuted maiden theme of the Greek love-novel and from the tradition of the conduct books. The psychological relevance of Richardson's fiction creates a new novelistic form; there is some consideration of epistolary form and style and some emphasis upon diction and punctuation as rhetorical devices.

639. Phelps, William Lyon. *The Advance of the English Novel*. New York: Dodd, Mead and Company, 1923.

A brief, general analysis of Richardson and Defoe as

the originators of the English novel; he suggests that,
finally, Richardson's novels are less didactic than
Fielding's.

640. Pollard, Arthur. "Samuel Richardson." In *Webster's
    New World Companion to English and American Litera-
    ture*. New York: World Publishing, 1973. Pp. 566-68.

    A brief, general evaluation.

641. Priestley, John Boynton. "The Eighteenth Century." In
    The English Novel. Nelson Classics. 1927; rpt. New
    York: Nelson, 1935. Ch. I, 21-25.

    A summary review of Richardson's writing.

642. ————. "The Novel." In *Literature and Western Man*.
    New York: Harper & Bros., 1960. Ch. 8, 85-95.

    A general summary, stressing Richardson's sensibility
    for sensibility's sake.

643. Quennell, Peter. "The Growth of the Novel." In *A
    History of English Literature*. Springfield, Mass.:
    G. & C. Merriam Company, 1973. Pp. 248-50.

    A brief look at Richardson's life and a summary of
    the novels.

644. Rogers, Pat. "Richardson." In *The Augustan Vision*.
    New York: Harper & Row, 1974. Pp. 267-74.

    A brief summary of Richardson's success as a novelist
    with three pages given to some clear analysis of *Clarissa*.

645. Saintsbury, George. *The English Novel*. 1913; rpt.
    St. Clair Shores, Mich.: Scholarly Press, 1971; New
    York: AMS Press, 1976. Ch. 3, 77-98.

    Special attention is given to *Pamela*; Richardson
    created a probable human being never so extensively
    worked out before.

646. Sampson, George. "Richardson." In *The Concise
    Cambridge History of English Literature*. 3rd edn.
    London: Cambridge Univ. Press, 1970. Pp. 418-20.

    Briefly discusses each novel.

647. Schirmer, Walter F. *Geschichte der englischen und
    amerikanischen Literatur von den Anfängen bis zur*

Gegenwart. 1937; rpt. Tübingen, 1968. Pp. 435-40.

Includes a chapter comparing Richardson's sentimentalism with Fielding's and Smollett's realism; considers
how the sentimental novel created by Richardson utilized
(like the pastoral novel) many episodes and persons,
love intrigues, abductions, and duels, and it intensi-
fied even more an analysis of emotion and praise of
good manners.

648.   Sherbo, Arthur. *Studies in the Eighteenth Century
       English Novel.* East Lansing: Michigan State Univ.
       Press, 1969. Pp. 184-87.

       Passing references to Richardson with some discussion
       of his description of character.

649.   Sherburn, George. "The Mid-Century Novel." In *The
       Restoration and Eighteenth Century 1660-1789.* Bk.
       III of *A Literary History of England.* Ed. Albert
       C. Baugh. Rev. D.F. Bond, New York: Appleton-Century
       Crofts, 1967. Pp. 952-55.

       One of the basic summaries of Richardson's life,
       novels, techniques, and reputation.

650.   Skilton, David. "Richardson and Fielding." In *The
       English Novel: Defoe to the Victorians.* New York:
       Barnes & Noble, 1977. Pp. 19-31.

       The chapter looks at Richardson's and Fielding's
       general achievement in separate sections, giving a very
       general summary of Richardson's novels and noting the
       most obvious merits of each; includes only passing
       comparisons between the two authors.

651.   Stevenson, Lionel. *The English Novel: A Panorama.*
       Boston: Houghton Mifflin, 1960. Pp. 79-86, 94-99,
       115-19.

       A general summary of Richardson in terms of the
       development of the novel.

652.   Stoddard, F.H. *The Evolution of the English Novel.*
       New York: Macmillan Company, 1900.

       Passing references to Richardson and *Pamela* in a
       general discussion of the evolution of the novel.

653.   Wagenknecht, Edward. "Psychological Realism Begins:
       Samuel Richardson." In *Cavalcade of the English*

Novel from Elizabeth to George VI. 1943; rpt. New
York: Holt, Rinehart and Winston, 1967. Pp. 46-57.

A general survey with special sections on "The Epistolary Method" and "Ancestors and Descendants."

654.   Ward, Alfred Charles. *Ben Jonson to Samuel Johnson.*
Vol. 2 of *Illustrated History of English Literature.*
3 vols. London: Longmans, Green, 1953-55. Ch. 10,
179-82.

A summary analysis with some commentary on the genuine
authenticity of Pamela's character.

655.   Whitcomb, Seldon L. *The Study of a Novel.* Boston:
D.C. Heath, 1905.

Refers to Richardson (and *Pamela* and *Clarissa*) to
illustrate the technique of the novel form; primarily
a text for a formal, rhetorical evaluation of the
novel.

656.   Williams, Harold. "Samuel Richardson." In *Two Centuries of the English Novel.* London: Smith, Elder
& Co., 1911. Pp. 32-52.

A summary analysis, noting Richardson's morality,
tedious prose, appeal to the emotions, psychological
detail, and lack of narrative interest.

C. GENERAL LITERARY AND BIOGRAPHICAL CRITICISM
IN PERIODICALS, FESTSCHRIFTS,
AND LITERARY STUDIES

657.   *Academy.* "The Richardson Revival," 61 (1901), 485-86.

A condescending evaluation of Richardson who is "not
for the wireless age"; agrees, however, that Richardson
created the first naturalistic novels: "unflinching,
complete and exact."

658.   Addleshaw, S. "A Pioneer--Samuel Richardson." *Church
Quarterly Review,* 110 (1930), 297-315.

A summary of Richardson's literary reputation with a
careful analysis of his kind of fiction and its strengths;
includes a brief summary of the novels.

659. Allen, Walter. "Letters As Literature: 3. The Virtues of the Epistolary Novel." *TLS*, 26 Jan. 1973, pp. 97-98.

A short, general summary and analysis of the epistolary form.

660. Allot, Miriam. *Novelists on the Novel*. New York: Columbia Univ. Press, 1959.

An index locates extracts from Richardson's correspondence and novels to illustrate his ideas on such items as "romantic extravagance," "moral purpose," amd "characterization."

661. Askew, H. "Samuel Richardson's Birthplace." *N&Q*, 169 (1935), 263.

Requests material regarding Richardson's birthplace (see #887).

662. Baker, C.H. Collins. "A Conversation Piece by Joseph Highmore." *Connoisseur*, 51 (1918), 183-88.

Three of the plates for *Pamela* are reproduced; the text argues that the *Conversation Piece* (a painting) is actually Highmore's, although it has been attributed to Jonathan Richardson.

663. ————. "Joseph Highmore, Samuel Richardson, and Lady Bradshaigh." *Huntington Library Quarterly*, 7 (1944), 316-19.

Primarily concerns the portrait of Richardson by Joseph Highmore, particularly regarding the relationship between Richardson and Lady Bradshaigh and the portrait.

664. Baker, Sheridan. "The Idea of Romance in the Eighteenth-Century Novel." *PMASAL*, 49 (1964), 507-22.

Although novelists are considered "realists," Richardson and his contemporaries "looked for qualities of romance in actual experience" and even "romanced their tales ... with the devices and formulas of their romantic predecessors."

665. Ball, Donald L. "Richardson's Resourceful Wordmaking." *SAQ*, 41 (1976), 56-65.

Further research on Richardson as a literary artist by focusing on his ability to coin new words and

develop compound words and phrases to fit into the
"expansive new world of fiction he was creating."

666.   Barker, Gerard A.   "The Complacent Paragon: Exemplary
       Characterization in Richardson."   *SEL*, 9 (1969),
       503-19.

       The traditional, Protestant belief in the validity of
       self-judgment is illustrated in Richardson's chief
       characters; a Pamela, Clarissa, or Sir Charles display
       their virtue through unhesitant approval of their own
       behavior.

667.   Barnett, George L., ed.   "Samuel Richardson."   In
       Eighteenth-Century British Novelists on the Novel.
       New York: Appleton-Century-Crofts, 1968.   Pp. 72-89.

       A brief summary of Richardson's novelistic techniques
       with a reprinting of the 1751 fourth edition Postscript
       to *Clarissa*.

668.   Beasley, Jerry C.   "English Fiction in the 1740's: Some
       Glances at the Major and Minor Novels."   *SNNTS*, 5
       (1973), 155-75.

       Discusses the nature and scope of the more popular
       eighteenth-century fiction and how in contrast we can
       better understand the freshness of Richardson.

669.   ————.   "Romance and the 'New' Novels of Richardson,
       Fielding, and Smollett."   *SEL*, N.S., 16 (1976), 437-
       50.

       Develops in some detail an analysis of "the climate"
       of the 1740's which spawned the great works of these
       novelists especially in terms of how they attracted
       their audience's attention through topical interests--
       a similarity they shared with popular romancers.

670.   Beer, Gillian.   "Richardson, Milton, and the Status of
       Evil."   *RES*, N.S., 19 (1968), 261-70.

       Explores Richardson's debt to Milton, especially in
       Clarissa, where he, too, justifies the ways of God to
       man and espouses the serious doctrine of virginity;
       characters become both models for mankind and for
       individuals--hence, their poignancy.

671.   Binkley, Harold C.   "A Novelist in Letters."   *PMASAL*,
       8 (1927), 333-40.

       An analysis of Richardson's epistolary technique.

672.   Birkhead, Edith. "Sentiment and Sensibility in the
       Eighteenth-Century Novel." *Essays and Studies by Mem-*
       bers of the English Association, 11 (1925), 92-116.

       An analysis of the two terms with references to
       Richardson's use and understanding of them in his novels;
       also refers to other novels of the period.

673.   Biron, Sir Henry Chartres. "The First English Novelist."
       Littell's Living Age, 303 (11 Oct. 1919), 98-106.

       A comparison of Richardson with Henry James; it in-
       cludes a close analysis of Clarissa and Lovelace.

674.   Black, Frank G. "The Technique of Letter Fiction from
       1740 to 1800." *Harvard Studies and Notes in Philology*
       and Literature, 15 (1933), 291-312.

       Discusses the influence of Richardson's epistolary
       techniques: informality, self-revelation, and the role
       of the confidant.

675.   Black, Sidney J. "Eighteenth-Century 'Histories' As a
       Fictional Mode." *Boston University Studies in*
       English, 1 (1955), 38-44.

       No direct references to Richardson, but valuable as a
       study of a fictional mode affecting the development of
       the novel as Richardson would write it.

676.   Blanchard, Frederic T. *Fielding the Novelist: A Study*
       in Historical Criticism. 1926; rpt. New York: Russell
       & Russell, 1966.

       Includes many references to comparisons between
       Richardson and Fielding; consult the index.

       Reviewed: *RES*, 3 (1927), 227-32.
                 YWES, 7 (1926), 238-40.

677.   Bond, Richmond P. "Eighteenth Century Correspondence:
       A Survey." *SP*, 33 (1936), 572-86.

       A survey of three primary types: (1) intimate, in-
       formal messages; (2) formal, "public" letters; and
       (3) fictitious letters as a literary device.

678.   *Book Prices Current*, 24 (1910), 66.

       Richardson's Notebook contained an account of the
       expenses of printing Sir William Keith's *History of the*
       British Plantations in America.

679. Boyce, Benjamin. *The Benevolent Man: A Life of Ralph
      Allen of Bath.* Cambridge, Mass., 1967.

      Notes information in passing regarding Richardson's
      knowledge of and acquaintance with Ralph Allen.

680. ————. "The Effect of the Restoration on Prose Fic-
      tion." *Tennessee Studies in Literature*, 6 (1961),
      77-83.

      Studies currents in Restoration fiction, such as
      the heroic mode, and concludes that a *Clarissa* might
      have been written sooner "in a middle-class society
      with more emphasis on social pressure and business and
      less on court pleasures."

681. Bradbrook, Frank W. "Samuel Richardson and Joseph
      Conrad." *N&Q*, N.S., 5 (1958), 119.

      Suggests three possible allusions in *Victory* to
      Pamela or *Clarissa* and notes the two authors' mutual
      interest in moral and psychological detail.

682. Braudy, Leo. "The Form of the Sentimental Novel."
      Novel, 7 (1973), 5-13.

      Passing references to *Clarissa* in a discussion of the
      sentimental novel——not in terms of the theater or
      philosophy, but in relation to the tradition as es-
      tablished by the novelists themselves.

683. Brewster, Dorothy. "Hill and Richardson." In *Aaron
      Hill, Poet, Dramatist, Projector*. 1913; rpt. New
      York: AMS Press, 1966. Pp. 239-74.

      Recounts Hill's relationship to Richardson, the basis
      of their friendship, and the substance of their concerns
      and correspondence.

684. Broadus, E.K. "Mr. Richardson Arrives." *London Mercury*,
      28 (1933), 425-35.

      A summary review of Richardson's career and ultimate
      success.

685. Cain, Roy E., and William C. Slattery. "Richardson's
      Role in an Attack on Hume and Bolingbroke." *PLL*, 4
      (1968), 330-34.

      Richardson was apparently successful in persuading
      Peckard to temper his criticism of the so-called deists,
      Hume and Bolingbroke.

686. Carroll, John. "Richardson on Pope and Swift." *UTQ*,
        33 (1963), 19-29.

        An analysis of Richardson's evaluations of Pope and
        Swift which is based upon one of Richardson's letters
        to Cheyne.

687. ————. "Samuel Richardson. A Biography." *RES*, N.S.,
        23 (1972), 504-08.

        A review of Eaves and Kimpel's biography (#537) which
        also considers Richardson's passionate commitment "to
        certain attitudes, certain beliefs," revealing his view
        of the nature of man, "a view that intermingles per-
        sonality, experience, daydreaming."

688. ————. *Samuel Richardson: A Collection of Critical
        Essays.* Englewood Cliffs, N.J.: Prentice-Hall, 1969.

        Provides a critical introduction to a reprinting of
        the following items: #44, #539, #577, #789, #795, #854,
        #941, #977, #1047, #1063, #1064, and #1116.

689. Champion, Larry ,S., ed. *Quick Springs of Sense: Studies
        in the Eighteenth Century.* Athens: Univ. of Georgia
        Press, 1974.

        Numerous references in several essays place Richardson
        in the traditions of sentimentalism, in the conventions
        of novelistic techniques, and in the social milieu;
        consult the index.

690. Chesterton, G.K. "England's Novelists in the National
        Portrait Gallery." *Bookman*, 14 (Jan. 1902), 465.

        Includes Highmore's portrait of Richardson; comments
        briefly on Richardson's features.

691. Clements, Frances M. "The Rights of Women in the
        Eighteenth-Century Novel." *Enlightenment Essays*,
        4 (1973), 63-70.

        Looks briefly at the conditions faced by women
        (domestic service, prostitution, housewifery) and their
        subordination to men; uses references from *Clarissa*
        and *Grandison* and other works of the time.

692. Cockshut, A.O.J. "Richardson and Fielding." In *Man
        and Woman: A Study of Love and the Novel 1740-1940.*
        London: Collins, 1977. Pp. 32-45.

        Compares the two authors by examining their moral

ethics and their portrayal of moral choice in their
novels; some important notice is given to the role
played by the double standard of sexual morality and
its consequences for understanding the characters of
Pamela and Clarissa.

693.   ————. "Sentimentality in Fiction." *Twentieth Cen-*
       tury, 161 (1957), 354-64.

The term "sentimentality" is considered very carefully and discussed in terms of many novels; *Pamela* is
sentimental because Richardson did not analyze his
heroine's motives thoroughly, but *Clarissa* is not:
"complete analysis of motive honestly carried out
precludes sentimentality altogether."

694.   Cohen, Richard. *Literary References and Their Effect*
       upon Characterization in the Novels of Samuel Richard-
       son. Husson College Monograph. Bangor, Me.: Husson
       College Press, 1970.

Considers Richardson's analyses of past and contemporary writers as well as his views on literary genres.

Reviewed: *PQ*, 50 (1971), 474.

695.   ————. "The Social-Christian and Christian-Social
       Doctrines of Samuel Richardson." *Hartford Studies*
       in Literature, 4 (1972), 136-46.

The novels as a whole reveal an interwoven relationship of Christian doctrines through which characters
may resolve their problems; the doctrines also reveal
an environment in which characters learn to instruct
themselves "in how one can properly evaluate himself
relative to life and death."

696.   Collins, A.S. "The Growth of the Reading Public during
       the Eighteenth Century." *RES*, 2 (1926), 284-94,
       428-38.

Richardson's novels are seen in the context of a
growing taste for reading, reflected in the development
and growth of literary periodicals and prose fiction.

697.   Collins, Norman. "The First Psychological Novelist."
       In *The Facts of Fiction*. New York: E.P. Dutton &
       Co., 1933. Pp. 15-37.

A brief discussion of the three novels with extracts
to illustrate major points; suggests, finally, that

there is "about the ceaseless striving of Richardson's
characters, the frantic, unearthly persistence of the
actors in a dream."

698. Copeland, Edward. "Samuel Richardson and Naive Allegory: Some Beauties of the Mixed Metaphor." *Novel*,
4 (1971), 231-39.

The more Richardson uses figurative language (especially mixed metaphors), the more it becomes "an integral
part of the emotional and psychological effects of his
novels"; points out the opposing interests of the
mimetic and didactic in his work.

699. Crane, Ronald S. "A Note on Richardson's Relation to
French Fiction." *MP*, 16 (1919), 495-99.

Disputes Macaulay's argument (#785) for Richardson's
indebtedness to French authors, based on the Preface
to the fourth volume of the first edition of *Clarissa*,
by establishing that the Preface was written by Warburton
and has "no value as a reflection of Richardson's
thought."

700. ————. "Richardson, Warburton and French Fiction."
MLR, 17 (1922), 17-23.

Further evidence that Richardson's alleged indebtedness to the French, suggested by the Preface to the
fourth volume of the first edition of *Clarissa*, is
inaccurate; the work was by Warburton; also clarifies
the argument which occurred between the two men.

701. Cross, Wilbur L. *The History of Henry Fielding*. 3
vols. 1918; rpt. New York: Russell & Russell, 1963.

Many comparisons are made between Richardson and
Fielding with a comment upon four character types that
Richardson drew.

Reviewed: *MLN*, 34 (1919), pp. 235-39.
          TLS, 26 June 1919, p. 350.
          Yale Review, N.S., 8 (1919), 415.

702. Culler, A. Dwight. "Edward Bysshe and the Poet's
Handbook." *PMLA*, 63 (1948), 858-85.

Indicates that Richardson borrowed from Bysshe's
Handbook to supply the characters of his novels with
appropriate sentiments on such subjects as "love, rape,
death, chastity and despair."

703. Daiches, David. "Samuel Richardson." In *Literary*
      Essays. 1956; rpt. Chicago: Univ. of Chicago Press,
      1967. Pp. 26-49.

      A short but incisive introduction to Richardson with
      an analysis of patterns and ideas in *Pamela* and *Clarissa*.

704. Dalziel, Margaret. "Richardson and Romance." *AUMLA*,
      33 (1970), 5-24.

      Richardson's novels have many similarities with the
      romances he despised; considers how he used "the *idea*
      of romance to aid his thinking about what he himself
      was doing."

705. Danielowski, Emma. "Die Grundlagen des Richardson'schen
      Romans." *Germanisch-romanische Monatsschrift*, 12
      (1924), 21-42, 88-110.

      Argues that Richardson's novelistic method of minute
      introspection can be found in the earlier Quaker auto-
      biographies; however, she does not claim any *direct* in-
      fluence.

706. Davis, Frank. "Pioneer Novelist and His Illustrator
      at Kenwood." *The Illustrated London News*, 243 (6
      July 1963), 24.

      Reviews Richardson's and Joseph Highmore's relation-
      ship; prints the portrait by Highmore and one of the
      painter's illustrations for *Pamela*.

707. Davis, Robert G. "The Sense of the Real in English
      Fiction." *CL*, 3 (1951), 200-17.

      Briefly asserts that Richardson used Aristotelian
      tragic theory in *Clarissa* and *Grandison*; primarily a
      discussion of how Aristotelian concepts are incorporated
      into the novel from Boccaccio to George Eliot.

708. Dawson, William James. "Richardson, and the Novel of
      Sentiment." In *The Makers of English Fiction*. New
      York: Fleming H. Revell, 1905. Pp. 12-29.

      A discussion which is critical of Richardson's per-
      sonality as well as of his writing style.

709. Day, Robert A. "Richardson, Aaron Hill, and Johnson's
      'Life of Savage.'" *N&Q*, N.S., 13 (1966), 217-19.

      Reviews the relationship between Richardson and

Johnson, suggesting that the former may have known
Johnson as early as 1744.

710. Detig, Joseph, S.V.D. "Samuel Richardson and His Modern
Critics." *Fu Jen Studies* (Republic of China), 1
(1968), 55-70.

Not examined.

711. Dibelius, Wilhelm. "Richardson." In *Englische Roman-
kunst. Die Technik des englischen Romans im achtzehnten
und zu Anfang des neuenzehnten Jahrhunderts.* Palaestra
92 and 98. Berlin: Mayer and Müller, 1910. Pp. 57-84.

Includes an analysis of the characters of Anna Howe
and Charlotte Grandison and their influence upon the
English novel; there are sections on the relationship of
the heroic novel to French literature, on characterization, structure, narrative form, and Richardson's didac-
ticism. The second volume considers Richardson's
relationship to his times as well as his influence upon
Maria Edgeworth and Jane Austen.

712. Digeon, Aurélien. "Autour de Fielding: I. Miss Fielding, son frère, et Richardson." *Revue Germanique*,
11 (1920), 209-19.

Considers the differences between the two authors
with comments upon the novels.

713. Dobson, Austin. *At Prior Park and Other Papers.* 1912;
rpt. London: Milford, 1925. Pp. 2, 29, 149.

Includes two anecdotes about Richardson concerning
(1) his pride at being admitted to the finest social
company, and (2) his likely response to a comment
written about him by Miss Margaret Collier.

714. ————. *Side-Walk Studies.* 1902; rpt. London: Oxford
Univ. Press, 1924. Pp. 44-45, 74, 75, 78.

Passing references to Richardson in relation to
Dobson's discussion of such topics as St. James Park,
The Covent-Garden Journal, Mrs. Delaney, and Dr.
Johnson.

715. Donaldson, Ian. "The Clockwork Novel: Three Notes on
an Eighteenth-Century Analogy." *RES*, N.S., 21
(1970), 14-22.

A comparison of Richardson and Fielding in terms of

clock imagery, an image which relates to art and the
presentation of time itself.

716. Dottin, Paul. "Samuel Richardson et le roman épis-
      tolaire." *RAA*, 13 (1936), 481-99.

      Discusses Richardson's epistolary technique, especial-
      ly noting that with *Clarissa* the form determines the
      narrative development.

717. Dussinger, John A. "Richardson and Johnson: Critical
      Agreement on Rowe's *The Fair Penitent*." *English
      Studies*, 49 (1968), 45-47.

      Johnson follows Richardson's criticism as expressed
      in Belford's letter to Lovelace [*Clarissa* (Shakespeare
      Head Edition), VII, 133-34 ("Thursday, Aug. 17")].

718. ⸺. "Richardson's 'Christian Vocation.'" *PLL*, 3
      (1967), 3-19.

      Richardson's "religious milieu has been largely ig-
      nored," yet it is crucial to an understanding of his
      literary achievement; examines his religious attitudes
      and how they function in the novels.

719. Eaves, T.C. Duncan. "Graphic Illustration of the Novels
      of Samuel Richardson, 1740-1810." *Huntington Library
      Quarterly*, 14 (1951), 349-83.

      The illustrations of the novels reveal not only that
      Richardson was a dramatist "of high rank" but that
      modern critics of the novels often fail to interpret
      them accurately. The later neglect by artists of
      Richardson's novels (as well as the decline in his
      reputation) lies not with his art but with changing
      attitudes toward Richardson himself.

720. ⸺. "'The Harlowe Family' by Joseph Highmore: A
      Note on the Illustration of Richardson's *Clarissa*."
      Huntington Library Quarterly, 7 (1943), 89-96.

      This painting, thought to be a Hogarth entitled
      The Green Room, Drury Lane, is really by Joseph High-
      more.

721. ⸺. "Joseph Highmore's Portrait of the Reverend
      Edward Young." *SP*, 43 (1946), 668-74.

      Richardson induced Young to sit for this portrait.

722. ————, and Ben D. Kimpel. "Richardsoniana." *SB*, 14 (1961), 232-34.

Describes seven items in a bound volume labeled "Richardsoniana," in the Forster Collection of the Victoria and Albert Museum. Item one provides proof that *Remarks on "Clarissa"* is by Sarah Fielding (see #145); item two is a copy of the catalogue of the Southgate sale of January 21-28, 1828, at which the Richardson material in the Forster Collection was purchased; item three describes the rare eleven-page pamphlet, *Answer to the Letter of a Very Reverend and Worthy Gentleman* (see #12); items four and five are clippings from the *Gentleman's Magazine* referring to *Clarissa* (see #149); and items six and seven are two printed letters of Richardson's concerning *Grandison* (see #51 and #60).

723. ————. "Richardson's Connection with *Sir William Harrington*." *PLL*, 4 (1968), 276-87.

Examines Richardson's detailed comments on this novel in order to throw more light on his moral and social principles as well as on his literary practice.

724. ————. "Samuel Richardson and His Family Circle." *N&Q*, N.S., 11 (1964), 212-18, 264-70, 300-04, 343-47, 362-71, 402-06, 467-69; 15 (1968), 448-50.

Discusses Richardson's connections with Wilde and Leake, his will, ancestors, parents, brothers and sisters, and his birthplace; corrects and supplements information initially considered by Reade (#833).

725. ————. "Samuel Richardson's London Houses." *SB*, 15 (1962), 135-48.

Indicates the various houses Richardson lived in and the periods during which he occupied them.

726. ————. "Two Notes on Samuel Richardson: Richardson's Chapel Rules; the Printer of the *Daily Journal*." *Library*, 5th ser., 23 (1968), 242-47.

Provides evidence that the rules are those of the journeymen in Richardson's own chapel; further evidence of Richardson's connection with the printing of the *Daily Journal*.

727. Enomoto, Futoshi. "Richardson no Atarashisa." *Eigo Seinen*, 114 (1968), 586-87.

Not examined.

728. ————. "Richardson's Theory of Fiction." *Studies in English Literature* (Tokyo), 43 (1967), 181-95.

Discusses how Richardson reveals his critical theory of fiction through the prefaces he wrote; although he reacted against a romance and epic tradition, being temperamentally attuned to a Puritan, realistic tradition, he developed a fiction of the internal heart closely allied with the romance of tradition.

729. Enright, D.J. "The Virtue of Verbosity." *Listener*, 19 Aug. 1971, pp. 245-46.

A review of Eaves and Kimpel's biography (#537) which briefly examines the merits of *Pamela* and *Clarissa*. Pamela is a character "who is sanctimonious, coy, vain, shifty, cunning, vulnerable and plucky--and inexorably present and real"; Clarissa is a great tragic character, and Richardson did well to adhere to his notion of writing a "Religious Novel" by refusing to wed her to Lovelace despite advice from such influential friends as Lady Bradshaigh.

730. Erämetsä, Erik. "Notes on Richardson's Language." *NM*, 53 (1952), 18-20.

Examples of newly-coined words like "out-argued" and "out-talented" in *Clarissa* are discussed as well as abusive terms Richardson enjoyed concocting and verbs normally used as nouns or adjectives.

731. Ernle, Rowland E.P., Lord. "Samuel Richardson." In *The Light Reading of Our Ancestors: Chapters in the Growth of the English Novel*. 1927; rpt. Freeport, N.Y.: Books for Libraries Press, 1970. Pp. 184-204. Originally published *Edinburgh Review*, 243 (Jan. 1926), 139-57.

Discusses Richardson in the context of his predecessors (Mrs. Behn or Eliza Haywood), considers his life and friends, briefly summarizes the novels, and notes their primary distinctions: for example, the character of Lovelace.

732. Follett, Wilson. "Sentimentalism." In *The Modern Novel. A Study of the Purpose and the Meaning of Fiction*. Rev. edn. New York: Alfred A. Knopf, 1923. Pp. 71-99.

Sentimentalism is defined in terms of self-righteousness, vanity, hypocrisy, and fashionable optimism;

Richardson, as a sentimentalist "incarnate," had a
disastrous effect upon the novel as a form which might
reveal and criticize the true values of life even though
he also increased the novel's scope by being "an incom-
parable anatomist of motive and feeling."

733. Forman, H. Buxton. "Richardson, Fielding, and the
      Andrews Family." *Fortnightly Review*, 76 (1901),
      949-59.

Discusses Richardson's shift from model letters to
epistolary fiction, concluding that *Pamela* reveals his
genius in observing the workings of the mind; suggests
that Richardson was attracted to rather than repulsed
by the "sexual misdemeanours" portrayed in the novels.

734. Frank, Frederick S. "From Boudoir to Castle ·Crypt:
      Richardson and the Gothic Novel." *Revue des Langues
      Vivantes* (Bruxelles), 41 (1975), 49-59.

The motifs of terror and pleasurable pain developed
by Richardson in his novels as well as the specific
sex contests in *Pamela* and *Clarissa* reveal that
Richardson is an important source for the rise of the
English Gothic novel.

735. Frye, Northrop. "Towards Defining an Age of Sensi-
      bility." In *Backgrounds to Eighteenth-Century Litera-
      ture*. Ed. Kathleen Williams. Scranton, Pa.:
      Chandler Publishing Company, 1971. Pp. 312-21.
      Originally published *ELH*, 23 (1956), 144-52.

Considers Richardson a writer more intent upon the
"process" of art than upon "story," a technical feature
of narrative closely allied to the emphasis in an age
of sensibility upon the personal and biographical.

736. Gallaway, W.F., Jr. "The Conservative Attitude toward
      Fiction 1770-1830." *PMLA*, 55 (1940), 1041-59.

General references to Richardson in an analysis of the
criticism of fiction; supplements work in #676 and #747.

737. Garnett, David. "Richardson, Fielding, and Smollett."
      In *The English Novelists. A Survey of the Novel by
      Twenty Contemporary Novelists*. Ed. Derek Verschoyle.
      1936; rpt. Folcroft, Pa.: Folcroft Press, 1969. Pp.
      71-82.

A study of Richardson's limitations and strengths;

emphasizes his middle-class tendencies, reviews the three novels, and considers Richardson to "have had but the slightest influence" on literature; praises the dramatic intensity of *Clarissa.*

738. Glättli, Walter. "Richardson." In *Die Behandlung des Affekts der Furcht im englischen Roman des 18. Jahrhunderts.* Zürich: Juris, 1949. Pp. 57-70.

Discusses Richardson's use of fear, especially as it is used in conjunction with the theme of persecuted innocence. The heroine's degree of apprehension oscillates repeatedly to produce a particularly strong effect.

739. Golden, Morris. "Richardson's Repetitions." *PMLA*, 82 (1967), 64-67.

Richardson employed similar character types in his novels and "involved them in similar situations ... more pervasively and significantly than has so far been noted"; includes a list of plot devices repeated in the novels and notes an attempt "to show the essential ambiguity of all moral actions."

740. Green, F.C. "Further Evidence of Realism in the French Novel of the Eighteenth Century." *MLN*, 40 (1925), 257-70.

Discusses Richardson's "realism" with regard to the criticism of Desfontaines.

741. Guilhamet, Leon M. "From *Pamela* to *Grandison*: Richardson's Moral Revolution in the Novel." In *Studies in Change and Revolution: Aspects of English Intellectual History 1640-1800.* Ed. Paul J. Korshin. Menston, Yorkshire: Scolar Press, 1972. Pp. 191-210.

Richardson writes neither social nor psychological realism; his characters are primarily moral exemplars: "The moral ideal he envisioned had a reality like that of the symbol for a Romantic poet."

742. ————. *The Sincere Ideal: Studies on Sincerity in Eighteenth-Century Literature.* Montreal: McGill-Queens Univ. Press, 1974. Pp. 287-99.

Includes an Appendix ("The Novel of Sincerity") in which Richardson is discussed in terms of the ideal of sincerity which spawned an intellectual and moral movement during the period.

743. Gwynn, Stephen. "Samuel Richardson." *Quarterly Review*,
      259 (1932), 315-30.

      A general, undiscerning summary of Richardson's life,
      briefly noting his achievement in *Pamela* and *Clarissa*.

744. H., A.J. "Lady Bradshaigh, Richardson's Correspondent."
      N&Q, 164 (1933), 192-93.

      Identifies Lady Bradshaigh as Dorothy Bradshaigh
      whose father was William Bellingham of Levens, Westmore-
      land.

745. Halsband, Robert. "Lady Mary Wortley Montagu and
      Eighteenth-Century Fiction." *PQ*, 45 (1966), 145-56.

      Considers Richardson's novels from Lady Mary's
      sophisticated experience as a writer of fiction.

746. ————. "Women and Literature in 18th Century
      England." In *Woman in the 18th Century and Other
      Essays*. Ed. Paul Fritz and Richard Morton.
      Toronto: Hakkert, 1976. Pp. 55-71.

      Two references to Richardson appear in this analysis
      of the prominence and activity of women in the literary
      life of the eighteenth century. Most novels published
      in this century were written by women, and because
      these were considered more salable, even men signed
      their works with female pseudonyms. One of the effects
      of this practice was "to encourage critics to define
      what they regarded as feminine qualities in litera-
      ture" and "to analyze what was distinctive in the mind
      and art of women writers."

747. Heidler, Joseph B. *The History from 1700 to 1800, of
      English Criticism of Prose Fiction*. University of
      Illinois Studies in Language and Literature, 13, No.
      2 (May, 1928). Urbana: Univ. of Illinois Press, 1928.

      Richardson and his novels are discussed in the context
      of the developing perception during the eighteenth cen-
      tury that the novel was not just "a pleasing diversion
      for women and children" but an artistic unit "which
      required the development of new critical standards."

748. Highet, Gilbert. "Fiction." In *The Classical Tradition:
      Greek and Roman Influences on Western Literature*.
      New York and London: Oxford Univ. Press, 1949. Pp.
      340-42.

      A brief, three-page reference to Richardson, suggesting

the influence of Greek and Roman romances on *Clarissa*
and *Pamela*.

749. Hillhouse, James T. *The Grub-Street Journal*. Durham,
     N.C.: Duke Univ. Press, 1928. Pp. 154, 157.

     Provides some brief information on Richardson's con-
     nection with his contemporary periodicals.

750. Hopkinson, Tom. "The English Novel--II. The Printer
     Who Wrote a Masterpiece." *Listener*, 43 (1950), 162-63.

     A brief look at Richardson's life and a summary analy-
     sis of *Pamela* and *Clarissa*.

751. Horn, András. "Byron's Don Juan and the Eighteenth-
     Century English Novel." *Swiss Studies in English*,
     51 (1962).

     This work is not specifically on Richardson, but
     studies the Byronic protagonist as it is derived from
     Fielding, Sterne, and Smollett; however, the discussion
     of social morality, subjectivism, and the picaresque
     provides relevant information for understanding the
     character of Lovelace.

752. Hornbeak, Katherine G. "The Complete Letter Writer in
     English, 1568-1800." *Smith College Studies in Modern
     Languages*, 15 (1934). Northampton, Mass.: Smith
     College, 1934.

     Richardson's letter writers are discussed from the
     perspective of the letter-writing tradition.

753. ————. "Richardson's 'Familiar Letters' and the
     Domestic Conduct Books; Richardson's 'AEsop.'" *Smith
     College Studies in Modern Languages*, 19 (1938), 1-50.
     Northampton, Mass.: Smith College, 1938.

     Demonstrates that the spirit and content of Richard-
     son's "complete letter-writer" are derived from the
     domestic conduct books; Richardson's *AEsop* reveals, in
     its comparison with Sir Roger L'Estrange's, Richardson's
     ideas and general attitude toward life, especially his
     stance as a moralist.

754. Horner, Joyce M. "The English Women Novelists and Their
     Connection with the Feminist Movement (1688-1797)."
     Smith College Studies in Modern Languages, 11 (1929-
     30). Northampton, Mass.: Smith College, 1929-30.

Discusses Richardson's attitude toward women and his
influence upon the women novelists who came after him.

755. Howells, W.D. "Editor's Easy Chair." *Harper's Monthly
      Magazine*, 105 (Aug. 1902), 479-83.

An analytical review of Richardson's achievement,
especially in *Clarissa*, stimulated by Phelps' edition
of the novels (#30).

756. Hudson, William H. "Samuel Richardson: The Father of
      the English Novel." *A Quiet Corner in a Library*.
      1915; rpt. Freeport, N.Y.: Books for Libraries Press,
      1968. Pp. 163-238.

A general and informal survey of Richardson and his
novels.

757. Hughes, Helen Sard. "An Early Romantic Novel." *JEGP*,
      15 (1916), 564-98.

Discusses the recently discovered novel by Mrs. Mary
(Mitchell) Collyer, *Felicia to Charlotte* (1749); suggests that the epistolary format reveals Richardson's
influence. Richardson and the author did share a common
friend, Miss Talbot.

758. ————. "English Epistolary Fiction Before *Pamela*."
      In *The Manly Anniversary Studies in Language and
      Literature*. Chicago: Univ. of Chicago Press, 1923.
      Pp. 156-69.

A survey of epistolary fiction before Richardson in
order to show how his works are part of a larger epistolary tradition; he "blended the self-revelation of
the letters of intrigue and the realism of the letters
of affairs" to create a new form aimed at instruction.

759. ————. "The Middle-Class Reader and the English
      Novel." *JEGP*, 25 (1926), 362-78.

References to Richardson's influence upon the growing
middle-class reader; primarily discusses "the growing
recognition of the merchant as a person of interest to
the reading public."

760. ————. "Translations of the *Vie de Marianne* and Their
      Relation to Contemporary English Fiction." *MP*, 15
      (1917), 491-512.

A discussion of the relation of Marivaux and Richardson

to the development of fiction prior to and at the time
of the appearance of *Pamela*.

761. Hughes, Leo. "Theatrical Convention in Richardson: Some
      Observations on a Novelist's Technique." In *Restora-
      tion and Eighteenth-Century Literature: Essays in
      Honor of Alan Dugald McKillop*. Ed. Carroll Camden.
      Chicago and London: Univ. of Chicago Press for William
      Marsh Rice Univ., 1963. Pp. 239-50.

      Richardson's use of "stage business" as it formulated
      and developed his dramatic method for displaying depth
      of feeling.

762. Humiliata, Sister M. "Standards of Taste Advocated for
      Feminine Letter Writing, 1640-1797." *Huntington
      Library Quarterly*, 13 (1950), 261-77.

      No references to Richardson, but valuable for under-
      standing how a tradition "of preciosity" stemmed from
      Balzac's *Letters* (1624) and Voiture's (1649) and thereby
      brought "elegant language" and "refined sentiment" to
      the attention of a middle-class audience.

763. Humphreys, A.R. "'The Friend of Mankind' 1700-60: An
      Aspect of Eighteenth-Century Sensibility." *RES*, 24
      (1948), 203-18.

      Provides significant background for understanding
      how intuition and emotion became more important as the
      century progressed; refers to *Grandison* as an example.

764. ————. "Richardson's Novels: Words and the 'Movements
      Within.'" *Essays and Studies by Members of the
      English Association*, N.S., 23 (1970), 34-50.

      "The syntax and style of *Pamela* and *Clarissa* are
      strangely acute transmitters of psychological idiosyn-
      crasies"; syntax recreates a psychological situation
      where "no fact *is*, but where all facts are resultants
      of attitudes."

765. Hunt, Russell H. "Johnson on Fielding and Richardson:
      A Problem in Literary Moralism." *The Humanities
      Association Review*, 27 (1976), 412-20.

      A comparison of the two authors based on Johnson's
      evaluations, noting Johnson's greater similarity to
      Fielding in art and morality, but determining that
      Fielding's ethic is finally based on emotion whereas

the seemingly sentimental Richardson has his ethic
soundly centered on reason.

766. Hunter, Jean E. "The 18th-Century Englishwoman: Ac-
     cording to the *Gentleman's Magazine*." In *Woman in
     the 18th Century and Other Essays*. Ed. Paul Fritz
     and Richard Morton. Toronto: Hakkert, 1976. Pp. 73-
     88.

     Not specifically on Richardson, but discusses how in-
     formation gleaned from the *Gentleman's Magazine* shows
     that traditional attitudes towards women (the "soft
     sex," incapable and helpless) were not as prevalent as
     often thought. Articles are generally supportive of
     women and sympathetic to their plight; knowledge of
     these facts is important for assessing Richardson's
     own treatment of his women characters.

767. *Illustrated London News*. "The Himalayan 'Yeti';
     London Kestrel, and a Novelist's Coffin," 221 (July
     12, 1952), 65.

     A photograph of Richardson's coffin; the latter was
     found during excavations of St. Bride's Church and also
     a bronze memorial tablet to him.

768. Jackson, Holbrook. "Samuel Richardson." In *Great
     English Novelists*. 1908; rpt. Folcroft, Pa.: Folcroft
     Press, 1972. Pp. 39-63.

     Summarizes Richardson's life and then evaluates the
     novels with an emphasis upon his gift for subjective
     development, storytelling, and epistolary style; notes
     his fondness for women whom he understood with "sym-
     pathetic intuition."

769. Johnson, Reginald Brimley. *Novelists on Novels: From
     the Duchess of Newcastle to George Eliot*. London:
     Noel Douglas, 1973. Pp. 35-45.

     Extracts Richardson's views on the novel from his
     novels and correspondence.

770. Jones, C.E. "The English Novel: A Critical View, 1756-
     86 (Notices of Fiction in the *Critical Review*.)"
     MLQ, 9 (1958), Pt. I, 147-59; Pt. II, 213-24.

     A general account of the *Critical Review*'s attitude
     toward the novel-reading public, publishers, and circu-
     lating libraries as well as notices of individual authors
     such as Richardson.

771. Jost, François. "L'Évolution d'un genre: le roman
      épistolaire dans les lettres occidentales." In
      Essais de littérature comparée. II, Europaeana.
      Fribourg: Éditions universitaires; Urbana: Univ. of
      Illinois Press, 1968. Pp. 89-179.

      Richardson's epistolary method is discussed in terms
      of the general evolution of this technique in Western
      literature. "Les germes de tendances nouvelles sont à
      chercher dans les traditions mêmes de chacune de ces
      littératures. Ce n'est point Richardson qui a inventé
      et promulgué le roman épistolaire, lequel demeure
      essentiellement une manifestation générale de la
      civilisation européene tout entière." An appendix also
      provides a catalogue of epistolary fiction from the
      time of Ovid to Juan Alonso (1966).

772. ———. "Le roman épistolaire et la technique narrative
      au XVIIIe siècle." *Comparative Literature Studies*, 3
      (1966), 397-427.

      Refers to Richardson as the father of the psychological
      novel based upon epistolary form; the novel of letters
      is considered as a special development of the eighteenth-
      century milieu.

773. Kearney, Anthony. "A Recurrent Motif in Richardson's
      Novels." *Neophilologus*, 55 (1971), 447-50.

      Richardson's metaphoric use of "the unwary bird
      threatened by the fowler's snare" is discussed as it
      appears in the three novels.

774. Kermode, Frank. "Richardson and Fielding." *Cambridge
      Journal*, 4 (1950), 106-14.

      Considers the reputation of the two novelists in
      their own time to the shift occurring with Coleridge.

775. Kinkead-Weekes, Mark. "Defoe and Richardson--Novelists
      of the City." In *Dryden to Johnson*. Ed. Roger
      Lonsdale. Vol. 4 of the *History of Literature in the
      English Language*. London: Barrie & Jenkins, 1971.
      Pp. 226-58.

      Both writers ordered experience according to their
      unique perspectives: Defoe is extensive, Richardson
      intensive; Defoe considered how situations determine
      action, and how economic behavior underlies feeling
      and consciousness whereas Richardson considered situa-

tions only as they provided a means for probing in
depth a personality, character, and consciousness.

776. Kirby, H.T. "Publishers and Booksellers in the
      National Portrait Gallery." *Bookman*, 84 (April 1933),
      24-26.

      Prints Highmore's portrait of Richardson and a one-
      paragraph comment on Richardson as a novelist and a
      generous man.

777. Klotman, Phyllis R. "Sin and Sublimation in the Novels
      of Samuel Richardson." *College Language Association
      Journal*, 20 (March 1977), 365-73.

      Discusses Richardson's Puritan and "inordinate fascina-
      tion" with sin, but argues that he controls it through
      detail and didactic purpose; Pamela and Clarissa as
      moralists are described and analyzed.

778. Konigsberg, Ira. "The Dramatic Background of Richard-
      son's Plots and Characters." *PMLA*, 83 (1968), 42-53.

      Discusses how Richardson was influenced by drama, con-
      cluding that he was probably indebted to plots and
      character types for his own fiction.

779. Lefever, Charlotte. "Richardson's Paradoxical Success."
      PMLA, 48 (1933), 856-60.

      Richardson desires to instruct in manners and morals
      as well as provide model letters for anyone who needs
      instruction; but when he fails in this dual purpose,
      he is most successful as a realist.

780. LeGates, Marlene. "The Cult of Womanhood in Eighteenth-
      Century Thought." *ECS*, 10 (1976), 21-39.

      Pamela, "virtuous unto marriage," and Clarissa,
      "virtuous unto death," become the models for a new
      definition of womanhood, replacing the earlier concept
      of "disorderly woman."

781. Liddell, Robert. *A Treatise on the Novel*. 1947; rpt.
      London: Jonathan Cape, 1963. Pp. 17-18, 108.

      Includes a brief comment on Richardson, claiming that
      the novel in England became the heir of creative minds
      once the drama died in 1700.

782. Logan, A.M. "Richardson Redivivus." *Nation*, 73 (1901),
      489-90.

      A review of Richardson's achievement in the light of
      the Chapman and Hall and Macmillan editions of Richard-
      son's work (#30 and #31).

783. Lubbock, Percy. *The Craft of Fiction.* 1921; rpt.
      New York: The Viking Press, 1964. Pp. 152-55.

      A brief discussion of *Clarissa* in terms of tech-
      nique with some comparisons with *The Ambassadors.*

784. McAdam, E.L., Jr. "A New Letter from Fielding." *Yale
      Review*, 38 (1948), 300-10.

      Richardson's and Fielding's relationship is further
      revealed through a letter from Fielding commenting on
      Clarissa; the text of the letter is given.

785. Macaulay, G.C. "Richardson and His French Predecessors."
      MLR, 8 (1913), 464-67.

      Studies the influence of Marivaux and Richardson upon
      each other: each deals with the romance of everyday
      life in much the same manner and develops a kind of
      writing that leads directly to the modern novel.

786. MacCarthy, D. "Richardson and Proust." In *Criticism.*
      London: Putnam, 1932. Pp. 210-15.

      Finds Richardson "repellent," but, like Proust,
      Richardson focuses attention upon the texture of ex-
      perience while extracting from it the contemporary
      values.

787. McCrae, Thomas. "George Cheyne, an Old London and
      Bath Physician." *Johns Hopkins Hospital Bulletin*,
      15 (March 1904), 1-29.

      Discusses the nature of Cheyne's correspondence
      with Richardson. For a fuller discussion of Cheyne
      see #75.

788. McKenna, Ethel M.M. Introduction to the Chapman and
      Hall Edition of the Novels. See #31, pp. ix-xxxii.

      Discusses how Richardson was an "Apostle of Feminism,"
      summarizes his life, notes the influence of Greek drama
      upon his art, considers his morality, and traces his
      influence on the Continent.

789. McKillop, Alan Dugald. "Epistolary Technique in
      Richardson's Novels." In *Studies in the Literature
      of the Augustan Age: Essays Collected in Honor of
      Arthur Ellicott Case.* Ed. Richard C. Boys. Augustan
      Reprint Society. Ann Arbor, Mich.: The George Wahr
      Publishing Co., 1952. Pp. 199-217. Originally pub-
      lished *The Rice Institute Pamphlet*, 38, No. 1 (April
      1951), 36-54.

      Discusses the art with which Richardson constructed
      his novel of letters to portray the "enmeshing com-
      plexities of life."

790. ――――. "Notes on Smollett ... II. Smollett and Richard-
      son." *PQ*, 7 (1928), 369-71.

      Reprints Smollett's concern about a "silly, mean Insin-
      uation against Mr. Richardson's Writings" and suggests
      the reference is to Greville's criticism appearing in
      the *Critical Review*; also notes Richardson's approval
      of Smollett as an historian.

791. ――――. "The Personal Relations Between Fielding and
      Richardson." *MP*, 28 (1931), 423-33.

      A reassessment of the relationship between the two
      authors, suggesting that "the malevolent passages
      against Fielding inevitably loom too large in a detailed
      account of Richardson's correspondence."

792. ――――. "Richardson, Young, and the *Conjectures*,"
      MP, 22 (1925), 391-404.

      An analysis of the Richardson-Young correspondence,
      revealing the history of the *Conjectures*.

793. ――――. "Richardson's Early Writings--Another Pamphlet."
      JEGP, 53 (1954), 72-75.

      Adds *A Seasonable Examination* ... to Richardson's
      canon.

794. ――――. "Richardson's Early Years as a Printer." *RES*,
      9 (1933), 67-70.

      Discusses Richardson's obscure years from 1715 to
      1725 when he became a freeman of the Stationer's Company
      until he was established as a master printer at Salis-
      bury Court.

795. ————. "Samuel Richardson." In *The Early Masters of
      English Fiction*. Lawrence: Univ. of Kansas Press,
      1956. Pp. 47-97.

      A careful study of the three novels; includes dis-
      cussion of the critical formulas of Richardson's age.

796. ————. "Samuel Richardson's Advice to an Apprentice."
      JEGP, 42 (1943), 40-54.

      Proof that the pamphlet, *The Apprentice's Vade Mecum*,
      was by Richardson.

797. ————. "Supplementary Notes on Samuel Richardson As
      a Printer." *SB*, 12 (1958), 214-18.

      Adds two titles to Sale's list of books printed by
      Richardson: *The Matchless Rogers* and Hervey's *Medita-
      tions among the Tombs, Reflections on a Flower-Garden*;
      includes some additional information on Richardson's
      printing business.

798. ————. "Two 18th Century 'First Works.'" *Newberry
      Library Bulletin*, 4 (1955), 10-13.

      Discusses Richardson's *Vade Mecum* as an example of
      the apprentice manual and of the cautionary tale; it
      is an early example of what he will later do with
      greater complexity in his novels.

799. *Macmillan's Magazine*. "Samuel Richardson and George
      Meredith," 85 (1901-02), 356-61.

      Contrasts Meredith's superior understanding of
      women as real and independent personalities with
      Richardson's portrayal of women constrained by con-
      vention and stereotype; but despite the prejudices of
      his time, Richardson did show an interest in women *as
      women* almost unknown in his age.

800. Martin, Burns. "Richardson's Removal to Salisbury
      Court." *MLN*, 45 (1930), 469.

      Cites evidence of the date Richardson moved from
      Fleet Street to Salisbury Court in 1723.

801. Maslen, Keith. "Samuel Richardson and Smith's
      Printer's Grammar." *Book Collector*, 18 (1969),
      518-19.

      Briefly discusses Richardson's self-interest in

publishing Smith's work; further identifies ornaments
from Richardson's press.

802. McWatters, K.G. "Stendhal, Richardson, et l'*Edinburgh
      Review*." *Stendhal Club*, 1 (1959), 229-30.

      Considers Stendhal's knowledge of Richardson's cor-
      respondence to be derived from his reading of Jeffrey's
      comments upon Mrs. Barbauld's edition (#62).

803. Michele, Laura di. "Il Realismo come expressione dei
      sentimenti e delle emozioni in S. Richardson." In
      *L'Educazione del Sentimento: La Crisi del Romanzo
      inglese fra Gotico a Sentimentale (1750-1800)*.
      Napoli: Istituto Universitario Orientale, 1977. Pp.
      66-92.

      Not examined.

804. Miles, Kathleen. "A Note on Richardson's Response to
      Fielding's Felon." *SNNTS*, 1 (1969), 373-74.

      Notes an oblique attack in *Clarissa* against Fielding's
      Jonathan Wild.

805. Miller, George Morey. "The Publisher of 'Pamela.'"
      TLS, 31 July 1930, p. 628.

      Corrects the account by Aitken in the *DNB* that an
      Osborne (Thomas) was one of the men responsible for
      influencing Richardson to write *Pamela*; the correct
      man was John Osborn of Paternoster Row.

806. Moers, Ellen. "Women's Liberator." *New York Review
      of Books*, 10 Feb. 1972, pp. 27-31.

      A review of Eaves and Kimpel's biography (#537) which
      considers the value of the epistolary form, especially
      in *Pamela*: "Clearly Richardson was obsessed with the
      power of letters to change the world, and with the
      imperative need for the unprotected female to express
      herself in letter form." Moers also considers that
      Richardson possessed "an almost fanatical zeal for
      change" in the relationship between the sexes; he made
      the English novel "the vehicle for sexual reform."
      There is further analysis of the difference between
      Richardson's and Fielding's treatment of the relation-
      ship between men and women.

807. Moore, John Robert. "Daniel Defoe: Precursor of Samuel
      Richardson." In *Restoration and Eighteenth-Century*

Literature: Essays in Honor of Alan Dugald McKillop.
Ed. Carroll Camden. Chicago and London: Univ. of
Chicago Press for William Marsh Rice University, 1963.
Pp. 351-69.

A careful comparison of Defoe and Richardson in terms
of background and narrative method.

808. —————. "The London Address of Samuel Richardson's
      Father." *N&Q*, 193 (1948), 166.

      Establishes the exact location of the elder Richard-
      son's house in London.

809. Moore, Robert E. "Dr. Johnson on Fielding and Richard-
      son." *PMLA*, 66 (1951), 162-81.

      A thorough analysis of Johnson's evaluation of the
      two novelists.

810. Mornet, Daniel. "Les enseignements des bibliothèques
      privées (1750-1780)." *Revue d'histoire littéraire
      de la France*, 17 (1910), 449-96.

      An analysis of French private libraries shows the
      abiding interest in English fiction by the number of
      copies found for various novels: *Pamela*--78; *Clarissa*--
      69; *Grandison*--44.

811. Moss, Mary. "Why We Read Richardson." *Lippincott's
      Magazine of Popular Literature and Science*, 69 (1902),
      489-91.

      Reviews Richardson's genius in light of the Richardson
      "boom" at the turn of the century by commenting upon
      his deserved reputation in spite of his exasperating
      "tedium, artificiality, and revolting impropriety."

812. Munro, James S. "Richardson, Marivaux and the French
      Romance Tradition." *MLR*, 70 (1975), 752-59.

      Suggests that Richardson and Marivaux both drew from
      a common source (hence the many similarities between
      them): the love romances of the seventeenth century
      developed techniques of analysis too easily forgotten
      today.

813. Murakami, Shiko. "The Father of the English Novel."
      Eigo Seinen, 117 (1971), 142-44.

      Not examined.

814. Nairn, J.A. "Samuel Richardson and Merchant Taylors'
     School." *N&Q*, 149 (1925), 421.

     Class lists show the name Samuel Richardson for 1701
     and 1702; the name does not appear in any other school
     list when he was supposed to have attended a London
     school.

815. Niklaus, R. "Crébillon fils et Richardson." In *Studies
     on Voltaire and the Eighteenth Century*, 89 (1972),
     1169-85.

     Both men dealt with the psychology of sexuality and
     seemingly shared an aura of libertinism in their novels.

816. *Notes and Queries*. "Memorabilia," 149 (1925), 361.

     Dr. Nairn of Merchant Taylors' School indicates that
     Joseph Highmore was educated there and first became
     acquainted with Richardson then.

817. Oka, Teruo. "Samuel Richardson's View of Moderate
     Rakery." *SEL* (Tokyo), 44 (1967), 15-24. [In Japanese.]

     A general discussion of Richardson's development of
     the rake, based upon the distinction between the re-
     formed rake and the penitent rake; suggests that Richard-
     son derived much from Cibber's sentimental comedy.

818. Park, William. "Fielding *and* Richardson." *PMLA*, 81
     (1966), 381-88.

     The common ground shared by the two novelists is
     explored and compared with other eighteenth-century
     novelists in terms of stock characters, persecutions,
     attempted rape as a prelude to marriage, and social
     ideals.

819. ————. "What Was New about the 'New Species of
     Writing'?" *SNNTS*, 2 (1970), 112-30.

     A brief survey of attitudes toward Richardson's work.

820. Parnell, Paul E. "The Sentimental Mask." *PMLA*, 78
     (1963), 529-35.

     A discussion of the "basic relationship between
     sentimentalism and virtue or morality," using a passage
     from *Clarissa* as one of the examples in the argument.

821. Paulson, Ronald. "All About Richardson." *SNNTS*, 5

(1973), 110-16.

A review of Eaves and Kimpel's biography (#537) which
adds some biographical information about Richardson's
fire insurance policy, about his further relationship
to George Faulkner and his possible influence for
denying Faulkner membership in the Society for the
Encouragement of Arts, and about Richardson's relationship to Hogarth. There is also a brief analysis of
Richardson's personality: "The small sobersides who
impersonated adults by writing pseudo-letters to
neighbors in need (he thought) of moral improvement
became the middle-aged man who spoke through Pamela
and Clarissa."

822. Peake, Charles. "Richardson and Wit." *Books, the
      Journal of the National Book League* (May-June 1961),
      83-87.

A defense of Richardson's "powerful intelligence dis-
played in the novels" in terms of wit: "Richardson
gives us wit as it appears in life and characters who
are witty in their own right."

823. Phelps, William Lyon. "Richardson." In *Essays on Books*.
      New York: Macmillan Company, 1922. Pp. 16-128.

Presents Richardson's life and character, the character-
istics of his genius (for example, his portrayal of
women), his circle of friends, and an analysis of the
three novels.

824. ———. "The Richardson Revival." *The Independent*,
      53 (1901), 2743-47.

A brief attempt to explain the renewed interest oc-
curring at the turn of the century with a short account
of Richardson's reputation and the impact of Joseph
Texte's study (#504); includes photographs: Richardson
reading *Grandison* and his house at Hammersmith.

825. ———. "Richardson's Place in the English Novel."
      See #30, XIII, ix-xvi.

Discusses briefly Richardson's "historical significance:
his claims to originality; the reasons for his peculiar
method; the nature of his art; his position as a
realist; and his final rank in British fiction."

826. ———. "Samuel Richardson." See #30, I, ix-xliii.

A biography of Richardson as an introduction to his works, including a commentary on his character, homes, and friends.

827. Pierce, Robert B. "Moral Education in the Novel of the 1750's." *PQ*, 44 (1965), 73-87.

Briefly notes Richardson's emotional feeling as a source for the minor novelists.

828. Pons, Christian. "Richardson en 1973: A Propos de 'S. Richardson. A Biography.'" *EA*, 26 (1973), 296-308.

A review of Eaves and Kimpel's biography (#537) which assesses as well Richardson's achievement as a novelist; Pons balances the biographers' critical judgments against those of such critics as Dorothy Van Ghent and Morris Golden.

829. Proper, Coenraad, B.A. "From Richardson to Holcroft." In *Social Elements in English Prose Fiction Between 1780 and 1832*. Amsterdam: H.J. Paris, 1929. Pp. 46-49.

A short analysis of Richardson's interest in the lower social orders as portrayed in the novels.

830. Rawson, C.J. "Language, Dialogue, and Point of View in Fielding: Some Considerations." In *Quick Springs of Sense*. Ed. L.S. Champion. Athens: Univ. of Georgia Press, 1974. Pp. 137-56.

Considers Richardson's coinage of words and standards of gentlemanly speech.

831. ————. "'Nice' and 'Sentimental': A Parallel Between 'Northanger Abbey' and Richardson's 'Correspondence.'" *N&Q*, N.S., 11 (1964), 180.

Tilney's ironic comments on *nice* in *Northanger Abbey* are compared with Lady Bradshaigh's comments to Richardson on the word *sentimental*.

832. Reade, Aleyn Lyell. "Samuel Richardson and Christ's Hospital." *N&Q*, 10th ser., 12 (1909), 301-03, 343-44.

These articles weigh evidence of Richardson's possible education at Christ's Hospital and reject this long lingering notion.

833. ————. "Samuel Richardson and His Family Circle."
      N&Q, 143 (1922), 181–83, 224–26, 263–64, 303–05, 342–
      44, 383–86, 425–27, 465–67, 506–08; 144 (1923), 6–8,
      44–47, 83–85, 126–30, 167–70, 209–11, 247–50, 287–89,
      329–30, 366–68, 410–11, 446–47, 469–72, 504–06.

      Discusses at varying length people in Richardson's
      family circle (see #723).

834. ————. "Samuel Richardson's Supposed Derbyshire
      Connections." *N&Q*, 11th ser., 3 (1911), 123–24.

      Refutes Dr. Cox's opinion that Richardson was born
      at Smalley.

835. ————. "Samuel Richardson's Supposed Kinsfolk at
      Derby." *N&Q*, 10th ser., 9 (1908), 261–63.

      Comments regarding Richardson's family tree, refuting
      that Cox is descended from Richardson.

836. Roddier, Henri. "Robert Challes inspirateur de Richard-
      son et de l'Abbé Prévost." *Revue de Littérature
      Comparée*, 21 (1947), 5–38.

      Suggests that Challes in *Illustres Françaises* created
      "l'origine de cette protestation passionée contre les
      règles étroites d'une société tyrannique où, sous le
      couvert de l'autorité paternelle, l'argent et la
      naissance étaient les principaux obstacles au libre
      choix des jeunes gens."

837. Rogers, Katherine. "Richardson's Empathy with Women."
      In *The Authority of Experience. Essays in Feminist
      Criticism*. Ed. Arlyn Diamond and Lee R. Edwards.
      Amherst: Univ. of Massachusetts Press, 1977. Pp. 118–
      36. Originally published "Sensitive Feminism vs.
      Conventional Sympathy: Richardson and Fielding on
      Women." *Novel*, 9 (1976), 256–70.

      Argues that Richardson conceived of women as indepen-
      dent, intelligent, and autonomous human beings, defending
      them against exploitation not only by selfish men but by
      a male-dominated and oriented society.

838. Rogers, Pat. "Samuel Richardson and Defoe's *Tour* (1738):
      The Evidence of Bibliography." *SB*, 28 (1975), 305–07.

      Dates Richardson's share in Defoe's *Tour* back to
      1738.

839. Rogers, Winfield H. "The Reaction Against Melodramatic Sentimentality in the English Novel, 1796-1830." *PMLA*, 49 (1934), 98-122.

An analysis primarily of the reactions against pseudo-Richardsonian and Gothic writers.

840. Ronte, Heinz. *Richardson und Fielding. Geschichte ihres Ruhms; literarsoziologischer Versuch.* Leipzig, 1935; rpt. New York: Johnson Reprint Corp., 1966.

In their work Richardson and Fielding represent two fundamental world forces, "Bihel und Mythos." Their relative reputations are derived from fluctuations in social history, fluctuations depending upon which force is most readily accepted at the time. Ronte then traces these authors' reputations through five cycles of historical time, beginning with their contemporary age and moving through the post-Victorian period.

841. Rousseau, G.S. "Nerves, Spirits, and Fibres: Towards Defining the Origins of Sensibility." In *Studies in the Eighteenth Century III*. Papers presented at the Third David Nichol Smith Memorial Seminar, Canberra, 1973. Ed. R.F. Brissenden and J.C. Eade. Toronto and Buffalo: Univ. of Toronto Press, 1976. Pp. 137-57.

Richardson is discussed in relation to the term "sensation," and to the revolution in physiology; Rousseau asserts that "no novel of sensibility could appear until a revolution in knowledge concerning the brain, and ... the nerves, had occurred."

842. Sacks, Sheldon. "Novelists as Storytellers." *MP*, 73 (May 1976), S 97-109.

Briefly mentions Richardson in a theoretical re-examination of the basic forms of storytelling.

843. Saintsbury, George. *A History of Criticism and Literary Taste in Europe.* 3 vols. 1900-04; rpt. New York: Humanities Press, 1961.

Considers Richardson as analyzed by Diderot, Madame de Staël, and Hazlitt.

844. Sale, William M., Jr. "Samuel Richardson's House at Fulham." *N&Q*, 169 (1935), 133-34.

Maintains that Richardson had single occupancy of one large house in Fulham and that he did not share a residence with his landlord.

845. ———. "Samuel Richardson and 'Sir William Harring-
      ton.'" *TLS*, 29 Aug. 1935, p. 537.

      Cites facts regarding the revision of *Harrington*.

846. Scholes, Robert, and Robert Kellogg. *The Nature of
      Narrative*. New York: Oxford Univ. Press, 1966.
      Pp. 100–05.

      Brief references concerning illustration as opposed
      to representation.

847. Schücking, Levin L. "Die Grundlagen des Richardson'schen
      Romans." *Germanisch-romanische Monatsschrift*, 12
      (1924), 21–42, 88–110.

      Considers Richardson to be one of the first novelists
      to probe how a social code determines the behavior of
      his characters; it is also argued that Richardson's
      heroines are derived from Puritan, didactic literature,
      and Clarissa is compared with the girl in the first
      dialogue of Defoe's *Religious Courtship* who rejects
      a lover preferred by her father because the man has
      questionable religious beliefs.

848. Schulz, Dieter. "The Coquette's Progress from Satire
      to Sentimental Novel." *Literatur in Wissenschaft und
      Unterricht*, 6 (1973), 77–89.

      Not specifically on Richardson, but provides a good
      background to the history of the coquette and the im-
      plications of sensibility as it interacts with feminism.

849. ———. "'Novel,' 'Romance,' and Popular Fiction in
      the First Half of the Eighteenth Century." *SP*, 70
      (1973), 77–91.

      The novels of Richardson, Defoe, and Fielding should
      be considered a reaction against current popular fiction
      and not against the tradition of "'high' romance
      represented by the heroic romances of the seventeenth
      century."

850. Sen, S.C. "Richardson and Fielding: Moral Sense and
      Moral Vision." *Bulletin of the English Department,
      University of Calcutta*, 2 (1961), 38–40.

      Not examined.

851. Sherbo, Arthur. "Anecdotes by Mrs. LeNoir." *Durham
      University Journal*, N.S. 26 (1965), 166–69.

Notes that *Clarissa* received as much notoriety in its
time as the Bible, and recalls some mannerisms of
Richardson.

852. Sherburn, George. "Samuel Richardson's Novels and the
      Theatre: A Theory Sketched." *PQ*, 41 (1962), 325-29.

Richardson was indebted to plays for a diversity of
techniques and materials, especially his vivid conversations and focus upon situations.

853. ————. "Writing to the Moment: One Aspect." In
      *Restoration and Eighteenth-Century Literature: Essays
      in Honor of Alan Dugald McKillop*. Ed. Carroll Camden.
      Chicago and London: Univ. of Chicago Press for
      William Marsh Rice Univ., 1963. Pp. 201-09.

Richardson's "naturally strong visual imagination"
contributed to his ability to create a vivid sense of
immediacy in his novels.

854. Smidt, Kristian. "Character and Plot in the Novels of
      Samuel Richardson." *Critical Quarterly*, 17 (1975),
      1955-66.

A general study of character portrayal with some
commentary on Richardson's sense of humor.

855. Smith, Warren H. *Architecture in English Fiction*.
      Yale Studies in English, Vol. 83. New Haven: Yale
      Univ. Press, 1934.

Imprisonment and descriptions in Richardson's novels
may have had some effect on later Gothic stories;
references especially to *Pamela* and *Clarissa*.

856. Spacks, Patricia Meyer. *The Female Imagination*. 1975;
      rpt. New York: Avon Books, 1976.

Explores how women have divergent world views and
interpretations of the values in our world; includes
passing comments on *Pamela* and *Clarissa*.

857. Spector, Robert D., ed. *Essays on the Eighteenth-
      Century Novel*. Bloomington and London: Indiana Univ.
      Press, 1965.

Reprints items #774; #977; and #1057.

858. Straus, Ralph. *Robert Dodsley*. London and New York,

1910. P. 355.

Prints two of Richardson's bills for printing: to Miller for *Night-Thoughts* and *Centaur Not Fabulous*.

859. Stewart, Keith. "History, Poetry, and the Terms of Fiction in the Eighteenth Century." *MP*, 66 (1968), 110-20.

Discusses whether the novelist is an historian or poet, depending upon whether he paints human nature as it is (history) or as it ought to be (poetry); Richardson considered the novel and history not simply in terms of probability but in terms of "an ideal presence."

860. Stone, Lawrence. *The Family, Sex and Marriage in England 1500-1800.* New York: Harper & Row, 1977.

Contains a number of passing references to Richardson, *Pamela*, and *Clarissa*, such as Richardson's portrayal of Lovelace as a perfect example of "bachelor morality" during the eighteenth century. Check the index for specific references.

861. Suzuki, Yoshizo. "Juhachi Seiki Eikoku Shosetsu Kenkyu." *Eigo Seinen*, 115 (1969), 298-99.

A study of the eighteenth-century novel with a focus upon Richardson.

862. Symonds, E.M. [pseud. George Paston.] *Sidelights on the Georgian Period.* London: Methuen & Co., 1902. Pp. 88-89, 91-92.

Brief comments on Richardson, who is placed in his social milieu, especially in reference to "The Ideal Woman."

863. Thomson, Clara. "An Historic House." *Athenaeum*, No. 3770 (27 Jan. 1900), 115.

A description of The Grange, where Richardson lived for sixteen years (based upon letters and information in the Forster Collection).

864. Thorne, W.B. "A Famous Printer: Samuel Richardson." *Library*, 2nd ser., 2 (1901), 396-404.

A biographical study concentrating on Richardson as a printer.

865. Tieje, Arthur J. "The Expressed Aim of the Long Prose
        Fiction from 1579 to 1740." *JEGP*, 11 (1912), 402-32.

    Although prefactory comment does not reveal a "sys-
    tematic 'criticism'" of fiction during this time, it
    does show a critical tradition too often ignored;
    Richardson and the mid-century novelists develop out
    of this tradition.

866. ————. "A Peculiar Phase of the Theory of Realism
        in Pre-Richardsonian Fiction." *PMLA*, 28 (1913),
        213-52.

    Analyzes direct remarks from prefaces to show the
    conscious efforts pre-Richardsonian novelists took
    "to gain the implicit credence of the reader," efforts
    resulting in "a striving toward a crude form of
    realism."

867. Tiemann, Franziska and Hermann. *Geschichte der Meta
        Klopstock in Briefen*. Bremen, [1962]. Pp. 473-74.

    An account of Major Hohorst's visit to Richardson;
    informed Richardson that in Germany his works were
    used as a moral system.

868. *Times Literary Supplement*. "Notes on Sales," 6 March
        1930, p. 196.

    A review of Mr. A. Edward Newton's facsimile repro-
    duction of the rare 1769 Newbery edition of *Pamela*,
    noting that this edition with its "six delightful
    little full-page illustrations" adds the name of John
    Lodge to the known list of Richardson illustrators.

869. ————. "Richardson's Illustrators," 16 Dec. 1920,
        p. 864.

    An account of the sale of Highmore's engravings of
    Pamela at Christie's in November, with a brief analysis
    of the relationship between the artist and novelist;
    a further note is included, giving other illustrators
    of the three novels.

870. Tucker, Susie I. "Predatings from Samuel Richardson's
        'Familiar Letters.'" *N&Q*, N.S., 8 (1961), 56-57.

    Refers to several words which are earlier in form
    or sense than those found in the *OED*'s earliest
    examples.

871.   ———.   "Richardsonian Phrases."   *N&Q*, N.S., 13 (1966),
       464-65.

       Notes Richardson's liking for the Biblical phrases
       "Tell it not in Gath" and "The Nature of the Beast."

872.   Turberville, A.S., ed.   *Johnson's England*.   2 vols.
       1933; rpt. Oxford: Clarendon Press, 1965.

       Passing references in various essays to Richardson,
       concerning *Clarissa* or Richardson in St. James Park;
       all references are indexed.

873.   Tynan, Katherine.   "The Romance of a Bookseller."
       Cornhill Magazine, N.S. 22 (1907), 678-89.

       A thinly fictionalized account of Richardson as a
       silly, pitiful, middle-class printer.

874.   Utter, Robert P.   "On the Alleged Tediousness of Defoe
       and Richardson."   *University of California Chronicle*,
       25 (1923), 175-93.

       The minuteness of Richardson's passages makes them
       lifelike and compels the reader to read on.

875.   Van Tieghem, Paul.   "Quelques aspects de la sensibilité
       pré-romantique dans le roman européen au xviii
       siècle."   *Edda*, 26 (1927), 146-75.

       Passing references to Richardson in a study (and a
       history) of the words "sensible" and "sentimental" as
       they appeared in England, France, and Germany.

876.   ———.   "Le roman sentimental en Europe de Richardson
       à Rousseau (1740-1761)."   *Revue de Litterature
       Comparée*, 20 (1940), 129-51.

       A discussion of the evolution of the sentimental
       novel on the Continent between 1740 and 1761, and a
       study of the effect Richardson's novels were having
       in England.

877.   ———   "La sensibilité et la passion dans le roman
       européen au 18e siècle."   *Revue de Litterature
       Comparée*, 6 (1926), 424-35.

       Places Richardson, especially *Clarissa*, in the
       development of European sensibility.

878.   Ward, H.G.   "Samuel Richardson and the English
       Philosophers."   *N&Q*, 11th ser., 3 (1911), 5-6.

Collects the references to English philosophers in
the novels: Shaftesbury, Mandeville, Berkeley, and
Locke.

879. ————. "Samuel Richardson's Birth." *N&Q*, 11th ser.,
(1911), 127.

A query, asking for information about his date and
place of birth.

880. Waterhouse, Osborn. "The Development of English
Sentimental Comedy in the Eighteenth Century."
Anglia, 30 (1907), 137–72, 269–305.

A brief study of Richardson as the creator of the
"novel of sentimental analysis" with *Pamela*, and of the
circumstances regarding *Clarissa*'s publication which
reveal the degree of sensibility possessed by his
readers; the long study also provides a good background
for an understanding of sentimentalism.

881. Watt, Ian. "Defoe and Richardson on Homer: A Study of
the Relation of Novel and Epic in the Early Eighteenth
Century." *RES*, N.S., 3 (1952), 325–40.

Neither writer concerns himself with epic geneology,
and their novels reveal their independence from epic
theory or practice.

882. ————. "The Naming of Characters in Defoe, Richardson,
and Fielding." *RES*, 25 (1949), 322–38.

Discusses Richardson's choice of names like Pamela
and Clarissa, places these names in the romance tradition of prose fiction, and suggests that "the complexity of Richardson's attitude to his characters"
can be traced to these names.

883. White, William. "Richardson: Idealist or Realist?"
MLR, 34 (1939), 240–41.

The model for a young woman's behavior, suggested
in *Familiar Letters*, is not followed by Pamela or
Clarissa; the contrast reveals the latter heroines'
essential selfishness.

884. ————. "Samuel Richardson." *American Book Collector*,
11 (1961), 11–20.

Reviews Richardson's life, summarizes the plots of
the novels, and briefly criticizes each book.

885. ————. "Samuel Richardson: Novelist of the Sewing
      Circles." *Today's Japan: Orient/West* (Tokyo), 5
      (1960), 65-74.

      Gives a general account of Richardson's influence and
      his achievements as a novelist.

886. Whitley, W.T. *Artists and Their Friends in England,
      1700-1799.* London, 1928. Pp. 47-50.

      Notes briefly Richardson's relationship to Highmore,
      especially in terms of the painter's pictures illus-
      trating *Pamela*; Richardson also introduced Highmore
      to Dr. Young who eventually sat for a portrait and
      then presented it to Richardson.

887. Williamson, F. "Samuel Richardson's Birthplace."
      N&Q, 169 (1935), 300-01.

      Refutes Dr. Cox's claim that his grandmother was a
      member of Richardson's family.

888. Wolff, Erwin. "Die gesellschaftliche Welt als Erlebnis:
      Samuel Richardson." In *Der englische Roman im 18.
      Jahrhundert: Wesen und Formen.* Göttingen: Vandenhoeck
      & Ruprecht, 1964. Pp. 39-48.

      Discusses Richardson in terms of the content and
      form of the social world he inhabited.

889. Wright, Walter F. "Richardson's Illustration of the
      Influence of Feeling upon Morals and Manners." In
      *Sensibility in English Prose Fiction, 1760-1814:
      A Reinterpretation.* Illinois Studies in Language and
      Literature, Vol. 22. Urbana: Univ. of Illinois
      Press, 1937.

      Richardson preferred moral sentiment to emotion for
      its own sake, yet the sentimental writers after 1760
      owe their inspiration directly to him; Lovelace and
      Sir Charles are models for later writers.

890. Zach, Wolfgang. "Richardson und der Leser." *Arbeiten
      aus Anglistik und Amerikanistik*, 1 (1976), 65-105.

      Not examined.

891. Zirkir, Malvin R., Jr. "Richardson's Correspondence:
      The Personal Letter As Private Experience." In *The
      Familiar Letter in the Eighteenth Century.* Ed. Howard

Anderson, Philip B. Daghlian, and Irvin Ehrenpreis.
Lawrence: Univ. of Kansas Press, 1966. Pp. 71-91.

Discusses Richardson's interest in letters, considers
his moral and didactic concerns, and evaluates his
impersonation in letters from imaginary personalities.

D. *PAMELA*

892.   Aldridge, Alfred Owen. "Polygamy and Deism." *JEGP*,
       48 (1949), 343-60.

       A brief, opening reference to Mr. B's repeated com-
       ments on polygamy in *Pamela II* introduces a lengthy
       analysis of the close connection between deism and
       polygamy discussed by such eighteenth-century writers
       as Swift, Delany, Lord Bolingbroke, and Hume.

893.   Allentuck, Marcia Epstein. "Narration and Illustration:
       The Problem of Richardson's *Pamela*." *PQ*, 51 (1972),
       874-86.

       Although Richardson was not satisfied with narration
       alone and had *Pamela* illustrated, the illustrations do
       not extend the inward life of the novel, but do provide
       "evidence for his fictive intentions on the conscious
       level."

*   Baker, Ernest A. "Richardson's *Pamela*." See #585, IV,
       13-32.

       Discusses the history of the novel as well as pro-
       viding a source for *Pamela* and a synopsis of the novel.

894.   Baker, Sheridan W., ed. "Introduction." In *Samuel
       Richardson's Introduction to "Pamela."* Augustan Re-
       print Society Publication, No. 48. Los Angeles:
       William Andrews Clark Memorial Library, Univ. of
       California, 1954. Pp. 1-16.

       The fullest text of Richardson's Introduction from
       the second edition, and a discussion by Baker of
       Richardson's many revisions.

895.   Ball, Donald L. "*Pamela II*: A Primary Link in Richard-
       son's Development as a Novelist." *MP*, 65 (1968), 334-42.

       Richardson used *Pamela II* to refine and develop tech-

niques used in *Pamela I* and to experiment with new ones
to be used in later novels.

*   Barker, Gerard A. "The Complacent Paragon: Exemplary
         Characterization in Richardson." See #666.

         Pamela reveals her virtue through her Protestant
         approval of her own behavior.

896.   Battestin, Martin C. "On the Contemporary Reputations
         of 'Pamela,' 'Joseph Andrews,' and 'Roderick Random':
         Remarks by an 'Oxford Scholar,' 1748." *N&Q*, N.S., 15
         (1968), 450-52.

         This review of *Pamela* shows the author distinctly in
         the anti-*Pamela* camp.

897.   Beckstein, Julius. *Richardsons "Pamela," nach ihrem
         Gedankengehalt betrachtet. Mit einem Anhang: Die
         Quellenfrage bei der "Pamela."* Bremen: H. Engelke,
         1929.

         This is a close look at the novel, considering such
         items as its spiritual and religious qualities, female
         respectability, and characterization; an appendix
         examines the origins of the novel with regard to
         Marivaux and the Puritan tradition.

898.   Beckwith, F. "The Anti-Pamelas." *TLS*, 19 Feb., 1931,
         p. 135.

         Brief questions and some commentary regarding three
         of the anti-*Pamela*s.

899.   Bell, Michael Davitt. "Pamela's Wedding and the
         Marriage of the Lamb." *PQ*, 49 (1970), 100-12.

         With *Pamela* Richardson developed a stereotype of
         romantic love derived from the eighteenth-century
         adoration of Christ.

900.   Bernbaum, Ernest. *The Drama of Sensibility.* 1915; rpt.
         Gloucester, Mass.: Peter Smith, 1958. Pp. 164-65.

         Notes an analogy between *Sylvia* and *Pamela* and the
         parallel between *Clarissa* and Charles Johnson's *Caelia*.

901.   Black, Frank G. "The Continuations of *Pamela*." *RAA*,
         13 (1936), 499-507.

         Discusses three continuations of *Pamela* acquired by

the Harvard College Library in terms of the light they shed on the quarrel between Richardson and the book-sellers.

902. Blondel, Madeleine. *Images de la femme dans le roman Anglais de 1740 à 1771.* 2 vols. Paris: H. Champion, 1976.

This is a discussion which analyzes whether Pamela and Clarissa are representative of eighteenth-century women insofar as women are actually portrayed in the major and minor novels of the period.

903. Bond, Richard P. *English Burlesque Poetry 1700-1750.* 1932; rpt. New York: Russell & Russell, 1964. Pp. 425-26.

Briefly discusses *Pamela: Or, the Female Imposter. A Poem, In Five Cantos* as a criticism of Richardson's novel.

904. Broich, Ulrich. "Fieldings *Shamela* und *Pamela or, The Fair Imposter*, zwei Parodien von Richardsons *Pamela*." *Anglia*, 82 (1964), 172-90.

The *Pamela* parodies are works of a transitional period rather than precursors of a new form; they are even more the rearguard production of conservative writers in retreat. Richardson's is actually the new form, breaking classical rules and bringing about a "democratization" of the literary aesthetic and of the sociological criteria which establish literary form.

905. Brooks, Douglas. "Richardson's *Pamela* and Fielding's *Joseph Andrews*." *Essays in Criticism* (Oxford), 17 (1967), 158-68.

Asserts that *Joseph Andrews* should not be read in terms of *Pamela*. For Kearney's comment on this article see 18 (1968), 105-07; a following argument can be found in subsequent volumes: 18 (1968), 348-49; 18 (1968), 479-80; 19 (1969), 348-51.

*   Brophy, Elizabeth. "*Pamela*: A New Species of Writing." See #527, pp. 53-71.

Studies the novel in terms of Richardson's artistic intentions, such as his belief in the necessity for verisimilitude, in order to judge its merits and weaknesses.

906. Bruce, H.L. "Voltaire on the English Stage." *University of California Publications in Modern Philology*, 8 (1918), 1-152.

Voltaire renames Pamela as Nanine in his adaptation of Richardson's story, and the character returns to England in Charles Maclin's *True-born Scotchman* (completed in 1764 but not performed until revised in 1781 as *The Man of the World*).

907. Brückmann, Patricia C. "The Settings in *Pamela*." *Transactions of the Samuel Johnson Society of the Northwest*, 6 (1973), 1-10.

Studies the growth of Pamela's character as she moves from the relative peace of B's pastoral home in Bedfordshire to the gloom and melancholy traditionally linked to Lincolnshire and B's home there.

908. Canby, Henry Seidel. "*Pamela* Abroad." *MLN*, 18 (1903), 206-13.

Traces the translations and stage adaptations of *Pamela* through Europe.

909. Chalker, John. "'Virtue Rewarded': The Sexual Theme in Richardson's 'Pamela.'" *Literary Half-Yearly* (Bangalore Central College, India), 2 (1961), 58-64.

Defends Richardson against charges of "moral obtuseness" by discussing *Pamela* as "a persuasive moral testimonial," one which promotes a personal, moral responsibility.

910. Chevalley, Abel. "Monsieur Psalmanazar." *RAA*, 5 (1927-28), 308n.

Seriously doubts Richardson's account of the origin of *Pamela*: "Ne sont-elle pas aussi l'imposture?" See Schulte, #981, for another analysis of Richardson's account.

*   Cockshut, A.O.J. "Richardson and Fielding." See #692.

Despite Fielding's censure in *Joseph Andrews* of Richardson's morality as portrayed through Pamela, Pamela's dilemma is real, complex, and imminently tragic.

*   _____. "Sentimentality in Fiction." See #693.

Pamela is a sentimental novel because Richardson did not analyze his heroine's motives thoroughly.

*   Copeland, Edward W. "Samuel Richardson and Naive
       Allegory: Some Beauties of the Mixed Metaphor." See
       #698.

       Includes some interesting references to *Pamela*, regard-
       ing Richardson's use of figurative language to establish
       the psychological and didactic centers of the novel.

911.   Costa, Richard H. "The Epistolary Monitor in *Pamela*."
       MLQ, 31 (1970), 38-47.

       Argues that Richardson's epistolary method is effective
       beyond the merits usually ascribed to it, especially
       when one considers the letters as Pamela's courtship
       letters "to the one person in whose hands her destiny
       lay."

912.   Cowler, Rosemary, ed. *Twentieth Century Interpretations
       of "Pamela." A Collection of Critical Essays.* Engle-
       wood Cliffs, N.J.: Prentice-Hall, 1969.

       Reprints selections from the following: #38; #526;
       #528; #532; #539; #577; #703; #753; #795; #818; #852;
       #882; #938; #941; #944; #951; #953; #971; #974; and
       #1048.

913.   Cruse, Amy. "Pamela: Joseph Andrews." In *English Litera-
       ture through the Ages: Beowulf to Stevenson*." London:
       George G. Harrap & Co., 1914. Pp. 321-32.

       A short summary of the novel, Richardson's writing of
       it, and its contemporary success.

*   Daiches, David. "Samuel Richardson." See #703.

       Includes an analysis of patterns and ideas in *Pamela*.

914. **Danielowski, Emma.** *Richardsons erster Roman. Entstehungs-
       geschichte.* Berlin, 1917.

       Considers especially the influence of *Marianne* and
       Familiar Letters upon the art of *Pamela*, and examines
       the motifs in characterization and plot found in other
       works of the time.

915.   Detig, Joseph E. "Pamela and Her Critics." *Leyte-Samar
       Studies*, 2 (1968), 242-49.

       A brief survey of *Pamela* criticism from 1936 to 1968,
       assessing the nature of the novel's modern critical
       reputation.

916. Digeon, Aurélien. *Les Romans de Fielding*. Paris: Hachette, 1923.

    Suggests that the opposition to Pamela reveals a "querelle de *Pamela*"; further points out that Richardson himself probably "était dupe de Pamela."

917. Donovan, Robert A. "The Problem of Pamela." In *The Shaping Vision: Imagination in the English Novel from Defoe to Dickens*. Ithaca, N.Y.: Cornell Univ. Press, 1966. Pp. 47-67. Originally published as "The Problem of Pamela, or Virtue Unrewarded." *SEL*, 3 (1963), 377-95.

    In all the argument over *Pamela*, "the essential fact about Richardson's novel has been missed"; the moral and artistic center of the novel lies in its complex social attitudes, not its relatively crude ethic.

*   Doody, Margaret Anne. *A Natural Passion*. See #534, pp. 14-98.

    Devotes three chapters to *Pamela*, including the sources for the novel, a consideration of the novel as pastoral comedy, and the failure of *Pamela II*.

918. Dottin, Paul. "L'accueil fait à Pamela." *RAA*, 7 (1930), 505-19.

    Discusses *Pamela*'s reception ("Pamela conquit le monde!"), and gives French translations of some of the poetic tributes to *Pamela*.

919. ———. "Les continuations de *Pamela*." *Revue de l'Enseignement des Langues Vivantes*, 47 (1930), 444-61.

    Discusses Richardson and the literary pirates of *Pamela*, Kelly and Chandler.

920. Druce, Robert. "Jane, Heiress to Pamela." *Dutch Quarterly Review of Anglo-American Letters*, 6 (1976), 164-90.

    Primarily a long study of *Jane Eyre* which briefly notes the similarity of plot structure between it and *Pamela*.

921. Duckworth, Colin. "Madame Denis's Unpublished *Pamela*: A Link between Richardson, Goldoni and Voltaire." In *Studies on Voltaire and the Eighteenth Century*. Ed. T. Besterman. Vol. 76. Genève: Institut et Musée Voltaire, 1970. Pp. 37-53.

Examines the unpublished text of Voltaire's niece's dramatic version of *Pamela* and discusses the importance of *Pamela* upon their lives.

922. Duncan-Jones, E.E. "Proposals of Marriage in 'Pride and Prejudice' and 'Pamela.'" *N&Q*, N.S., 4 (1957), 76.

Darcy's phrase "In vain have I struggled" is considered an echo of B's sentiment in his letter to Pamela.

923. Dussinger, John A. *The Discourse of the Mind in Eighteenth-Century Fiction*. Studies in English Literature, 80. The Hague: Mouton, 1974.

Uses material from philosophical and medical writers to examine the questions of the changing conceptions in the eighteenth century toward knowledge, reality, and the status of the individual; includes a chapter on *Pamela*.

924. ————. "What Pamela Knew: An Interpretation." *JEGP*, 69 (1970), 377-93.

Although Pamela's quest for an identity marks the central action of the novel, Richardson's epistolary method renders her subjective reality subtly, revealing her "perceptions, analyses, and judgments at each stage of her narrative."

925. Eaves, T.C. Duncan. "An Unrecorded Children's Book Illustrated by Thomas Bewick." *Library*, 5th ser., 5 (1951), 272-73.

A description of an abridged but illustrated edition of *Pamela* (c. 1779), identifying the woodcuts as those probably made by Bewick.

926. ————, and Ben D. Kimpel. Introduction to the Houghton-Mifflin Edition of *Pamela*. See #39, pp. v-xvi.

Discusses Richardson as a literary artist, provides a brief biography and analysis of *Pamela*'s contemporary reception, considers how the novel fits into the sentimental tradition, and evaluates Richardson's morality.

*   ————. "Pamela." See #537, pp. 100-18.

A critical examination of the novel in terms of style, structure, and characterization, noting the primary critical evaluations.

927. ————. "The Publisher of *Pamela* and Its First
        Audience." *BNYPL*, 64 (1960), 143-46.

        Establishes the nature of the business relationship
        of the novel's first publishers and identifies Miss
        Midwinter as the young lady who, with Richardson's
        wife, heard the first installments of the novel as it
        was written.

928. ————. "Richardson's Revisions of *Pamela*." *SB*, 20
        (1967), 61-88.

        A collation of the some twelve editions of the novel,
        determining the extent of the various revisions and
        concluding that both the first edition and the 1801
        revision are necessary to students and best reveal
        Richardson's intentions.

929. Engel, Claire-Elaine. "English Novels in Switzerland
        in the XVIIIth Century." *Comparative Literature
        Studies*, 14 & 15 (1944), 2-8.

        Points out the reviews of Richardson's novels during
        the eighteenth century in Switzerland, such as those
        in the *Mercure Suisse*, and gives a close discussion of
        the novel and analyses of it (*Pamela*) in the Dutch
        Bibliothèque Raisonée.

930. Erickson, Robert A. "Mother Jewkes, Pamela, and the
        Midwives." *ELH*, 43 (1976), 500-16.

        Especially concerns the Lincolnshire section of
        Pamela, and how Richardson utilized the folklore of
        midwifery and witchcraft from which to develop the
        characters of Mrs. Jewkes and Pamela.

931. Facteau, Bernard Anthony. *Les romans de Richardson sur
        la scène française*. Paris: Les Presses Universitaires
        de France, 1927.

        Considers *Pamela*'s progress on the French and Con-
        tinental stage.

932. Folkenflik, Robert. "A Room of Pamela's Own." *ELH*,
        39 (1972), 585-96.

        Considers the importance of "place" and privacy in
        Pamela to be central to the problem of woman's self-
        determination in the novel.

*   Frank, Frederick S. "From Boudoir to Castle Crypt:
        Richardson and the Gothic Novel." See #734.

        Discusses the sex debate in the novel and links it
        to the development of the Gothic novel.

*   Golden, Morris. "Richardson's Repetitions." See #739.

        A specific analysis of *Pamela* in terms of character
        types which Richardson goes on to use in other novels.

933.   Grimm, Charles. "Encore une fois la question Marivaux-
        Richardson." *Revue de Littérature Comparée*, 4 (1924),
        590-600.

        Argues that Richardson was inspired to write *Pamela*
        after reading *Vie de Marianne* in November of 1739.

934.   H., C. "Another Pamela." *TLS*, 12 Dec. 1936, p. 1035.

        Notes the similarity of a section in *Dear Miss Heber*
        to *Pamela*.

935.   Hartveit, Lars. "Samuel Richardson, *Pamela I*. The Im-
        pact of Moral Exemplum: the Dilemma of the Didactic
        Writer." In *The Art of Persuasion: A Study of Six
        Novels*. Bergen: Universitetsforlaget, 1977. Pp. 14-32.

        Although *Pamela* is written in traditional language of
        moral instruction, it transcends this inherent limita-
        tion. Richardson's dilemma was to teach and instruct
        and at the same time respect "the 'rights' of his
        heroine as an 'independent' fictitious character"; he
        does not thoroughly solve the problem, but does develop
        his protagonist so that conventional, religious, and
        moral values are tested meaningfully.

936.   Hulme, William H. "Shenstone on Richardson's *Pamela*."
        MLN, 26 (1911), 158-59.

        Notes how a Shenstone letter in Dodsley's edition
        seems to suggest the novel was in circulation as early
        as July, 1739. (See #1003 for a refutation.)

*   Humphreys, A.R. "Richardson's Novels: Words and the
        'Movements Within.'" See #764.

        Considers syntax and style in *Pamela* as factors which
        create complex psychological situations.

937. Jeffrey, David K. "The Epistolary Format of *Pamela* and
      Humphry Clinker." In *A Provision of Human Nature:*
      Essays on Fielding and Others in Honor of Miriam
      Austin Locke. Ed. Donald Kay. University: Univ. of
      Alabama Press, 1977. Pp. 145-54.

      Considers the similarities and differences between
      the two novels and examines, especially, how the epis-
      tolary form places the letter writer close to the
      reality he has experienced but conscious at the same
      time of his distance from it, making the letter writer
      both "isolated and unreliable."

938. Jenkins, Owen. "Richardson's *Pamela* and Fielding's
      'Vile Forgeries.'" *PQ*, 44 (1965), 200-10.

      A reexamination of Richardson's achievement in *Pamela*,
      the validity of Fielding's criticism, and Richardson's
      reply in *Pamela II*.

939. Kaul, A.N. *The Action of English Comedy; Studies in*
      the Encounter of Abstraction and Experience from
      Shakespeare to Shaw. New Haven and London: Yale Univ.
      Press, 1970. Pp. 163-68.

      Primarily a study of Fielding's comedy with a note
      for the reasons underlying Fielding's parody of *Pamela*
      in *Shamela* and *Joseph Andrews*.

940. Kay, Donald. "Pamela and the Poultry." *Satire News-*
      letter, 10 (1972), 25-27.

      Bird imagery in *Pamela* creates a microcosm accentuating
      character interaction.

941. Kearney, Anthony M. "Richardson's *Pamela*: The Aesthetic
      Case." *REL*, 7 (1966), 78-90.

      Sets aside the question of Pamela's psychological
      motivations and looks at the novel in terms of the
      special problems raised by style and narration.

942. Kinkead-Weekes, Mark. Introduction to the Everyman
      Edition of *Pamela*. See #38, pp. v-xiii.

      Provides a brief biographical sketch, discusses the
      novel's contemporary reception and Richardson's repu-
      tation, and looks at his dramatic technique.

*   ————. *Samuel Richardson*. See #544, pp. 7-120.

      Devotes four chapters to *Pamela*, emphasizing Richard-

son's dramatic art which projects several points of view
and reveals his conscious artistry, which delineates
character and plot development and which reveals the
ethical basis for the novel.

943. Kitchin, George. *A Survey of Burlesque and Parody in
      English.* 1931; rpt. New York: Russell & Russell,
      1967. Pp. 166-69.

      A brief commentary on *Joseph Andrews* and *Shamela* as
      parodies of *Pamela*, with *Shamela* being perhaps the best
      prose parody before *Northanger Abbey*.

*   Klotman, Phyllis R. "Sin and Sublimation in the Novels
      of Samuel Richardson." See #777.

      Pamela is discussed in her role as a self-conscious
      letter writer concerned with morality.

944. Kreissman, Bernard. *"Pamela-Shamela": A Study of the
      Criticisms, Burlesques, Parodies, and Adaptations of
      Richardson's "Pamela."* Univ. of Nebraska Studies,
      N.S., No. 22. Lincoln: Univ. of Nebraska Press, 1960.

      A full study of the *Pamela* phenomena, including
      criticism of Richardson's ethical philosophy and artis-
      tic capability which in part stimulated so much furor.

      Reviewed: *CE*, 22 (1961), 205.
               JEGP, 61 (1962), 410-13.
               PQ, 40 (1961), 421.

945. Krutch, Joseph Wood. "Samuel Richardson." *Atlantic
      Monthly*, 146 (1930), 50-59.

      Discusses Richardson's life briefly, especially as
      the details of his life led to the writing of *Pamela*;
      provides plot summary and brief critical analysis of
      Pamela as well as commentary on Richardson's character
      after the novel was well received.

946. **Lathrop, Henry Burrowes.** *The Art of the Novelist.* New
      York: Dodd, Mead and Company, 1919.

      Uses illustrative examples from *Pamela* and *Clarissa*
      to define "characterization" and the distinction of
      tragedy from comedy.

947. Leed, Jacob. "Pa-mé-la--Pám-e-la." *JNL*, 27 (1967), 11.

      A note suggesting that Richardson changed the pronun-
      ciation to make the name more like his own.

948. ————. "Richardson's Pamela and Sidney's." *AUMLA*, 40
      (1973), 240-45.

      The importance of the link to Sidney's *Arcadia* for
      the name, Pamela, is again argued; Richardson was not
      always negative toward earlier romance fiction.

*   LeGates, Marlene. "The Cult of Womanhood in Eighteenth-
      Century Thought." See #780.

      Notes how Pamela, "virtuous unto marriage," becomes a
      model for a new definition of eighteenth-century
      womanhood.

949. Lesser, S.O.A. "A Note on 'Pamela.'" In *The Whispered
      Meanings; Selected Essays*. Ed. Robert Sprich and
      Richard W. Noland. Boston: Univ. of Massachusetts
      Press, 1977. Pp. 14-19. Originally published *CE*,
      14 (1952), 13-17.

      Sets up the Cinderella motif as the basis for under-
      standing the novel.

950. Levin, Gerald. "Richardson's *Pamela*: 'Conflicting
      Trends.'" *American Imago*, 28 (1971), 319-29.

      A discussion of masochistic traits in Pamela and B.

951. Lyles, Albert M. "Pamela's Trials." *College Language
      Association Journal*, 8 (1965), 290-92.

      Because Mr. B is a justice of the peace, the legal
      metaphor provides Richardson an opportunity to emphasize
      the relationship of both melodramatic and comic scenes
      to the theme of virtue rewarded.

952. Lynch, Kathleen M. "*Pamela Nubile*, '*l'Écossaise*,' and
      The English Merchant." *MLN*, 47 (1932), 94-96.

      Suggests how Voltaire was influenced by Goldoni's
      dramatic adaptation of *Pamela*, and how the altered
      heroine returned to England through a translation of
      Voltaire by George Colman.

953. McIntosh, Carey. "Pamela's Clothes." *ELH*, 35 (1968),
      75-83.

      Allusions to clothes represent a unifying leitmotif
      in the novel, leading to moral evaluation of character,
      often (though not exclusively) linked to distinctions
      of social class.

954. Mack, Edward C. "Pamela's Step-daughters: The Heroines of Smollett and Fielding." *CE*, 8 (1947), 293-301.

The later heroines are evaluated against the eighteenth-century ideal woman as characterized and portrayed by Pamela.

955. McKillop, Alan Dugald. "The Mock Marriage Device in *Pamela*." *PQ*, 26 (1947), 285-88.

Notes how the marriage project borders on a direct transcript from contemporary social conditions, but is also derived from the sensationalism of *chronique scandaleuse* and drama.

956. ————. "Wedding Bells for Pamela." *PQ*, 28 (1949), 323-25.

A discussion of Sir John Herschel's anecdote of villagers ringing out church bells upon reading of Pamela's eventual marriage.

957. Manheim, Leonard H. "The Absurd Miss Pamela and the Tragic Miss Clarissa: A Brief Study of Samuel Richardson as a Developing Artist." *Nassau Review* (Nassau [N.Y.] Community College), 2 (1970), 1-10.

A brief look at *Pamela* as an absurd story, revealing Richardson's deficient understanding of psychology.

*   May, Georges Claude. *Le dilemme du roman au XVIIIe siècle.* See #554.

Numerous specific references to *Pamela* in terms of the general attack upon the aesthetics and morality of the novel during the eighteenth century.

958. Monteser, Frederick. *The Picaresque Element in Western Literature.* Studies in the Humanities, No. 5. University: Univ. of Alabama Press, 1975.

Contends with F.W. Chandler that *Pamela* cannot be classified as picaresque because Pamela is a heroine in service.

959. Morton, Donald E. "Theme and Structure in *Pamela*." *SNNTS*, 3 (1971), 242-57.

Argues that "balance, proportion, order, and harmony" are the distinctive features of the novel which support the theme of virtue rewarded and minimize the significance of the novel's so-called tedious plot.

960. Muecke, D.C. "Beauty and Mr. B." *SEL*, 7 (1967), 467–74.

Richardson's imagination was "engaged at the fairy story/romance level" and if characters and events were not consciously a part of his artistic creations, they were never far away; parallels are established between *Pamela* and fairy tales, especially "Beauty and the Beast."

961. Needham, Gwendolyn B. "Richardson's Characterization of Mr. B. and the Double Purpose in *Pamela*." *ECS*, 3 (1970), 433–74.

A close examination of the novel, refuting traditional criticisms by asserting that the characterization of Mr. B. is realistic and a thoroughly successful creation.

962. Newlin, Claude M. "The English Periodicals and the Novel, 1709–40." *PMASAL*, 16 (1932), 467–76.

A survey of stories in the periodicals, revealing similar subject matter and moralizing upon which Richardson would capitalize in *Pamela*.

963. Olivier, Theo. "'Pamela' and 'Shamela': A Reassessment." *English Studies in Africa*, 17 (1974), 59–70.

Although usually contrasted, Richardson and Fielding were not as different regarding their principles and methods as is often claimed: Richardson, besides being a moralist, constructed *Pamela* in terms of suspense and for values of entertainment.

964. Parker, Dorothy. "The Time Scheme of *Pamela* and the Character of B." *TSLL*, 11 (1969), 695–704.

The time scheme in the novel alters the black and white interpretation of B, provides greater narrative complexity and psychological validity, and reveals a new aspect of Pamela's role as a reporter.

*   Phelps, William Lyon. *Essays on Books*. See #823.

A thorough examination of *Pamela* in terms of characterization, structure, and theme.

965. ———. "Pamela." See #30, I, xliii–lvi.

Summarizes the origin and composition of the novel, analyzes briefly its artistic merits and faults, and criticizes its morality.

966. Pons, Christian. *Samuel Richardson. "Pamela."* Paris: Armand Colin, 1970.

    A biographical sketch of Richardson, leading to a thorough literary criticism of the novel and including a study of sources and the literary and moral traditions.

967. Purdie, Edna. "Some Adventures of *Pamela* on the Continental Stage." In *German Studies Presented to Professor H.G. Fielder.* Oxford: Clarendon Press, 1938. Pp. 352-84.

    Considers the influence of *Pamela* on the Continental drama.

968. Rader, Ralph W. "Defoe, Richardson, Joyce, and the Concept of Form in the Novel." In *Autobiography, Biography, and the Novel.* Papers read at a Clark Library Seminar, May 13, 1972. Ed. William Matthews and Ralph W. Rader. Los Angeles: William Andrews Clark Memorial Library, Univ. of California, 1973. Pp. 31-72.

    Discusses a theory of novelistic form which may resolve some of the controversy regarding the structure of *Pamela* as compared with *Moll Flanders.*

969. Randall, D.A., and J.T. Winterich. *"Pamela." Publishers Weekly,* 138 (17. Aug. 1940), 492-94.

    A descriptive, bibliographic note of a *Pamela* edition; includes a background note on Richardson.

970. Reade, Aleyn Lyell. "Richardson's Pamela: Her Original." *N&Q,* 10th ser., 9 (1908), 361-63, 503-05.

    Two articles trying to identify the original for Pamela, refuting any claims for Lady Gainsborough or Lady Hazlerigg, but failing to find any original.

971. Reid, B.L. "Justice to *Pamela*." In *The Long Boy and Others.* Athens: Univ. of Georgia Press, 1969. Pp. 31-51. Originally published *Hudson Review,* 9 (1957), 516-33.

    Defends the novel against two charges: that it is "fatally sentimental and artificial," and that its moralizing is "vicious and false."

972. Riva, S. *"Pamela* e Venezia." In *Annuario 1933-4 del R. Istituto Tecnico Provinciale Pareggioto Jacopo*

Riccotti de Treviso. Treviso, 1934.

Not examined.

*   Romberg, Bertil. "Clarissa." See #1102.

Considers *Pamela* in light of narrative techniques, points of view, and the role of multiple narrators.

973.   Roussel, Roy. "Reflections on the Letter: The Reconciliation of Distance and Presence in *Pamela*." *ELH*, 41 (1974), 375-99.

The letter format develops the characterization of Pamela and B through the tension between the writer's "presence and absence" or his commitment to being in "company or retirement"; this tension underlies the conflict between love and society which informs the novel's plot.

974.   Sacks, Sheldon. *"Fiction" and the Shape of Belief: A Study of Henry Fielding, with Glances at Swift, Johnson and Richardson.* Berkeley and Los Angeles: Univ. of California Press, 1964. Pp. 236-42.

A thoughtful consideration of how Richardson's intentions are related to the represented action in *Pamela*, concluding that an evaluation of its "morality" must isolate the latter through a series of inferences "about what Richardson must have believed in order to evaluate as he did the characters, actions, and thoughts represented in the work"; passing references to the relation between Fielding and Richardson.

Reviewed: *CE*, 27 (1966), 654.
           JEGP, 65 (1966), 602-04.
           Yale Review, 55 (1965), 126-30.

*   Saintsbury, George. *The English Novel.* See #645.

Special attention is given to *Pamela* in which Richardson created a probable human being as no character had been worked out before.

975.   ———. Introduction to the Everyman Edition of *Pamela*. See #36, pp. v-ix.

A brief analysis of the novel placing it in its historical context.

*   ———. *The Peace of the Augustans.* See #564.

Pamela is discussed in terms of the eighteenth-century "nascent taste for 'sensibility.'"

976. Sale, William M., Jr. "The First Dramatic Version of *Pamela*." *Yale University Library Gazette*, 9 (1935), 83-88.

Looks at the first, early stage comedies of *Pamela* in the Yale library; provides evidence for the popularity of the novel.

977. —————. "From *Pamela* to *Clarissa*." In *The Age of Johnson: Essays Presented to Chauncey Brewster Tinker*. New Haven: Yale Univ. Press, 1949. Pp. 127-38.

Discusses how Richardson's fiction "rendered the conflicts he saw in his own society," revealing the meaning his novels had for his contemporaries and what they still mean today.

978. —————. Introduction to the Norton Edition of *Pamela*. See #37, pp. v-xiv.

Considers the eighteenth-century milieu which helped to formulate Richardson's fiction, and looks at the biographical background immediately preceding publication of *Pamela*.

979. Schleck, Florian J. "Richardson on the Index." *TLS*, 25 April 1935, p. 272.

Dates the placing of the French translation of *Pamela* on the Index of Prohibited Books in 1744, four years after its initial publication (see #998).

980. Schroers, Carola. "Ist Richardsons *Pamela* von Marivauxs *Vie de Marianne* beeinflusst?" *Englischen Studien*, 49 (1916), 220-54.

Endorses Macaulay's claim that Richardson owed a debt to authors of French fiction; especially attempts to show that the action of *Pamela* follows the first three parts of *Marianne*.

981. Schulte, Edvige. "Pamela e le sue origini." *Annali Istituto Universitario Orientale, Sezione Germanica*, 7 (1964), 143-74.

Argues at length that Defoe was the "friend" Richardson referred to in his letter to Hill when the novelist wrote about how he originated the *Pamela* story; Defoe

deeply influenced Richardson's art and morality:
Richardson conceived the epistolary form from Defoe's
The Family Instructor; chastity is only a physical at-
tribute for Richardson—as it was for Defoe; and Richardson closely follows the moral lesson of Defoe although
his morality is more refined.

982. Schulz, Dieter. "Samuel Richardson." In *Studien zur
      Verführungsszene im englischen Roman (1660-1760)*.
      Marburg: Erich Mauersberger, 1968. Pp. 119-82.

      This is a discussion which analyzes *Pamela* and the
      problem of "lascivious images."

983. Scouten, Arthur H., ed. *The London Stage, 1660-1800*.
      Part 3: 1729-47. Carbondale: Univ. of Southern
      Illinois Press, 1961. II, 929, 941-46, 948, 951-52,
      971.

      Considers the dramatic adaptation of *Pamela*.

984. Scrutton, Mary. "Bourgeois Cinderellas." *Twentieth
      Century*, 155 (1954), 351-55.

      A brief analysis of *Pamela* as the archetypal story of
      a woman marrying above her station, but the fable does
      not fit the moral structure of the book.

985. Senex. "Richardson and Philology." *N&Q*, 182 (1942),
      120.

      Disdains Richardson's cavalier treatment of philology
      as indicated by a passage in *Pamela*.

986. Sharrock, Roger. "Richardson's *Pamela*: The Gospel and
      the Novel." *Durham University Journal*, N.S., 27
      (1966), 67-74.

      Pamela is a supremely Christian heroine whose heroism
      "satisfies the new demands of the emerging novel form";
      the Christian heroine is compared with more conventional
      types.

987. Shepperson, Archibald Bolling. "Richardson and Fielding:
      Shamela and *Shamelia*." In *The Novel in Motley: A
      History of the Burlesque Novel in English*. 1936; rpt.
      New York: Octagon Books, 1967. Pp. 9-38.

      A summary review of the early anti-*Pamela*s from Povey
      to Fielding; a description of some burlesques of Field-
      ing's novels as well.

988.   Shipley, John B.   "Samuel Richardson and 'Pamela.'"
       N&Q, N.S., 1 (1954), 28-29.

       Prints Richardson's petition for a royal license
       giving him exclusive printing rights to *Pamela*.

989.   Shuman, R. Baird.   "Censorship As a Controlling Theme
       in 'Pamela' and 'Clarissa.'"   *N&Q*, N.S., 3 (1956),
       30-32.

       Suggests that censorship over a character's writing
       becomes a major symbol in *Pamela*, emphasizing Richardson's
       belief in personal freedom.

*   Smith, Warren H.   *Architecture in English Fiction*.   See
       #855.

       Considers how the theme of imprisonment and Richard-
       son's descriptions in *Pamela* affected the development
       of later Gothic stories.

*   Spacks, Patricia Meyer.   *The Female Imagination*.   See
       #856.

       Considers Pamela as a character who reveals how dif-
       ferently a woman views or interprets the values of our
       world.

990.   ————.   "The Sense of Audience: Samuel Richardson,
       Colley Cibber."   In *Imagining a Self: Autobiography
       and Novel in Eighteenth-Century England*.   Cambridge:
       Harvard Univ. Press, 1976.   Pp. 193-226.

       A study of *Pamela* in terms of the implications of
       Pamela's conscious knowledge of her literary effort;
       the writing has significance as pleasure, as control,
       and as important action.

991.   Spearman, Diana.   "Richardson."   In *The Novel and
       Society*.   London: Routledge and Kegan Paul, 1966.
       Pp. 173-98.

       Compares the novelistic worlds of *Pamela* and *Clarissa*
       against the known reality of eighteenth-century life
       as depicted in letters and memoirs, suggesting that
       Richardson's novels do not accurately picture the age.

992.   Steeves, Edna L.   "Pre-Feminism in Some Eighteenth-
       Century Novels."   *Texas Quarterly*, 16 (1973), 48-57.

       References to Pamela as an example of Richardson's
       assumption that women are naturally subordinate to men.

993. Steeves, Harrison R. "Virtue Rewarded (Samuel Richard-
      son)." In *Before Jane Austen: The Shaping of the
      English Novel in the Eighteenth Century*. New York:
      Holt, Rinehart and Winston, 1965. Pp. 53-87.

      Primarily a plot discussion of *Pamela* with some
      general evaluation.

994. Stein, William B. "*Pamela*: The Narrator as Unself-
      Conscious Hack." *Bucknell Review*, 20 (1972), 39-66.

      Pamela's sincerity must be judged by the reigning ethos
      of her time or one violates the integrity of Richardson's
      imaginative world.

995. Strandberg, Victor H. "A Palm for Pamela: Three Studies
      in the Game of Love." *Western Humanities Review*, 20
      (1966), 37-47.

      Pamela's "mercantile virtue" is defended by comparing
      the love game in the novel to those created by some of
      the world's experts on love: in the Hindu *Shakuntala*,
      in Shakespeare's *Romeo and Juliet*, and in Hemingway's
      A Farewell to Arms.

996. Swaen, A.E.H. "Marianne--Pamela." *Neophilologus*, 23
      (1937), 409-11.

      Reviews the critical positions taken toward the
      emergence of these two novels at nearly the same time,
      noting the major disagreement between English and Con-
      tinental critics; the former look for specific models
      and influences, whereas the latter are more interested
      in stylistic and cultural parallels. Swaen aligns him-
      self with Jusserand (#445) and Seccombe (#490).

997. Ten Harmsel, Henrietta. "The Villain-Hero in *Pamela* and
      Pride and Prejudice." *CE*, 23 (1961), 104-08.

      Jane Austen builds her novel from the same base as
      Richardson did his: will the "low" heroine catch the
      noble hero? The social distinctions create the ob-
      stacles, and in the social struggle which ensues, the
      hero actually plays the part of the villain.

998. Thornton, Richard H. "English Authors, Placed on the
      Roman 'Index' (1600 to 1750)." *N&Q*, 11th ser., 12
      (1915), 333.

      Notes 1745 as the date *Pamela* was condemned and
      "listed" (see #979).

999.   *Times Literary Supplement.* "Newbery's Edition of
        'Pamela,' 1769," 6 March 1930, p. 196.

        A note describing Newbery's illustrated and abridged
        edition.

1000.   Utter, Robert P., and Gwendolyn B. Needham. *Pamela's
        Daughters.* New York: Macmillan Company, 1936.

        A study of *Pamela* in terms of contemporary social
        conventions and novelistic practices; considers such
        items as the love plot, delicacy, prudery, tears and
        hysteria, virginity, the wages of sin, and the Cin-
        derella motif. Takes the subject through the reign of
        Victoria.

*   Waterhouse, Osborn. "The Development of English Sen-
        timental Comedy in the Eighteenth Century." See
        #880.

        Briefly considers that *Pamela* is the first "novel of
        sentimental analysis."

*   Watt, Ian. "Love and the Novel: *Pamela*." See #577, pp.
        135-73.

        Studies the novel in terms of its structure: unity
        through a single action, courtship; examines the ques-
        tion of love in the novel and the contemporary milieu,
        and in terms of Richardson's essentially "feminine
        perspective."

1001.   ————. "The Novelist as Innovator: Samuel Richardson."
        Listener, 73 (1965), 177-80.

        Discusses *Pamela* in terms of Richardson's conscious
        artistry, and the effect of its technique on the
        development of the novel form.

1002.   Wells, John Edwin. "The Dating of Shenstone's Letters."
        Anglia, 35 (1912), 429-52.

        Reviews again that Richardson wrote *Pamela* between
        10 Nov. 1739 and 10 Jan. 1740, commenting that Hulme
        (#936) errs in thinking the "1739" date of Letter II
        in Dodsley's edition is accurate; the date should be
        1741. Also see #1003.

1003.   ————. "'Pamela' and Shenstone's Letters." *Nation*,
        93 (10 Aug. 1911), 120.

        Points out the probable misdating of a Shenstone

letter which otherwise seems to show a published version of *Pamela* as early as July 1739. See #936 and
#1002.

*   Whitcomb, Seldon L. *The Study of a Novel.* See #655.

Pamela is considered in terms of a formal, rhetorical
evaluation of the novel form.

*   White, William. "Richardson: Idealist or Realist?"
      See #883.

The model for a young woman's behavior, suggested
in *Familiar Letters*, is not followed by Pamela; the
contrast reveals Pamela's selfish nature.

1004.   Whiteford, Robert N. "Samuel Richardson, Henry Field-
        ing, Sarah Fielding, and Tobias Smollett." In
        Motives in English Fiction. New York: Putnam's Sons,
        1918. Pp. 86-118.

A short discussion of Pamela, Clarissa, Harriet Byron,
and Clementina, analyzing their characterization.

1005.   Wiles, R.M. *Serial Publication in England before 1750.*
        Cambridge: Cambridge Univ. Press, 1957. Pp. 162-68.

Includes information regarding Richardson's fight to
protect his rights to *Pamela*.

1006.   Wilson, Colin. *The Craft of the Novel.* London: Victor
        Gollancz, 1975.

Pamela is briefly considered in terms of Richardson's
genius for freeing "the human imagination"; comparisons
made with Defoe, Cleland, Smollett, and Rousseau.

1007.   Wilson, Stuart. "Richardson's *Pamela*: An Interpreta-
        tion." *PMLA*, 88 (1973), 79-91.

The novel has powerful psychological unity, and
Pamela is neither an adventuress nor "a paragon of
virtue"; she is, rather, a complex character, moving
from "a naive adolescence to a composed maturity."

*   Wolff, Cynthia Griffin. "Pamela." See #582, pp. 58-
      73.

Studies characterization in the novel from two perspectives: (1) why *Pamela* is still felt to possess
creative "force," and (2) why our expectations are
eventually disappointed.

1008. Wolff, Renate C. *"Pamela* as Myth and Dream." *Costerus,*
       7 (1973), 223-35.

       Develops the idea that *Pamela* is most fruitfully ap-
       proached as a "consistent and revealing dream fantasy."

1009. Wolff, Samuel Lee. *The Greek Romances in Elizabethan
       Prose Fiction.* 1912; rpt. New York: Burt Franklin,
       1961. P. 463n.

       Notes Richardson's several debts to Sidney and the
       Arcadia, especially in connection with Pamela's name.

1010. Woods, Charles B. "Fielding and the Authorship of
       Shamela." PQ, 25 (1946), 248-72.

       Considers *Pamela* while assessing Fielding's authorship
       of the satire.

                         E. *CLARISSA*

1011. Abraham, David. "Clarissa and Tess: Two Meanings of
       Death." *Massachusetts Studies in English,* 1 (1968),
       96-99.

       Analyzes Clarissa's death as a "consummation of
       Christian ethics."

1012. Adams, Henry H., and Baxter Hathaway. "Samuel Richard-
       son: *Clarissa,* Postscript." In *Dramatic Essays of
       the Neoclassic Age.* 1947; rpt. New York: Benjamin
       Blom, 1965. Pp. 324-27.

       Excerpts from the 1748 edition with a brief, two-
       paragraph introduction given to Richardson.

*   Allen, B. Sprague. *Tides in English Taste, 1619-1800.*
       See #520.

       Places *Clarissa* into the milieu of its times.

1013. Anderson, Howard. "Answers to the Author of *Clarissa*:
       Theme and Narrative Technique in *Tom Jones* and *Tristram
       Shandy." PQ,* 51 (1972), 859-73.

       Fielding and Sterne reject the "costly self-reliance"
       of Clarissa, establishing instead the necessity of
       mutual trust.

1014.   Babb, Howard S. "Richardson's Narrative Mode in
          Clarissa." *SEL*, 16 (1976), 451-60.

          Examines the narrative technique in the novel in
          terms of Richardson's setting up of alternatives and
          of the controlled rate at which the story unfolds.

*   Baker, Ernest A. "Clarissa." See #585, IV, 33-54.

          Discusses the publication of *Clarissa* and provides
          a plot summary and critical analysis.

1015.   Barker, Gerard A. "Clarissa's 'Command of her Passions':
          Self-Censorship in the Third Edition." *SEL*, 10 (1970),
          525-39.

          Although Richardson changed his novel in an attempt
          to reinforce Clarissa's exemplary character (regarding
          her feelings toward Lovelace), the changes actually
          undermine her struggle with herself and make her self-
          reproach after the rape seem "inordinate and prudish."

*   ————. "The Complacent Paragon: Exemplary Characteriza-
          tion in Richardson." See #666.

          Clarissa reveals her virtue through her Protestant
          approval of her own behavior.

*   Barnett, George L., ed. "Samuel Richardson." See
          #667.

          Includes a printing of the 1751 fourth edition Post-
          script to *Clarissa*.

*   Beer, Gillian. "Richardson, Milton, and the Status of
          Evil." See #670.

          Clarissa is examined in the light of the serious doc-
          trine of virginity.

1016.   Bennett, Arnold. *Books and Persons*. New York, [1917].
          P. 139.

          Notes briefly that *Clarissa* is "the greatest realistic
          novel in the world."

*   Bernbaum, Ernest. *The Drama of Sensibility*. See #900.

          Discusses a parallel between *Clarissa* and Charles
          Johnson's *Caelia*.

1017.   Biron, Sir Henry Chartres. "Clarissa Harlowe." In
        Pious Opinions. London: Duckworth & Co., 1923.
        Pp. 1-19.

        Studies Clarissa's real tragedy as one of her dual
        nature: a saint betrayed by her temperament.

1018.   Blake, H.M. "Miss Howe--Pioneer." *Harper's Weekly*,
        61 (2 Oct. 1915), 332-33.

        In Anna Howe, Richardson created a model of the
        truly "eternal feminine," only later understood and
        developed by Meredith; Miss Howe is "courageous, high
        spirited, independent" and "she thinks deep and sees
        clear, realizing her own power."

*   **Blondel, Madeleine.** *Images de la femme.* **See #902.**

        Considers whether Clarissa is actually representative
        of eighteenth-century women as they are portrayed in
        the fiction of the period.

*   Braudy, Leo. "The Form of the Sentimental Novel."
        See #682.

        Clarissa is used to illustrate how sentimentalism
        developed out of a novelistic tradition and not from
        either the theater or philosophy.

1019.   ————. "Penetration and Impenetrability in *Clarissa*."
        In *New Approaches to Eighteenth-Century Literature*.
        Ed. John Phillip Harth. English Institute Essays for
        1972, 1973. New York: Columbia Univ. Press, 1974.
        Pp. 177-206.

        Analyzes and compares the cultural milieu which
        provoked Pope's satirical attack upon sexual assault
        in *The Rape of the Lock* with Richardson's tragic por-
        trayal of repressed sexuality in *Clarissa*; especially
        considers self-willed isolation in the novel as a
        security against an evil world.

1020.   Brissenden, R.F. "*Clarissa*: The Sentimental Tragedy."
        In *Virtue in Distress: Studies in the Novel of
        Sentiment from Richardson to Sade*. New York: Mac-
        millan Co., 1974. Pp. 159-86.

        Defines the novel of sentiment in earlier chapters,
        and then shows how the struggle between Clarissa and
        Lovelace is crucial because the former "is the feminine
        embodiment of the sentimental virtues and ideals."

1021.   ————. "Introduction." In *Samuel Richardson, "Claris-*
         sa": Preface, Hints of Prefaces, and Postscript.
         Augustan Reprint Society, Pub. 103. Los Angeles:
         William Andrews Clark Memorial Library, Univ. of
         California, 1964. Pp. i-vii.

         Richardson's revisions to his Preface and Postscript
         represent his most elaborate and extensive theory of
         fiction. *Hints of Prefaces* includes two critical
         assessments by Philip Skelton and Joseph Spence not
         published before.

1022.   ————. "Le Philosophie dans le boudoir; or, *A Young*
         Lady's Entrance into the World." In *Studies in*
         Eighteenth-Century Culture: Irrationalism in the
         Eighteenth Century. Ed. Harold E. Pagliaro. Vol. 2.
         Cleveland and London: The Press of Case Western
         Reserve Univ., 1972. Pp. 113-41.

         A connection is made between the sentimental novelists,
         Clarissa, and the novels of the Marquis de Sade.

*   Brophy, Elizabeth. "*Clarissa*: My Favorite Clarissa."
         See #527, pp. 91-107.

         An analysis of the novel in terms of Richardson's
         artistic theory, showing that his theories accurately
         describe the structure of the novel and account for
         its success.

1023.   Brown, Herbert B. "Richardson and Sterne in the *Massa-*
         chusetts Magazine." *New England Quarterly*, 5 (1932),
         65-82.

         Traces Richardson's influence upon the theme of
         seduction in this magazine and the many references to
         Lovelace or Clarissa in the eight volumes of the
         periodical, 1789 to 1796.

1024.   Brownstein, Rachel Mayer. "'An Exemplar to Her Sex':
         Richardson's Clarissa." *Yale Review*, 67 (1977),
         30-47.

         An analysis of Clarissa's character (and Lovelace's)
         in terms of imagery (imprisonment, houses, clothes), an
         imagery which reveals some of the mythic elements of
         Clarissa's desperate attempt to escape from those who
         have power over her and who wish to exercise it.

1025.   Bundy, Jean. "Fréron and the English Novel." *Revue de*
         Littérature Comparée, 36 (1962), 258-65.

A brief mention of Fréron's admiration for Richardson's ability to portray verisimilitude in *Clarissa*.

1026. Burrell, John. Introduction to the Modern Library Edition of *Clarissa*. See #43, pp. v-xiv.

Discusses Richardson's achievement as a literary artist and his epistolary technique, and provides a brief biography. For an evaluation of this edition see #1091.

1027. Butt, John. Introduction to the Everyman Edition of *Clarissa*. See #44, pp. v-xv.

Summarizes the novel and discusses background material and Richardson's epistolary technique.

1028. Carroll, John. "Annotating *Clarissa*." In *Editing Eighteenth Century Novels*. Ed. G.E. Bentley, Jr. Toronto: Hakkert, 1975. Pp. 49-66.

Considers the difficulties and challenges facing an annotator of the novel.

1029. ————. "Lovelace as Tragic Hero." *UTQ*, 42 (1972), 14-25.

A careful study of Lovelace as a complex but extraordinarily magnetic personality imbued with Faustian qualities.

1030. ————. "Richardson at Work: Revisions, Allusions, and Quotations in *Clarissa*." In *Studies in the Eighteenth Century, II: Papers Presented at the Second David Nichol Smith Memorial Seminar*. Canberra, 1970. Ed. R.F. Brissenden. Toronto: Univ. of Toronto Press, 1973. Pp. 53-71.

Revisions in the novel's text are discussed in relation to Richardson's narrative and didactic problems; quotations reveal much about his reading and knowledge.

1031. Carter, A.E. "The Greatest English Novelist (On the Occasion of the Bicentenary of *Clarissa*, 1748)," *UTQ*, 17 (1948), 390-97.

Richardson's powers of characterization and psychological insight are most demonstrated in *Clarissa*; but Clarissa is more an unsatisfactory character than is Lovelace.

1032. ———. "The Most Audacious Novel." *UTQ*, 24 (1954),
       46-55.

       Suggests that Laclos' *Les Liaisons dangereuses* had
       its source in *Clarissa*, but indicates how different
       Mme. de Merteuil is from the more conventional
       eighteenth-century heroine.

*   Clements, Frances M. "The Rights of Women in the
       Eighteenth-Century Novel." See #691.

       Uses references from *Clarissa* to reveal the conditions
       faced by women: domestic service, prostitution, house-
       wifery.

*   Cockshut, A.O.J. "Richardson and Fielding." See #692.

       Clarissa, like Amelia and the heroines of Emily Brontë
       and George Eliot, shares "with men the whole range of
       moral choices, a moral arena as wide as life."

*   ———. "Sentimentality in Fiction." See #693.

       Argues that *Clarissa* is not a sentimental novel
       because a thorough analysis of Clarissa's motives pre-
       cludes sentimentality.

1033. Cohen, Steven M. "*Clarissa* and the Individuation of
       Character." *ELH*, 43 (1976), 163-83.

       Richardson employs the epistolary convention to ex-
       plore complex human personalities, revealing a dual
       perspective of character as both type and individual.

1034. Collins, R.L. "Moore's *The Foundling*--an Intermediary."
       PQ, 17 (1938), 139-43.

       Richardson's *Clarissa* is the basis for Moore's play:
       Fielding's response to both works is considered.

1035. Copeland, Edward. "Allegory and Analogy in *Clarissa*:
       The 'Plan' and 'No-Plan.'" *ELH*, 39 (1972), 254-65.

       The two figurative strategies, allegory (rhetoric)
       and analogy (logic), move in opposite directions in the
       novel and hence inspire the "myriad interpretations of
       the novel's meaning."

1036. ———. "*Clarissa* and *Fanny Hill*: Sisters in Distress."
       SNNTS, 4 (1972), 343-52.

       Discusses the conventions shared by the two novels,

suggesting the sexual energy in the terminology of
Clarissa and the implications of the "essentially her-
metic nature of sentimental fiction" must be understood
in order to view the novel correctly.

*   ————. "Samuel Richardson and Naive Allegory: Some
           Beauties of the Mixed Metaphor." See #698.

           Includes some interesting references to *Clarissa*, re-
           garding Richardson's use of figurative language to
           establish the psychological and didactic centers of
           the novel.

*   Daiches, David. "Samuel Richardson." See #703.

           Includes an analysis of patterns and ideas in
           Clarissa.

1037.   Danziger, Marlies K. "The Eighteenth-Century Novel:
           A Comparative Approach." *CE*, 23 (1962), 646-48.

           Puts *Clarissa* into a discussion of an eighteenth-
           century novel course for undergraduates based upon com-
           parative and general literature.

*   Davis, Robert G. "The Sense of the Real in English
           Fiction." See #707.

           Discusses how Richardson applied Aristotelian tragic
           theory to *Clarissa*.

1038.   de Castro, J. Paul. "Ursula Fielding and 'Tom Jones.'"
           N&Q, 178 (1940), 164.

           Notes how this other sister of Fielding (like Sarah)
           admired *Clarissa*.

1039.   Detig, Joseph, S.V.D. "Clarissa and Her Modern Critics."
           Leyte-Samar Studies, 4 (1970), 131-38.

           Briefly classifies modern criticism of *Clarissa* under
           various headings, such as myth, Puritanism, social caste,
           family life, and sexuality.

*   Dibelius, Wilhelm. "Richardson." See #711.

           Gives special attention to the characterization of
           Anna Howe.

*   Doody, Margaret Anne. *A Natural Passion*. See #534,
           pp. 99-240.

           Includes five chapters on the novel, dealing with

earlier novels of love and seduction, the tragic
themes and influence of the drama, deathbed themes,
and recurring and thematic imagery.

*   Dottin, Paul. "Samuel Richardson et le roman épisto-
        laire." See #716.

        The epistolary form in *Clarissa* determines the nar-
        rative development.

1040.   Drew, Elizabeth. "Samuel Richardson: Clarissa." In
        *The Novel: A Modern Guide to Fifteen English Master-
        pieces*. New York: Norton, 1963. Pp. 39-58.

        A very general introduction to the novel.

1041.   Dussinger, John A. "Conscience and the Pattern of
        Christian Perfection in *Clarissa*." *PMLA*, 81 (1966),
        236-45.

        Studies in detail how Clarissa is the martyr-heroine
        in a religious novel aimed at reviving Christianity;
        Clarissa is the prototype for the principal doctrines
        espoused by Richardson.

*   ———. *The Discourse of the Mind*. See #923.

        Includes a chapter on *Clarissa* relating the novel to
        eighteenth-century conceptions of knowledge, reality,
        and the status of the individual.

1042.   ———. "Richardson's Tragic Muse." *PQ*, 46 (1967),
        18-33.

        Discusses Richardson's interest in the drama to
        clarify the tragedy of *Clarissa*.

1043.   Eaves, T.C. Duncan. "Amelia and Clarissa." In *A
        Provision of Human Nature: Essays on Fielding and
        Others in Honor of Miriam Austin Locke*. Ed. Donald
        Kay. University: Univ. of Alabama Press, 1977. Pp.
        95-110.

        Notes how *Clarissa* probably influenced Fielding's
        novel.

*   ———, and Ben D. Kimpel. "Clarissa." See #537, pp.
        235-84.

        A critical examination in terms of style, structure,
        and characterization, noting the primary critical
        evaluations of the novel.

1044. ————. "The Composition of *Clarissa* and Its Revision
       Before Publication." *PMLA*, 83 (1968), 416-28.

       Arranges the evidence in order and determines the
       chronology of the novel's composition and the kinds of
       revisions Richardson made before its publication.

1045. ————. "Richardson's Helper in Creating the Character
       of Elias Brand." *N&Q*, N.S., 14 (1967), 414-15.

       Conjectures that a Mr. R. Smith was Richardson's
       corrector of the press and helped with creating the
       Brand letters in *Clarissa* as well as with other matters
       requiring a classical education.

1046. Enomoto, Futoshi. "Clarissa Harlowe's Pursuit of
       Happiness." *Studies in English Literature* (Tokyo),
       40 (1964), 167-84.

       The dominant ideas lying behind Clarissa's search for
       happiness are based on Puritan attitudes.

*   Erämetsä, Erik. "Notes on Richardson's Language."
       See #730.

       Cites examples from *Clarissa* of newly-coined words
       used by Richardson.

*   Ernle, Rowland E.P., Lord. "Samuel Richardson." See
       #731.

       Discusses the character of Lovelace.

1047. Farrell, William J. "The Style and the Action in
       Clarissa." *SEL*, 3 (1963), 365-75.

       Argues against Ian Watt's thesis that Richardson
       did not rely upon earlier prose conventions by demon-
       strating how the latter used traditional styles to
       affect a reader's response to characters and incidents.

1048. Fiedler, Leslie A. "Richardson and the Tragedy of
       Seduction"; "*Clarissa* in America: Toward *Marjorie
       Morningstar*"; "Good Good Girls and Good Bad Boys:
       Clarissa as a Juvenile." In *Love and Death in the
       American Novel*. Rev. edn. New York: Stein and Day,
       1966. Chs. 2, 7, 8.

       An analysis of the archetypal and the mythic in
       Clarissa and Richardson's embodiment of "the bourgeois
       Liebestod" in his fiction and its impact upon American

fiction. There was no prototype which affected
American fiction so thoroughly as the sentimental
tale of seduction.

1049.   ————. "Richardson und die Tragödie der Verführung."
        Die Neue Rundschau, 75 (1964), 441–51.

        Primarily a discussion of the seduction theme in
        Clarissa.

1050.   ————. "Le Viol des temple: de Richardson à Faulk-
        ner." *Preuves*, 12 (1962), 75–81.

        Clarissa is discussed as the Bible of sentimental
        love and as the repository of a secret bourgeois
        religion in which the pure young maiden was defiled
        and represented as a "savior"; marriage is considered
        the basis for salvation, and the seducer is equated
        with the devil himself, seduction being an ultimate
        blasphemy.

1051.   Fougères, Michel. *La Liebestod dans le roman français,
        anglais et allemand au XVIIIe siècle*. Preface by
        Jean-Pierre Monnier. Collection études, 4. Sher-
        brooke, Quebec: Naeman, 1974.

        Considers the theme of fatal love, its ancestry and
        distinctive nature; uses *Clarissa* as one of the five
        basic stories discussed.

*   Frank, Frederick S. "From Boudoir to Castle Crypt:
        Richardson and the Gothic Novel." See #734.

        Discusses the sex debate in the novel and links it
        to the development of the Gothic novel.

1052.   Friedman, Arthur. "Aspects of Sentimentalism in
        Eighteenth-Century Literature." In *The Augustan
        Milieu: Essays Presented to Louis A. Landa*. Ed.
        Henry Knight Miller, Eric Rothstein, and G.S.
        Rousseau. Oxford: Clarendon Press, 1970. Pp. 247–
        61.

        Uses Goldsmith's distinction between laughing and
        sentimental comedy to isolate two aspects of sentimen-
        talism; briefly looks at *Clarissa* in order to demon-
        strate how a sentimental plot is "softened" through
        Christian doctrine.

*   Golden, Morris. "Richardson's Repetitions." See #739.

A specific analysis of *Clarissa* in terms of character types which Richardson used in his novel.

1053. Goldknopf, David. "The Meaning of the Epistolary Format in *Clarissa*." In *The Life of the Novel*. Chicago: Univ. of Chicago Press, 1972. Pp. 59–78.

The *writing* of the letters themselves frees the characters from the "banality of their inner life and allows them to project their desires upon an outer world."

1054. Gopnik, Irwin. "An Analysis of the Verbal Structure in *Clarissa*"; "Verbal Structure and the Role of 'Editor' in *Clarissa*." In *A Theory of Style and Richardson's "Clarissa*." The Hague: Mouton, 1970.

Investigates key phrases and terms like "generosity" in the novel to show Richardson's manipulation of language; based upon the theories of the Prague Linguistic Circle, the study is perhaps too heavily theoretical and spends too much time defining "formal realism."

1055. Greiner, Walter F., ed. *English Theories of the Novel*. Vol. II of *Eighteenth Century*. English Texts 7. Tübingen: Max Niemeyer, 1970. Pp. 69–75.

Reprints selections from Richardson's Preface to *Clarissa* (4th edn., 1751) and Postscript.

1056. Griffith, Philip Mahone. "Fire-Scenes in Richardson's *Clarissa* and Smollett's *Humphry Clinker*: A Study of a Literary Relationship in the Structure of the Novel." *Tulane Studies in English*, 11 (1961), 39–51.

Smollett may well have recalled the famous fire-scene in *Clarissa*, but in his novel he uses the situation for comic purposes, ridiculing not only Richardson's tedious style but his "morality" as well.

1057. Gwynn, Stephen. "The Eighteenth Century Novelists." In *The Masters of English Literature*. London: Macmillan Co., 1904. Pp. 212–30.

Discusses the plot of *Clarissa* and Richardson's treatment of the feminine temperament; includes an extract from one of Clarissa's letters and one from Lovelace to Belford.

1058. Halsband, Robert. "Samuel Richardson." *TLS*, 6 Aug.
       1971, p. 945.

       Notes George Sherburn's reason for his tardy
       abridgement of *Clarissa*: he had difficulty staying
       awake.

1059. Hardwick, Elizabeth. "Seduction and Betrayal." In
       Seduction and Betrayal: Women and Literature. New
       York: Random House, 1974. Pp. 175-208.

       Discusses *Clarissa* as "a disturbing mixture of wit
       and sentiment, of surface and disguise"; examines
       Lovelace and his motives as well as Clarissa's.

1060. **Heilbrun, Carolyn G. "The Woman As Hero." In** *Toward*
       a Recognition of Androgyny. 1973; rpt. New York:
       Harper Colophon Books, 1974. Pp. 59-62.

       Clarissa represents "the first cry of outrage against
       the almost total betrayal of the androgynous ideal."

1061. Herrick, Robert. "The First English Novelist." *The*
       Dial, a Semi-Monthly Journal of Literary Criticism,
       Discussion, and Information, 32 (1902), 243-44.

       A brief analysis of Richardson's achievement in
       Clarissa, emphasizing its unity, comprehensiveness,
       and "dramatic relationship of values."

1062. Heyningen, Christina van. *"Clarissa," Poetry and*
       Morals. Pietermaritburg: Univ. of Natal Press, 1963.

       This discussion of the novel in Part I is an un-
       critical re-reading of *Clarissa*.

1063. Hill, Christopher. "Clarissa Harlowe and Her Times."
       In *Puritanism and Revolution. Studies in Interpreta-*
       tion of the English Revolution of the 17th Century.
       1958; rpt. New York: Schocken Books, 1964. Originally
       published *Essays in Criticism*, 5 (1955), 315-40.

       Especially considers the period's economic background
       and its relevance to an understanding of the novel's
       structure.

1064. Hilles, Frederick W. "The Plan of *Clarissa*." *PQ*, 45
       (1966), 236-48.

       Argues that Richardson did work from a "very full
       sketch" of the novel.

1065. Hohendahl, Peter U. "Empfindsamkeit und gesellschaft-
       liches Bewusstsein: Zur Soziologie des empfindsamen
       Romans am Beispiel von *La vie de Marianne*, *Clarissa*,
       Fräulein von Sternheim, und *Werther*." *Jahrbuch der
       deutschen Schiller-Gesellschaft*, 16 (1972), 176-207.

       Discusses sentimentality and social conscience in
       Clarissa.

1066. Hopkinson, H.T. "Robert Lovelace, the Romantic Cad."
       Horizon, 10 (1944), 80-104.

       A critical analysis of the character of Lovelace in
       terms of his attitude toward women: they are considered
       a natural prey.

*   Howells, William Dean. "Editor's Easy Chair." See
       #755.

       Discusses *Clarissa* in terms of Richardson's general
       achievement.

1067. ————. "Some Nineteenth-Century Heroines in the
       Eighteenth Century." In *Heroines in Fiction*. 2 vols.
       New York: Harper and Brothers, 1901. I, 1-12.

       Howells especially applauds Clarissa's naturalness of
       characterization.

1068. Hughes, Helen Sard. "Characterization in *Clarissa Har-
       lowe*." *JEGP*, 13 (1914), 110-23.

       A review of Clarissa's "naturalness" as evaluated by
       critics from Dr. Johnson to W.D. Howells, with a further
       comparison of Clarissa (as well as Lovelace and Anna
       Howe) with the heroines and characters in other eigh-
       teenth-century novels and in the dramas.

1069. ————. "Richardson and Warburton." *MP*, 17 (1919),
       45-50.

       Discusses possible reasons why Richardson eliminated
       the Warburton Preface to the fourth volume of the first
       edition of *Clarissa* from subsequent editions.

*   Humphreys, A.R. "Richardson's Novels: Words and the
       'Movements Within.'" See #764.

       Considers syntax and style in *Clarissa* as factors
       which create complex psychological situations.

1070. Johnson, Clifford R. "*Clarissa*." In *Plots and Charac-
       ters in the Fiction of Eighteenth-Century English
       Authors*. Hamden, Conn.: Archon Books, 1977. Pp.
       18-42.

       A volume-by-volume plot summary of the novel with a
       list of characters.

1071. Jones, Louis Clark. *The Clubs of the Georgian Rakes*.
       New York: Columbia Univ. Press, 1942.

       Not specifically on Richardson, but it provides
       valuable background to an understanding of Lovelace
       and his cohorts in *Clarissa*.

1072. Kaplan, Fred. "'Our Short Story': The Narrative
       Devices of *Clarissa*." *SEL*, 11 (1971), 549-62.

       Richardson's use of narrative devices such as the
       flashback, delayed details, or editorial summary plays
       an important role in the development of themes like
       isolation or Christian salvation.

1073. Karl, Frederick. "Samuel Richardson and *Clarissa*."
       In *The Adversary Literature. The English Novel in
       the Eighteenth Century: A Study in Genre*. New York:
       Farrar, Straus and Giroux, 1974. Pp. 99-145.

       The development of English fiction beginning with
       Richardson is away from picaresque episodes towards
       "the two person, interior scene," utilizing such
       elements as irony, concealment, vanity, and innocence.

1074. Kearney, Anthony M. "*Clarissa* and the Epistolary
       Form." *Essays in Criticism*, 16 (1966), 44-56.

       The emphasis on the shared experience generated by
       the epistolary form should not distract one from the
       unified vision of life Richardson achieved through the
       artistic structure of the novel.

1075. ————. *Samuel Richardson: "Clarissa."* Studies in
       English Literature, No. 55. General ed. David
       Daiches. London: Edward Arnold, 1975.

       An analysis of the novel with specific chapters on
       (1) "Design and Movement," (2) "Clarissa and Love-
       lace," (3) "Supporting Roles," and (4) "Styles and
       Voices."

1076. Keast, William R. "The Two *Clarissa*s in Johnson's

　　　　Dictionary." *SP*, 54 (1957), 429-39.

　　　　Richardson received special attention in Johnson's
work, being quoted some 96 times: one group of 18
references reveals only that Richardson was innovative
with language, but the remaining 78 quotations reveal
how thoroughly Johnson recognized that the novelist
conveyed an unequalled knowledge of the human heart.

1077.　Kinkead-Weekes, Mark. "*Clarissa* Restored?" *RES*, N.S.,
　　　　10 (1959), 156-71.

　　　　Suggests that some of the material added to later
editions was dictated by Richardson's responses to
interpretations of his work, making the third edition
considerably different and less effective than the
first.

*　　　　————. *Samuel Richardson.* See #544, pp. 123-276.

　　　　Three chapters on *Clarissa* analyze how the novel "is
actually three novels in one, each with a different
focus": (1) the social, (2) the ethical, and (3) the
religious.

*　　　　Klotman, Phyllis R. "Sin and Sublimation in the Novels
　　　　of Samuel Richardson." See #777.

　　　　Clarissa is given considerable analysis as a self-
conscious letter writer who achieves her didactic
purpose despite the Puritan concern for sin.

1078.　Knight, Charles A. "The Function of Wills in Richard-
　　　　son's *Clarissa*." *TSLL*, 11 (1969), 1183-90.

　　　　Around the social problem of marriage are grouped
the three conflicting attitudes in the novel represented
by the Harlowe family, Clarissa, and Lovelace; a pattern
of wills, heirs, and executors reveals social attitudes
in the novel.

*　　　　Konigsberg, Ira. "The Tragedy of Clarissa." See #545,
　　　　pp. 74-94.

　　　　Considers the novel a formal tragedy constructed according to "neoclassic concepts of poetic justice, the
tragic hero, and unity of action."

1079.　Krutch, Joseph Wood. "Samuel Richardson and His *Claris-
　　　　sa*." *Atlantic Monthly*, 146 (1930), 205-15.

　　　　Krutch is critical of Richardson as a man, but notes

"an astonishing power" in the novel (though rarely
read now) which is then given some critical analysis;
Clarissa becomes the model for all subsequent sentimental fiction.

*   Lathrop, Henry Burrowes. *The Art of the Novelist.* See
       #946.

       Uses examples from *Clarissa* to define the distinction
       of tragedy from comedy.

*   LeGates, Marlene. "The Cult of Womanhood in Eighteenth-
       Century Thought." See #780.

       Notes how Clarissa, "virtuous unto death," becomes a
       model for a new definition of eighteenth-century woman-
       hood.

1080. Leibowitz, Judith. "The Poetics of Salvation in *Claris-*
       sa, *La nouvelle Héloïse*, and *Die Leiden des jungen*
       Werther." In *Proceedings: Pacific Northwest Con-*
       ference on Foreign Languages. Ed. Walter C. Kraft.
       Corvallis: Oregon State Univ. Press, 1974. Pp. 242-
       45.

       Clarissa achieves salvation solely through her own
       feelings, illustrating the shift in the eighteenth cen-
       tury from salvation through abnegation to salvation
       through asserting a passionate individualism.

1081. Levin, Gerald. "Lovelace's Dream." *Literature and*
       Psychology, 29 (1970), 121-27.

       Lovelace's dream of sleeping with Clarissa merges
       into a miscomprehension of waking reality, revealing a
       particular kind of "moral" masochism.

1082. MacAndrew, Elizabeth. "Courtly-Genteel or Moral-Didac-
       tic?--A Response to Carey McIntosh." In *Studies in*
       Eighteenth-Century Culture. Ed. Harold E. Pagliaro.
       Vol. 4. Madison: Univ. of Wisconsin Press for the
       American Society for Eighteenth-Century Studies, 1975.
       Pp. 155-59. See #1084.

       Argues that analysis of style depends largely on an
       understanding of a novel's themes; only the meaning
       determines the effect of a particular stylistic ar-
       rangement.

1083. McCullough, Bruce. "The Novel of Sentiment. Samuel

Richardson: *Clarissa*." In *Representative English
Novelists: Defoe to Conrad*. New York: Harper and
Brothers, 1946. Pp. 23-41.

Richardson discovered his primary inspiration in
Puritan sentimentalism; a general study with comparisons
with Defoe and special attention given to violence com-
mitted against a "somewhat romanticized Puritan conscience" in *Clarissa*.

1084. McIntosh, Carey. "Quantities of Qualities: Nominal
Style and the Novel." In *Studies in Eighteenth-
Century Culture*. Ed. Harold E. Pagliaro. Vol. 4.
Madison: Univ. of Wisconsin Press for the American
Society for Eighteenth-Century Studies, 1975. Pp.
139-53.

An analytical study of language and style in *Clarissa*.
Objections to McIntosh's conclusions are found in #1082.

* McKillop, Alan Dugald. "A Letter from Samuel Richardson to Alexis Claude Clairaut." See #80.

Provides more details of Richardson's concern over
the foreign translations of *Clarissa*.

* Manheim, Leonard H. "The Absurd Miss Pamela and the
Tragic Miss Clarissa." See #957.

Clarissa is considered as a "sincere work," reflecting the manners and morals of the period.

1085. Miller, Nancy K. "Novels of Innocence: Fiction of
Loss." *ECS*, 11 (1978), 325-39.

Considers Clarissa as one of the unambiguous "avatars"
of innocence; her loss of innocence creates a "ricochet"
effect, whereby her antagonists only learn to under-
stand her (and themselves) correctly after she has
died.

1086. Moynihan, Robert D. "Clarissa and the Enlightened
Woman as Literary Heroine." *Journal of the History
of Ideas*, 36 (1975), 159-66.

Changing values and patterns toward women in the
eighteenth century reflected in contemporary writings
are an essential ingredient to an understanding of
structure and theme in *Clarissa*.

1087. Nachtigall, Elsbeth. *Die "Memoires" der Marguerite*

de Valois als Quelle zu Samuel Richardsons "Clarissa."
Romanistische Versuche und Vorarbeiten, 5 (1960). Bonn:
Romanisches Seminar an der Universität.

In a first section, Nachtigall reviews the literary
research which refers to Richardson and French literature, discusses the sociological hypothesis underlying
Richardson's art, considers his merits as a moral
preacher, and studies his achievement as a narrative
writer; in a second section, Nachtigall studies the
special significance of the "Memoires" for Richardson,
examining closely the connection between it and *Clarissa*
and providing parallel passages for discussion.

1088.   Napier, Elizabeth R. "'Tremble and Reform': The In-
version of Power in Richardson's *Clarissa*." *ELH*,
42 (1975), 214-23.

The question of power is central to the novel's plot
and theme, and the eventual "balance of Richardson's
fictional world" is largely determined by the degree
and extent of power Clarissa ultimately attains at
the end of the novel.

1089.   New, Melvyn. "'The Grease of God': The Form of
Eighteenth-Century English Fiction." *PMLA*, 91
(1976), 235-44.

Clarissa is cited as an example of how the providen-
tial view did not necessarily determine characterization, that radical individualism was part of Richardson's focus in the novel; his fiction shows the two
"in uneasy and temporary alliance."

1090.   Noble, Yvonne. "*Clarissa*: Paradise Irredeemably Lost."
In *Transactions of the Fourth International Congress
on the Enlightenment*. (SVEC 154.) Oxford: Voltaire
Foundation, 1976. Pp. 1529-45.

Richardson vividly imagines "the divisive principle
of the Fall," but he does not follow Milton to then
assert any "life-renewing alternative"; a study of the
novel in terms of the mythic patterns also found in
Paradise Lost. But whereas Milton affirms that in life
"good must be redeemed," Richardson portrays a world
which "relentlessly extrudes its goodness." *Clarissa*
is "a myth of life as unliveable."

*   Noyes, Robert G. *The Neglected Muse*. See #557.

Considers the specific effect of *The Fair Penitent*
upon *Clarissa*.

1091. Palmer, William J. "The Abridgements of *Clarissa*."
      JNL, 32 (1972), 8-9.

      Evaluations of three modern editions: Modern Library
      (1950), Riverside (1962), and Rinehart (1971).

1092. ———. "Two Dramatists: Lovelace and Richardson in
      Clarissa." *SNNTS*, 5 (1973), 7-21.

      Argues that Lovelace is the controlling agent in
      the novel.

1093. Park, William. "*Clarissa* As Tragedy." *SEL*, 16 (1976),
      461-71.

      A thorough discussion of the novel as tragedy: "in-
      verted values, pathology, and catastrophe," innocence
      destroyed, the actual virtues of the protagonist abet-
      ting her destruction—all these characterize the novel.

*   Parnell, Paul E. "The Sentimental Mask." See #820.

      Uses a passage from *Clarissa* to present his analysis
      of the relationship between sentimentalism and morality.

1094. Phelps, William Lyon. "Clarissa." See #30, V, ix-
      xxxiii.

      Discusses Richardson's influence and critically
      examines the novel.

*   ———. *Essays on Books*. See #823.

      A thorough examination of *Clarissa* in terms of
      characterization, structure, and theme.

*   Poetzsche, Erich. *Samuel Richardsons Belesenheit*.
      See #560.

      Considers the influence of dramatic literature upon
      Clarissa.

1095. Poovey, Mary. "Journeys from This World to the Next:
      The Providential Promise in *Clarissa* and *Tom Jones*."
      ELH, 43 (1976), 300-15.

      Discusses the differences between Richardson and
      Fielding, emphasizing the dissimilarities between their
      didactic conceptions of art and the world, though
      beginning with the assertion that both novels express
      a fictionalized Christian epic.

1096. Praz, Mario. "The Shadow of the Living Marquis." In
       The Romantic Agony. Trans. Angus Davidson. 2nd
       edn. London: Oxford Univ. Press, 1970. Pp. 95-186.

       Richardson (especially with *Clarissa*) is considered
       in the tradition of "the unfortunate, persecuted
       maiden"; comparisons are made with other eighteenth-
       century works such as Diderot's *Religieuse* and Laclos'
       Les Liaisons dangereuses.

1097. Preston, John. "*Clarissa* (i): A Process of Estrange-
       ment"; "*Clarissa* (ii): A Form of Freedom." In *The
       Created Self: The Reader's Role in Eighteenth-Cen-
       tury Fiction*. New York: Barnes & Noble, 1970. Pp.
       38-62; 63-93.

       The epistolary form of the novel reveals a continuing
       existential crisis leading to personal isolation; the
       reader must evaluate the process of the form itself,
       the *whole* story, and he becomes a collaborator in the
       fiction.

1098. Price, Martin. "Clarissa and Lovelace." In *To the
       Palace of Wisdom. Studies in Order and Energy from
       Dryden to Blake*. Garden City: Doubleday & Company,
       1964. Pp. 276-84.

       The divided or unexamined heart is shown to have
       tragic consequences for both characters.

1099. Pritchett, V.S. "*Clarissa*." In *The Living Novel &
       Later Appreciations*. 1947; rpt. with additions,
       New York: Random House, 1964. Pp. 11-20.

       Richardson was preoccupied with sex, and *Clarissa*
       "is a novel written about the world as one sees it
       through the keyhole."

1100. Rabkin, Norman. "*Clarissa*: A Study in the Nature of
       Convention." *ELH*, 23 (1956), 204-17.

       As a novel proclaiming conventional morality,
       Clarissa is unsuccessful. The actual center of action
       is the contest between "the free force of instinct" and
       the "decorum" one is forced to construct in order to
       live with others.

1101. Ray, J. Karen. "The Feminist Role in *Robinson Crusoe,
       Roxana*, and *Clarissa*." *Emporia State Research
       Studies*, 24 (1976), 28-33.

Compares the position of women in the three novels,
defined by the "tensions created by rigid restrictions
and the rejection of and struggle against them"; these
tensions provide "major formative devices" in each
of the novels.

*   Roddier, Henri. *J.J. Rousseau en Angleterre.* See
    #1201.

    Includes a special section comparing *Clarissa* with
    Héloïse.

1102. Romberg, Bertil. "*Clarissa*." In *Studies in the
       Narrative Technique of the First-Person Novel.*
       Trans. Michael Taylor and Harold B. Borland.
       Stockholm: Almqvist & Wiksell, 1962. Pp. 117-235.

       An analysis of Richardson's narrative technique,
       considering the distribution of letters and point of
       view in the novel, the editor's function, and the par-
       ticular narrators themselves.

1103. Sacks, Sheldon. "*Clarissa* and the Tragic Traditions."
       In *Studies in Eighteenth-Century Culture: Irrational-
       ism in the Eighteenth Century.* Ed. Harold E. Pag-
       liaro. Vol. 2. Cleveland and London: The Press of
       Case Western Reserve Univ., 1972. Pp. 195-221.

       A study of tragic action, catastrophe, and "poetical
       justice."

1104. Sale, William M., Jr. "A Bibliographical Note on
       Richardson's *Clarissa*." *Library*, 4th ser., 16
       (1936), 448-51.

       Examines volumes of the first edition of *Clarissa*
       to show how printers practiced economy with their
       materials.

*   ———. "From *Pamela* to *Clarissa*." See #977.

    Discusses how Richardson's fiction "rendered the
    conflicts he saw in his own society," revealing the
    meaning his novels had for his contemporaries and
    what *Clarissa* may still mean today.

1105. Schmitz, Robert M. "Death and Colonel Morden in
       Clarissa." *SAQ*, 69 (1970), 346-53.

       Studies the prominence of Colonel Morden in the
       death symbolism of the novel.

1106.   ————, and Judith Wilt. "Lovelace and Impotence."
         PMLA, 92 (1977), 1005-06.

         An exchange, based on Wilt's arguments in #1127, on
         Lovelace's presumed impotence.

*   Schulz, Dieter. "Samuel Richardson." See #982.

         Discusses the problem of "lascivious images" in
         Clarissa.

1107.   Sherbo, Arthur. "Time and Place in Richardson's
         Clarissa." *Boston University Studies in English*,
         3 (1957), 139-46.

         Discusses the time period Richardson utilized for
         his novels, especially *Clarissa*; was Richardson faith-
         ful to this time scheme, and how did it affect his
         readers?

1108.   Sherburn, George. Introduction to the Riverside
         Edition of *Clarissa*. See #45, pp. v-xiv.

         Examines in some detail the psychology, morality,
         and themes of the novel, the composition of *Clarissa*,
         and Richardson's dramatic technique. For an evaluation
         of this edition see #1091.

1109.   Sherwood, Irma Z. "The Novelist As Commentator." In
         *The Age of Johnson: Essays Presented to Chauncey
         Brewster Tinker*. New Haven: Yale University Press,
         1949. Pp. 113-25.

         Discusses the digressive moralizing in eighteenth-
         century novels like *Clarissa* and *Tom Jones*.

1110.   Shipman, Carolyn. "A Dissection of the Female Heart."
         Book Buyer, 23 (1901-02), 29-30.

         A summary analysis of *Clarissa* with comment on
         Clarissa's and Lovelace's character, the one gentle,
         proud, and firm, the other witty, versatile, and
         adroit.

*   Shuman, R. Baird. "Censorship As a Controlling Theme
         in 'Pamela' and 'Clarissa.'" See #989.

         Suggests that censorship of a character's writing
         becomes a major symbol in *Clarissa*, emphasizing
         Richardson's belief in personal freedom.

*   Smith, Warren H. *Architecture in English Fiction*.
       See #855.

       Considers how the theme of imprisonment and
       Richardson's descriptions in *Clarissa* affected the
       development of later Gothic stories.

1111. Southam, B.C. "Jane Austen and 'Clarissa.'" *N&Q*,
       N.S., 10 (1963), 191-92.

       Suggests a parallel between Mr. Collins and the
       Rev. Elias Brand.

*   Spacks, Patricia Meyer. *The Female Imagination*.
       See #856.

       Considers Clarissa as a character who reveals how
       differently a woman views or interprets the values
       of our world.

*   Spearman, Diana. "Richardson." See #991.

       Compares the novelistic world of *Clarissa* against
       the known reality of eighteenth-century life as depic-
       ted in letters and memoirs, suggesting that the novel
       does not accurately picture the age.

1112. Stevick, Philip. Introduction to the Rinehart Edition
       of *Clarissa*. See #46, pp. vii-xxviii.

       Provides a brief biographical sketch, looks at the
       narrative form of the novel, and includes a collection
       of critical reactions toward Richardson from Johnson
       to the present. For an evaluation of this edition
       see #1091.

1113. Traugott, John. "*Clarissa*'s Richardson: An Essay to
       Find the Reader." In *English Literature in the Age
       of Disguise*. Ed. Maximillan E. Novak. Los Angeles:
       Univ. of California Press, 1977. Pp. 157-208.

       An analysis of the novel with regard to the "con-
       sciousness" of the author as he becomes an author, to
       the imagination of the man who possessed on one hand
       "such dubious personality and such silly postures,"
       and to the presence of the author in this work; in-
       cludes sections on "The Composer's Dream"; "Absolutism
       in Comedy and Realism"; and "Rewards and Punishments."

1114. Ulmer, Gregory L. "*Clarissa* and *La Nouvelle Héloïse*."

Comparative Literature, 24 (1972), 289-308.

Considers Rousseau's originality, uncompromised by his knowledge of Richardson; a comparison of the two authors in order to reveal Rousseau's genius.

1115.   Van Ghent, Dorothy. "Clarissa and Emma as Phèdre."
        Partisan Review, 17 (1950), 820-33.

Discusses the love-myth in the three works and its "archaic, sacramental significance"; suggests that *Clarissa* should therefore be read not as a tragedy but as a "divine comedy."

1116.   ⸺⸺. "On *Clarissa Harlowe*." In *The English
        Novel: Form and Function*. 1953; rpt. New York: Holt,
        Rinehart and Winston, 1964. Pp. 45-63.

Special attention is given to images and symbols in the novel, leading to a psychological analysis of the "myth" of the novel.

1117.   Van Marter, Leslie E. "Whole and Part: A Problem in
        the Philosophy of Art and Criticism." *Bucknell Re-
        view*, 16 (1968), 123-32.

Uses *Clarissa* as a focus for discussing how an unwarranted concentration on part of a novel or on individual scenes diminishes one's sense of artistic wholeness.

1118.   Van Marter, Shirley. "Richardson's Debt to Hester
        Mulso Concerning the Curse in *Clarissa*." *PLL*, 14
        (1978), 22-31.

Explores in some detail how Hester Mulso's conception of Clarissa's innocence and her right to refuse to marry Solmes and to defy her parents contributed to Richardson's revisions of his novel.

1119.   ⸺⸺. "Richardson's Revisions of *Clarissa* in the
        Second Edition." *SB*, 26 (1973), 107-32.

An analysis of the first set of revisions Richardson made in print, including a commentary upon the effect they had on characterization, narrative method, and style.

1120.   ⸺⸺. "Richardson's Revisions of *Clarissa* in the
        Third and Fourth Editions." *SB*, 28 (1975), 119-52.

An analysis of the revisions with an emphasis upon

those which crucially affect characterization, narrative style, or thematic patterns; a discussion as well
of the relative merits of the first edition as compared with the others.

*   Van Tieghem, Paul. "La sensibilité et la passion dans
le roman européen au 18e siècle." See #877.

Particularly considers how *Clarissa* fits into the
development of European sensibility.

1121.   Ward, H.G. "Anna Howe and Charlotte Grandison." *N&Q*,
11 ser., 3 (4 March 1911), 164-65.

Calls attention to the two characters' similarities
in *Grandison*; considers Lady Mary Wortley Montagu's
similar observations.

1122.   ———. "Richardson's Character of Lovelace." *MLR*,
7 (1912), 494-98.

Works out in detail the parallels between Lovelace
and Lothario in Rowe's *The Fair Penitent*.

1123.   Warde, William B., Jr. "Revisions of the Published
Texts of Samuel Richardson's Preface to *Clarissa*."
South Central Bulletin, 30 (1970), 232-34.

Extensive revisions in the Preface reveal "in micro-
cosmic form" the similar care Richardson took with
the novel's structure, characterization, and dramatic
quality.

*   Waterhouse, Osborn. "The Development of English
Sentimental Comedy." See #880.

Considers the circumstances of *Clarissa*'s publication
which reveal the degree of sensibility possessed by
Richardson's readers.

*   Watt, Ian. "Richardson As Novelist: *Clarissa*." See
#577, pp. 208-38.

Examines the epistolary form as it contributed to
plot, characterization, and themes in the novel; sees
how "family authority" and "attitudes of economic
individualism" create the primary obstacles for
Clarissa to surmount.

1124.   Wendt, Allan. "Clarissa's Coffin." *PQ*, 39 (1960),
481-95.

The symbol of the coffin dominates the book, drama-

tizing moral problems of Richardson's society and establishing an ethical point of view not thoroughly
explored until generations later.

*   Whitcomb, Seldon L. *The Study of a Novel*. See #655.

        Clarissa is considered in terms of a formal,
        rhetorical evaluation of the novel.

*   White, William. "Richardson: Idealist or Realist?"
        See #883.

        The model for a young woman's behavior, suggested in
        Familiar Letters, is not followed by Clarissa; the con-
        trast reveals her essential selfishness.

*   Whiteford, Robert N. "Samuel Richardson ..." See
        #1004.

        An analysis of Clarissa's characterization.

1125.   Wilson, Angus. "Evil in the English Novel." *Listener*,
        68 (1962), 1079-80.

        A very brief look at the "supernatural" power of
        Clarissa, suggesting that Clarissa is a citadel be-
        sieged, a citadel of three kinds: sexual innocence,
        social dignity, and a country way of living; Lovelace
        is the evil which corrupts all three.

*   Wilson, Colin. *The Craft of the Novel*. See #1006.

        Clarissa is briefly considered in terms of Richard-
        son's genius for freeing "the human imagination."

1126.   Wilson, Stuart. "The First Dramatic Version of
        Clarissa." *ELN*, 2 (1964), 21-25.

        Discusses the text of a play of *Clarissa* by Robert
        Porrett written in 1788.

1127.   Wilt, Judith. "He Could Go No Farther: A Modest
        Proposal about Lovelace." *PMLA*, 92 (Jan. 1977),
        19-32.

        Suggests that Lovelace was in fact impotent and ex-
        plores the consequences of such an interpretation to
        an understanding of *Clarissa*, especially by examining
        the relationship between Clarissa and Mrs. Sinclair
        and the significance of their symbolic functions. For
        a rebuttal see #1106.

1128.   Winner, Anthony. "Richardson's Lovelace: Character and
        Prediction." *TSLL*, 14 (1972), 53-75.

Richardson's faith in Providence contains Lovelace,
but the latter nevertheless nearly triumphs both as
demonic commentator and demon.

*   Wolff, Cynthia Griffin. "Clarissa and Her Family";
      "Clarissa and Lovelace"; "Clarissa Triumphant."
      See #582, pp. 74-99; 100-51; 152-73.

Three chapters explore Clarissa's development in the
changing circumstances of her family relationships,
of her growing awareness that there is no "moral and
social order informing" Lovelace's character or behavior, and of her longing for death "born of despair
and selfcondemnation."

1129.   Wolpers, Theodor von. "Clarissa." In *Der englische
       Roman: Vom Mittelalter zur Moderne.* Ed. Franz K.
       Stanzel. 2 vols. Dusseldorf: August Bagel, 1969.
       I, 144-231.

A formal analysis of Richardson and *Clarissa* from
the perspective of an intellectual concept of sensibility. Sensibility is a unifying motif in the novel,
creating an inner form which structures characterization, plot, and theme.

*   Wurzbach, Natascha, ed. *The Novel in Letters.* See
      #583.

Uses examples from *Clarissa* to discuss the letter
as a literary convention.

1130.   Wyndham, Maud. *Chronicles of the Eighteenth Century,
       Founded on the Correspondence of Sir Thomas Lyttleton
       and His Family.* 2 vols. London: Hodder and
       Stoughton, 1924.

Reports that Lyttleton did press Richardson to make
Clarissa end happily; quotes from Young's letter to
the Duchess of Portland.

F. *SIR CHARLES GRANDISON*

*   Allen, B. Sprague. *Tides in English Taste, 1619-
      1800.* See #520.

Richardson scoffed at "the passion for porcelain"
during his time by ridiculing it in *Grandison.*

*   Baker, Ernest A. "Sir Charles Grandison." In *The His-*
         tory of the English Novel. See #585, pp. 55-76.

         A general summary of the novel, noting that Grandi-
         son is a male counterpart of Clarissa.

1131.   Bander, Elaine. "The Case for *Sir Charles Grandison*:
         A Note on Barbara Reynold's 'The Origin of Peter
         Wimsey.'" *Sayers Review*, 1 (1977), 8-9.

         Argues briefly that Sir Charles, "Richardson's
         eponymous hero," is the source and model for Lord
         Peter Wimsey.

*   Barker, Gerard A. "The Complacent Paragon: Exemplary
         Characterization in Richardson." See #666.

         Sir Charles reveals his virtue through his Protestant
         approval of his own behavior.

*   Brophy, Elizabeth. "*Pamela II* and *Sir Charles Grandi-*
         son: Delicacies Arise on Delicacies." See #527, pp.
         72-90.

         Studies the novel in terms of Richardson's artistic
         intentions, finding Sir Charles' virtue so flawless
         that "moral tension important to Richardson's design
         is almost entirely lacking."

*   Clements, Frances M. "The Rights of Women in the
         Eighteenth-Century Novel." See #691.

         Uses references from *Grandison* to reveal the con-
         ditions faced by women in the eighteenth century:
         domestic service, prostitution, housewifery.

*   Davis, Robert G. "The Sense of the Real in English
         Fiction." See #707.

         Discusses how Richardson applied Aristotelian tragic
         theory to *Grandison*.

1132.   *The Dial, a Semi-Monthly Journal of Literary Criticism,*
         Discussion, and Information. "Grandisonian Manner,"
         45 (Aug. 16, 1908), 75-77.

         Suggests that a re-reading of *Grandison* might provide
         a corrective for the bad manners developing in the
         twentieth century; examples extracted to show Sir
         Charles' unfailing graciousness.

*   Dibelius, Wilhelm. "Richardson." See #711.

Gives special attention to the characterization of Charlotte Grandison.

1133.   Dircks, Richard J. "Cumberland, Richardson, and Fielding: Changing Patterns in the Eighteenth-Century Novel." *Research Studies* (Washington State University), 38 (1970), 291-99.

Considers Richardson's influence upon Cumberland, especially *Sir Charles Grandison* as a model for *Arundel*.

*   Doody, Margaret Anne. "'A Fiddle and a Dance': Patterns of Imagery in *Sir Charles Grandison*." See #534, pp. 340-67.

Explores how the imagery in the novel reinforces the theme of true courtship and "leads to the ceremony of marriage, to joy and fruition."

1134.   Duncan-Jones, E.E. "The Misses Selby and Steele." *TLS*, 10 Sept. 1964, p. 485.

Reveals the likeness between Lucy and Nancy Selby and their counterparts in Austen's *Sense and Sensibility*.

1135.   Eaves, T.C. Duncan, and Ben D. Kimpel. "Cowper's 'Ode on Reading Mr. Richardson's *History of Sir Charles Grandison*.'" *PLL*, 2 (1966), 74-75.

Notes the variations in Cowper's ode (possessed by Richardson) with references to the novel.

*   ————. "*Sir Charles Grandison*." See #537, pp. 387-400.

A critical examination of the novel in terms of style, structure, and characterization, noting the primary critical evaluations given the book.

1136.   Fischer, Walther. "Ein unbekannter Brief David Garricks an Samuel Richardson." *Anglia*, 63 (1939), 436-44.

Discusses *Grandison* and the Dublin pirates, based on a letter from David Garrick.

1137.   Gassenmeier, Michael. *Der Typus des Man of Feeling;*

*Studien zum sentimentalen Roman des 18. Jahrhunderts
in England*. Tübingen: M. Niemeyer, 1972.

This is an analysis which includes an examination of
Grandison in a discussion of eighteenth-century novels.

1138. Gibson, S., and William Holdsworth. "The Case of
        Samuel Richardson, of London, Printer." *Oxford
        Bibliographical Society*, 2 (1929), 320-25.

        A reprint of "Appendix II" of *Grandison*, concerning
        the dispute between Richardson and the Dublin pub-
        lishers; includes George Faulkner's comment from *The
        Dublin Journal* (3-6 Nov. 1753) on Richardson's delay
        in sending printer's sheets for the novel.

*   Gosse, Edmund. "Samuel Richardson." See #614.

        Includes a facsimile of Richardson's letter to Dr.
        Cox Macro, answering the latter's criticism of
        Grandison.

1139. Harris, Jocelyn. Introduction to the Oxford Edition
        of *Grandison*. See #48, pp. vii-xxxvii.

        Notes the construction of the novel, volume by
        volume, considers the novel's impact on its own times
        and Richardson's reputation, and considers the style,
        characterization, and theme of the novel; provides an
        analysis of the novel's text and a list of editions,
        translations, and abridgements.

1140. ―――. "The Reviser Observed: The Last Volume of
        Sir Charles Grandison." *SB*, 29 (1976), 1-31.

        The "distressed and distressing compromises" in
        Volume VII of the novel are examined in light of Rich-
        ardson's desire for advice from his friends about the
        conclusion of the book.

1141. ―――. "Twenty-eight Volumes of *Sir Charles Grandison*."
        N&Q, N.S., 20 (1973), 18-19.

        Identifies the rumored twenty-eight volumes of the
        novel as the manuscript volumes of the text, four
        manuscripts per seven printed volumes.

1142. Hilson, J.C., and Rosalind Nicol. "Two Notes On 'Sir
        Charles Grandison.'" *N&Q*, N.S., 22 (1975), 492-93.

        The source for the character and name of Richardson's

"good man" is possibly derived from the Earl of
Grandison as described by Ogilvie's dedication to his
translation of Giannone's *The Civil History of the
Kingdom of Naples*; they also note a possible source
for Richardson's account of the crossing of Mont Cenis
in the novel.

* Humphreys, A.R. "'The Friend of Mankind' 1700-60: An
Aspect of Eighteenth-Century Sensibility." See #763.

Uses *Grandison* as an example of how intuition and
emotion become increasingly important as the century
progresses.

* Kinkead-Weekes, Mark. *Samuel Richardson*. See #544, pp.
279-391.

Two chapters on *Grandison* study the art of the novel
in terms of Richardson's emphasis upon ethics and
debate: "he expected his readers to examine their
conduct in minute detail, and continually to raise the
question, 'Given the circumstances, did he (or she)
do right?'"

1143. Kurth, Lieselotte E. *Die zweite Wirklichkeit: Studien
zum Roman des achtzehnten Jahrhunderts*. University
of North Carolina Studies in the Germanic Languages
and Literature, 62. Chapel Hill: Univ. of North
Carolina Press, 1969.

Studies the relationship between the fictive and
real worlds, treats the reception of the eighteenth-
century novel in Europe, and summarizes theories of
the novel; some information on Richardson, such as
Wieland's dramatization of an episode from *Grandison*.

1144. Levin, Gerald. "Character and Fantasy in Richardson's
Sir Charles Grandison." *Connecticut Review*, 7 (1973),
93-99.

Explores in some detail the fantasy in Sir Charles
of "physical mastery" and "polygamy" hidden in the
narrative where a number of love-stricken women are
fated to share him only as "sisters."

1145. McKillop, Alan Dugald. "Introduction." In *Critical
Remarks on "Sir Charles Grandison," "Clarissa," and
Pamela" (1754)*. Augustan Reprint Society Pub. 21.
Los Angeles: William Andrews Clark Memorial Library,

Univ. of California, 1950. Pp. i–v.

McKillop rejects Dr. John Free as the probable author of this pamphlet, summarizes the author's attack on the novel, and notes the criticism which judges Richardson's emphasis upon sex; sees that *Grandison* duplicates some of the principal characters in *Clarissa*, and emphasizes the character of Charlotte rather than the other characters.

*   ———. "A Letter from Samuel Richardson to Alexis Claude Clairaut." See #80.

Includes information regarding the foreign translations of *Grandison*.

1146. Merington, Marguerite. "A Literary Love." *Lamp; a Review and Record of Current Literature*, 26 (1903), 136–41.

An enthusiastic summary of Cooke's edition of *Grandison*, applauding the angelic nature of Harriet Byron and the manly virtue of Sir Charles.

1147. Noel-Bentley, Elaine. "An Allusion to 'Sir Charles Grandison' in Jane Austen's Letters." *N&Q*, N.S., 24 (1977), 321.

Adds a third reference to Richardson in Chapman's edition of Austen's *Letters*; further reveals how thoroughly Austen knew the novel when she could refer to such an obscure passage.

*   Phelps, William Lyon. *Essays on Books*. See #823.

A thorough analysis of *Grandison* in terms of characterization, structure, and theme.

1148. ———. "Sir Charles Grandison." See #30, XIII, ix–xxxiii.

Discusses Richardson's achievement and reputation as well as the novel.

1149. Pierson, Robert C. "The Revisions of Richardson's *Sir Charles Grandison*." *SB*, 21 (1968), 163–89.

Provides an analysis of the four editions of the novel, concluding that Richardson's intentions are best served by an edition incorporating the substantive changes in the second, third, and 1810 edition as well as those which occur in Volume VII of the fourth edition.

1150. Roddier, Henri. *L'Abbé Prévost, l'homme et l'oeuvre.* Paris: Hatier-Boivin, 1955.

    Discusses the direct influence of *Grandison* upon *La Nouvelle Héloïse.*

*   Romberg, Bertil. "*Clarissa*." See #1102.

    Considers *Grandison*, briefly, in terms of narrative techniques, points of view, and the roles of multiple narrators.

1151. Sale, William M., Jr. "The Singer Copy of *Sir Charles Grandison*." *Library Chronicle* (Univ. of Pennsylvania), 3 (1935), 42-45.

    Discusses a copy of *Grandison* in the Singer Collection which helps resolve the question of Richardson's revision of Letter 37, Volume II.

1152. ————. "*Sir Charles Grandison* and the Dublin Pirates." *Yale University Library Gazette*, 7 (1932), 80-86.

    Concerns the pirated editions of *Grandison* which appeared in Dublin, and Richardson's attempt to deal with this invasion of his property.

1153. Shaw, Edward P. "Malesherbes, the Abbé Prévost and the First French Translation of *Sir Charles Grandison*." *MLN*, 49 (1954), 105-09.

    Correspondence reveals the difficulties Bruyset faced in not receiving permission to publish a translation of the novel.

1154. Steele, F.M. "Catholicism and English Literature in the Eighteenth Century." *The American Catholic Quarterly Review*, 36 (1911), 634-59.

    Discusses the problem of Clementine's Catholic religion in *Grandison* as a force separating her from Sir Charles with resulting tragic consequences; considers Richardson's portrayal of Catholicism just and sensitive.

1155. Tallmadge, Abby L. "Jane Austen's Letters." *TLS*, 19 Jan. 1933, p. 40.

    Identifies the James Selby in a letter of 14 Sept.

1804 as a reference to the character in *Grandison*, a cousin of Harriet Byron's who thinks travel alone will make him a Sir Charles.

*   Ward, H.G. "Anna Howe and Charlotte Grandison." See #1121.

Calls attention to the two characters' similarities in *Grandison* and considers Lady Mary Wortley Montagu's similar observation.

1156. ————. "Samuel Richardson and the Methodists." *N&Q*, 11 ser., 3 (18 Feb. 1911), 124.

Cites and comments upon the references to Methodism in *Grandison*.

*   Whiteford, Robert N. "Samuel Richardson." See #1004.

An analysis of the characterization of Harriet Byron and Clementina.

*   Wolff, Cynthia Griffin. "Sir Charles Grandison." See #582, pp. 174–229.

Discusses characterization in the novel from the perspective of Richardson's desire to create his hero in order "to formulate a coherent social expression of moral worth."

1157. Zach, Wolfgang. "Richardson and the Dedication to the Earl of Grandison in Ogilvie's *Civil History of the Kingdom of Naples*." *Archiv für das Studium der neueren Sprachen und Literaturen*, 213 (1976), 343–45.

Argues that Richardson would have known of this man and his principles since he printed Ogilvie's work.

V.
Richardson's Influence
and the General Foreign Reception
of His Novels

1158. Boas, F.S. "Richardson's Novels and Their Influence."
      In *From Richardson to Pinero. Some Innovators and
      Idealists*. London: John Murray, 1936. Pp. 6–46.

      Discusses epistolary technique and Richardson's in-
      fluence on eighteenth-century literature.

1159. Bradbrook, Frank W. *Jane Austen and Her Predecessors*.
      Cambridge: Cambridge Univ. Press, 1966.

      Richardson and his novels were a model for Jane
      Austen and hers, not so much in his portrayal of morals
      as in his capacity for presenting detailed states of
      mind and feeling.

      Reviewed: *JEGP*, 66 (1967), 271–74.
               NCF, 21 (1967), 387–88.
               RES, N.S., 18 (1967), 469–71.

1160. Brown, Herbert R. "The Elegant Epistolarians." In
      The Sentimental Novel in America 1789-1860. 1940;
      rpt. New York: Pageant Books, 1959. Pp. 52–73.

      Considers the influence of Richardson's epistolary
      technique upon authors in America.

1161. ———. "Richardson and Seduction." See #1160, pp.
      28–51.

      Considers at some length how Richardson's motifs
      influenced the development of American fiction.

1162. Cecil, David, Lord. "Fanny Burney's Novels." In
      *Essays on the Eighteenth Century Presented to David
      Nichol Smith*. 1945; rpt. New York: Russell &
      Russell, 1963.

      Includes a brief discussion of Richardson's influence
      upon Fanny Burney.

1163. Coe, Ada M. "Richardson in Spain." *Hispanic Review*,

3 (1935), 56–63.

Discusses Richardson's reputation and influence in Spain; argues that Richardson was introduced not in direct translation from the English, but first through Italian and then French texts. Provides a bibliography for articles appearing in Spain from 1785 to 1847 in the notes.

1164. Cordasco, Francesco. "La fortuna di Samuel Richardson in Italia." *Revista Universitaria*, 1 (1943), 37–58.

Not examined.

1165. Cru, R. Loyalty. *Diderot as a Disciple of English Thought*. 1913; rpt. New York: AMS Press, 1966.

Fully discusses Diderot's relationship to Richardson.

1166. Donner, J.O.E. "Richardson in der deutschen Romantik." *Zeitschrift für vergleichende Literaturgeschichte*, N.S., 10 (1896), 1–16.

Discusses Richardson's influence on two authors of the German Romantic period, Ludwig Tieck and Achim von Arnim.

1167. Erämetsä, Erik. "Der sprachliche Einfluss Richardson auf Goethes *Werther*." *NM*, 57 (1955), 118–25.

Discusses the likenesses between language used by Richardson and that used by Goethe in *Werther*.

1168. ———. "Über den englischen Einfluss auf den deutschen Wortvorrat des 18. Jahrhunderts." *NM*, 49 (1958), 34–40.

Examples are given from *Clarissa* and *Grandison*.

1169. Etienne, Servais. *Le genre romanesque en France depuis l'apparition de la "Nouvelle Héloïse" jusqu'aux approches de la révolution*. Paris: A. Colin, 1922.

Considers Richardson's influence upon French novelists, believing that it is minimal and that a wide gap exists between Richardson's reputation and actual influence in France.

1170. Fabian, Bernhard. "English Books and Their Eighteenth-Century German Readers." In *The Widening Circle: Essays on the Circulation of Literature in Eighteenth-*

Century Europe. Ed. Paul J. Korshin. Philadelphia: Univ. of Pennsylvania Press, 1966. Pp. 119-96.

Richardson's position in the contemporary reading scene in eighteenth-century Germany is assessed by examining subscription lists, the relation of English literature to the general reader of the period, and the emergence of the reading public that actually read English.

*   Facteau, Bernard Anthony. *Les romans de Richardson sur la scène Français.* See #931.

Traces *Pamela*'s adaptation on the French and Continental stage.

1171.   Foster, James R. "The Abbé Prévost and the English Novel." *PMLA*, 42 (1927), 443-64.

Considers Richardson's influence upon the development of the sentimental novel.

1172.   Ghijsen, H.C.M. "Wolff en Dekens romans uit haar bloetijd." *De Gids*, 87 (1922), 114-39, 241-64.

A lengthy study of Richardson's influence upon the two Dutch novelists; *Clarissa* was especially important as an influence, but Wolff and Deken possess a more modern, tolerant, and humanistic morality. Their novels do not, however, have the same intensity since they lack Richardson's dramatic strength and his emphasis upon violent conflict.

1173.   Graf, Arturo. *L'Anglomania e l'influsso inglese in Italia nel secolo xviii.* Turin, 1911.

This is primarily a literary survey; chapter twelve briefly looks at the influence of English writers such as Akenside, Johnson, Fielding, Richardson, Gray, Young, and Sterne.

1174.   Green, F.C. *French Novelists, Manners and Ideas from the Renaissance to the Revolution.* New York: D. Appleton and Company, 1929. Esp. pp. 164-73.

Analyzes the influence of Richardson upon French novelists and regards Joseph Texte's assertion that Richardson determined the development of the French novel until the Revolution to be highly exaggerated.

1175.   ————. *Minuet: A Critical Survey of French and*

English Literary Ideas in the Eighteenth Century.
1935; rpt. as *Literary Ideas...*, New York: F. Ungar,
1966.

A reconsideration of Richardson's influence upon the
French novel and of the French upon Richardson: the
question of *La Vie de Marianne* and *Pamela* is resolved,
concluding that the two are distinctly different "in
conception, in style, in plot."

1176. Irving, William H. *The Providence of Wit in the English
        Letter Writers.* Durham, N.C.: Duke Univ. Press,
        1955.

Briefly discusses Richardson's influence upon the
sentimental writers of the latter half of the eighteenth
century.

1177. Jost, François. "Prévost Traducteur de Richardson."
        In *Expression, Communication and Experience in Litera-
        ture and Language.* Ed. Ronald G. Popperwell. London:
        Modern Humanities Research Assn., 1972. Pp. 297-300.

Prévost's translation of *Clarissa* changes the heroine
from a Richardsonian Englishwoman to one acceptable to
French society; Richardson's influence upon French
narrative art is placed in three categories: (1) the
organization of the correspondence, (2) the technique
of reporting events, and (3) the elimination of the
omniscient narrator.

1178. ———. "Richardson, Rousseau et le roman épistolaire."
        *Cahiers de l'Association Internationale des Études
        Françaises*, 29 (1977), 172-85. [Also a discussion,
        later, pp. 353-55.]

A reassessment of Rousseau's debt to Richardson and
an evaluation of the two novelists' styles.

1179. Lanzisera, Francesco. "I romanzi de Samuele Richardson
        in Italia." *Annali del R. Istituto Orientale de
        Napoli (1928-29).* Napoli: Cimmaruta, 1929. Pp. 148-
        79.

Richardson revived the novel in Italy; the critic,
Bareti, openly encouraged imitation of Richardson, and
with Veri and Foscolo (the latter was especially influenced by *Clarissa*), the Italian novel reached a new
level of dignity. There is also a section on Richardson's influence upon the Italian theater.

1180. Liljegren, Sten Bodvar. *The English Sources of Goethe's Gretchen Tragedy: A Study on the Life and Fate of Literary Motives.* Lund: C.W.K. Gleerup, 1937.

Primarily an account of Richardson's influence on German, eighteenth-century literature; Goethe handled Richardsonian motifs originally and brilliantly whereas the minor novelists followed along mechanically imitative lines. Looks at some of the following kinds of motifs: the Faust-Gretchen theme; virtue; the idyll; the seduction; the summer house; the duel; women in love and insanity; and the dying saint.

1181. Lynch, Lawrence W. "Richardson's Influence on the Concept of the Novel in Eighteenth-Century France." *Comparative Literature Studies*, 14 (1977), 233-43.

Re-affirms Texte's basic formulation of Richardson's influence upon the French novel, especially emphasizing his impact upon the theory of the novel.

1182. May, Georges. "The Influence of English Fiction on the French Mid-Eighteenth-Century Novel." In *Aspects of the Eighteenth Century.* Ed. Earl R. Wasserman. Baltimore: Johns Hopkins Press, 1965. Pp. 265-80.

A careful, probing discussion of the effect of English fiction upon the French novel; considers such problems as popular success and critical assessments in determining the actual impact of the English novel upon the French.

1183. Mayo, Robert D. *The English Novel in the Magazines, 1740-1815.* Evanston, Ill.: Northwestern Univ. Press, 1962.

The effect of Richardson's technique and the success of his novels are discovered in the periodical literature of the eighteenth century; fully indexed references to Richardson.

1184. Miller, Meta Helena. *Chateaubriand and English Literature.* The Johns Hopkins Studies in Romance Literatures and Languages, Vol. 4. Baltimore: The Johns Hopkins Press, 1925.

Includes passing references to Richardson as a literary influence upon Chateaubriand.

1185. Mitrani, Charles. "Richardson and Madame de Souza."

West Virginia University Bulletin, Ser. 37, 1 (Oct. 1936), 28-35.

Briefly suggests Richardson's influence, particularly that of *Clarissa*, upon the French novels of Madame de Souza.

1186. Mojašević, Milka. "Richardsonovi romani i Goethor 'Werther.'" *Filologija*, 3 (1962), 97-108.

Suggests that Goethe, like Richardson, focused particularly upon a personality in conflict, and that Goethe derived from Richardson this fundamental problem: the dilemma wherein one must choose between one's natural, human inclinations and those more conservative viewpoints sanctioned by one's social environment.

1187. Monglond, André. *Le Préromantisme français*. 2 vols. 1930; rpt. Paris: Corti, 1965-66.

Richardson's influence needs to be re-examined in the light of romanticism as a natural development within French literature.

1188. Moquette, H.C.H. *Over de Romans van Wolff en Deken, beschouwd in Verband met de romantische Scheppingen van Richardson*. Rotterdam, 1898.

Considers what debt Wolff and Deken owe to Richardson with regard to epistolary form, to the practices they borrowed, and to their achievement compared with his romantic novels; includes an assessment of some parallel passages.

1189. Mornet, Daniel, ed. "L'Introduction." In *La Nouvelle Héloïse*. 4 vols. Paris: Librairie Hachette, 1925. I, 7-305.

Traces, again, the influence Richardson had upon Rousseau.

1190. Newcomb, Robert. "Franklin and Richardson." *JEGP*, 57 (1958), 27-35.

Both men used proverbs, maxims, and aphorisms in their writing; Franklin borrowed directly from Richardson for "over twenty of Poor Richard's sayings for the *Almanak* of 1752."

1191. Petersen, Carl S., and Vilhelm Andersen. *Illustreret Dansk Litteraturhistorie*. Copenhagen: Gyldendalske Boghandel, 1934. II, 581-84.

Provides a general account of Richardson's novels as they were received in Denmark.

1192. Phelps, William Lyon. "Richardson's Influence." See #30, V, ix-xvi.

Pamela not only initiated the parody of sentimental fiction in a work like *Joseph Andrews*, but Richardson "was responsible for something worse," namely the works of Sterne and Mackenzie; discusses as well Richardson's influence upon such German and French writers as Lessing, Goethe, and Rousseau.

1193. Pons, Christian. "Richardson et la *Nouvelle Héloïse*." *Etudes Anglaises*, 14 (1961), 350-51.

A response to Roddier (#1150), who claims a direct influence of *Grandison* upon the novel, arguing that concerning their "morales" or their "sensibilités," their differences are greater than their similarities.

1194. Price, Lawrence Marsden. "On the Reception of Richardson in Germany." *JEGP*, 25 (1926), 7-33.

Examines the translations of Richardson's novels into German.

1195. ————. "Richardson and the Moralizing Novel." In *The Reception of English Literature in Germany*. Berkeley: Univ. of California Press, 1932. Pp. 190-215.

Reviews and imitations of Richardson's novels in Germany are carefully considered.

Reviewed: *MLN*, 48 (1933), 547-50.
           MLR, 28 (1933), 390-93.
           RES, 10 (1934), 244-45.

1196. ————. "Richardson in the Moral Weeklies of Germany." *University of Wisconsin Studies in Language and Literature*, 22 (1925), 169-83.

Examines how Richardson was received in Germany: the principles of his art were of secondary concern to the issue of his moral values.

1197. ————. "Richardson, Wetzlar and Goethe." In *Mélanges d'histoire littéraire générale et comparée offerts à Fernand Baldensperger*. 2 vols. Paris: Champion,

1930. II, 174-87.

Discusses Richardson's influence on Goethe during the
Wetzlar period when German writers were living and
thinking according to their perception of a Richardsonian "code."

1198. Price, Mary Bell and Lawrence M. *The Publication of
       English Literature in Germany in the Eighteenth
       Century*. Berkeley: Univ. of California Press, 1934.

       The introduction and bibliography include informa-
       tion on Richardson.

1199. Prinsen, J. *De Roman in de 18e Eeuw in West-Europa*.
       Groningen, 1925.

       Considers the influence of Richardson upon the novels
       of Wolff and Deken.

1200. Reynaud, Louis. *Le Romantisme: ses origines anglo-
       germaniques; influences étrangères et traditions
       nationales; le réveil du génie français*. Paris: A.
       Colin, 1926.

       Follows Text's earlier analysis that Richardson's
       strain of sentiment and romance intruded upon French
       literature and triumphed over traditional classicism.

*   Roddier, Henri. *L'Abbé Prévost, l'homme et l'oeuvre*.
       See #1150.

       Discusses the direct influence of *Grandison* upon *La
       Nouvelle Héloïse*.

1201. ————. *J.-J. Rousseau en Angleterre au XVIIIe siècle.
       L'Oeuvre et l'homme*. *Études de littérature étrangère
       et comparée*, 21. Paris: Boivin, 1950.

       Notes that *Julie* was preferred to *Clarissa* by some
       contemporary English critics on the grounds that a way
       was shown to "regain esteem after a capital fault";
       numerous references to Richardson (indexed) with a
       special section comparing *Clarissa* with Rousseau's
       novel.

1202. Slattery, William C. "From Richardson to Wolff and
       Deken: Comic Devices in Willem Leevend." *Reisgidsen
       vol Belluno's en Blauwbaarden: Opstellen over S.
       Vestdijk en anderen aangeboden aan Dr. H.A. Wage*.

Leiden: Vakgroep Naderlandse Taal- en Letterkunde, 1976.

Not examined.

1203.   ———. "Samuel Richardson and the Netherlands: Early Reception of His Work." *PLL*, 1 (1965), 20-30.

Considers Richardson's relationship with the first Dutch translator of *Clarissa* and a summary of typical evaluations of the novels in Dutch periodicals.

1204.   Streeter, Harold W.   "The Vogue of Richardson's Novels in France."   In *The Eighteenth Century English Novel in French Translation: A Bibliographical Study*. 1936; rpt. New York: Benjamin Blom, 1976.   Pp. 91-105.

The French reaction to Richardson's novels in reviews is provided as well as a discussion of Richardson's imitators; includes lists of the French translations and a classification of those novels into kinds, such as "sentimental," "historical," or "philosophical."

1205.   Taupin, Rene.   "Richardson, Diderot, et l'art de conter."   *French Review*, 12 (1939), 181-94.

Compares the methods of Diderot in *La Religieuse* with those of Richardson in *Pamela* and *Clarissa*.

1206.   Tompkins, J.M.S.   *The Popular Novel in England 1770-1800*.   1932; rpt. Lincoln: Univ. of Nebraska Press, 1961.

Briefly traces Richardson's influence on later novelists.

1207.   Trahard, Pierre.   *Les maîtres de la sensibilité française au XVIIIe siècle (1715-1789)*.   4 vols.   Paris: Boivin, 1931-32.

Discusses Richardson's influence on sensibility and romanticism; both need to be examined in the context of their natural development in French literature.

1208.   Van Tieghem, Paul.   "The Novel of the Eighteenth Century."   In *Outline of the Literary History of Europe since the Renaissance*.   Trans. A.L. McKenzie. Preface Ronald S. Crane.   New York: The Century Co., 1930.   Pp. 180-90.

A brief summary of Richardson's contribution to the

novel with some indication of his influence upon such
writers as Goethe, Rousseau, and Wolff and Deken.

1209. Weinstein, Leo. *The Metamorphoses of Don Juan*. Palo
       Alto: Stanford Univ. Press, 1959.

       An analysis of Lovelace in the Don Juan tradition
       and of Lovelace's influence upon the protagonists in
       later novels.

1210. Wilcox, Frank Howard. *Prévost's Translations of
       Richardson's Novels*. *University of California Pub-
       lications in Modern Philology*, 21 (1927), 341-411.

       The characteristics of eighteenth-century taste are
       indicated by the changes Prévost introduced into the
       translations of Richardson's novels.

VI.
Theses